READING/LEARNING DISABILITY

An Ecological Approach

READING/LEARNING DISABILITY

An Ecological Approach

JILL BARTOLI
MORTON BOTEL

TEACHERS COLLEGE/COLUMBIA UNIVERSITY
New York and London

Published by Teachers College Press, 1234 Amsterdam Avenue,
New York, NY 10027

Charts 1, 2, 3 (pp. 30, 31, 32) and Figures I, II, III (pp. 2, 66, 164) were prepared by Donna J. Hoffman. Used with permission.

Library of Congress Cataloging-in-Publication Data

Bartoli, Jill.
  Reading/learning disability.
  Bibliography: p. 251
  Includes index.
    1. Learning disabled children—United States—
Education—Reading. 2. Reading—United States—
Language experience approach. 3. Language arts—United
States. I. Botel, Morton. II. Title.
LC4705.B37 1988   371.9′044   87-33615
ISBN 0-8077-2905-1
ISBN 0-8077-2904-3 (pbk.)

Manufactured in the United States of America

93 92 91 90 89 88   1 2 3 4 5 6

Contents

Foreword

Over the past half century, educators and society at large have debated the causes of reading failure and the potential of various interventions to improve reading skills. No area of human learning has been investigated as thoroughly as reading acquisition. During this period, understandings of reading failure have shifted. At first, low intelligence and lack of school attendance or lack of motivation were understood to be the sources of reading failure. Over time these etiologies were rejected as the basis for most reading failure, and understandings that implicated environmental disadvantages and cultural deprivation were accepted. More recently, understandings of reading failure as based in a neurological or physiological deficit, associated with a specific learning disability, have become widely accepted. As our understanding has changed, so have our labels for those children who found learning to read difficult (McGill-Franzen, 1987).*

Amidst these changing understandings, several things have remained unchanged. First, we have tended to situate the source of the failure with the individual learner—a sort of "blame the victim" mentality. Whether we called them "slow learners" (1945–60), "culturally disadvantaged" (1960–75), or "learning disabled" (1975–present), we invariably sought to identify the deficit inherent in the *learner*. Second, in our attempts to understand or intervene we rarely questioned the nature of the instructional environment that had been unsuccessful in developing literacy skills. A working assumption was that all children received adequate, appropriate, and timely literacy instruction, but that some failed to benefit from that instruction. Third, regardless of which treatment or intervention was popular and elected, there is virtually no evidence that our solutions solved the reading problems of the children served. For instance, we have good evidence that retention in grade does not solve reading problems. Children who are promoted, even when experiencing reading problems, read

---

*McGill-Franzen, Anne. (1987) Failure to learn to read: Formulating a policy problem. *Reading Research Quarterly, 22.*

better in the future than those retained. Remedial reading programs offer little evidence of any widespread success. Chapter I programs serve the same clients year after year; few earn their way out. Special education programs for the learning disabled and others designated as mildly handicapped simply add more students each year, with only a scant few clients ever declassified because their reading failure was resolved. The final constant has been the approach used to solve reading failure, regardless of the label attached to the child. In every era, across the several understandings of reading failure, we have applied a reductionist framework in our assessments, instruction, and evaluations. After a half century of substantial failure it seems time to consider alternatives.

In this book, Jill Bartoli and Morton Botel offer an alternative. Their well-reasoned and field-tested "ecological model" has been shaped by recent advances in fields that traditionally have not been part of the educational mainstream. They offer substantial arguments for their view and point to the evidence that has undermined the traditional diagnostic-prescriptive subskills approach to understanding reading failure. Their evidence is quite overwhelming in the aggregate. As with any new view, it is bound to attract skeptics, critics, and outright foes. Their rejection of most traditional understandings may make many uncomfortable and others even angry.

However, unlike many persistent critics of the educational scene, Bartoli and Botel offer an alternative that has demonstrated success. Their ecological view of learning to read emphasizes literacy as a thinking process and the acquisition of literacy through engagement in real reading and writing activities. Their ecological view of reading failure emphasizes understanding the reader's reading behavior in the larger contexts of classroom, school, and community. As one reads this book, whether beginner or expert, the sensibleness of the argument comes through. The question is: Why have we been so slow to recognize that which is so obvious and has been for so long?

Richard Allington
SUNY Albany, New York

Introduction

If we look at reading and learning disability through an ecological lens, some broader areas of interest take on new light and suggest potential for both prevention and remediation of reading and learning problems. In this book we begin to ask questions that explore how the ecological process is working to label more students as disabled. Such questions as the following suggest a need to look beyond the narrow view of a deficient student to a broader understanding of the wider ecology in which the student's problem occurs. The first four questions have been the subject of considerable research. The last three, addressed by the case studies in this book, deserve more attention and study.

- What is the nature of the population that is most often labeled as disabled? Research points to an overrepresentation of poor and minority students.[1]
- What is the nature of the curriculum wherein the student's problem arises? Studies by Goodlad (1984) and Oakes (1985) have documented an overdependence on fragmented subskill methods and materials to the exclusion of whole language learning in meaningful contexts.
- What is the nature of the diagnostic and evaluative techniques that are used to determine the disability of the student? Coles (1978, 1983) has documented the inadequacy of the disability tests; Kamin (1974) and Gould (1981) have demonstrated the cultural bias of supposedly objective measures of intelligence.
- What is the process by which a student comes to be labeled as reading or learning disabled? The social nature of the process of labeling the student, which has very little to do with any biological/neurological deficiency in the student, has been documented.[2]

---

[1]See Rist, 1970; Rivers, 1975; Mercer, 1973; Cummins, 1986; Hobbs, 1975, 1978.
[2]See Rist and Harrell (1982), McDermott (1974), Hobbs (1975, 1978), Mercer (1973), and Bart (1984).

- What is the nature of the interaction between the home and the school in the creation, perpetuation, labeling, and remediation of the student's problem?
- What is the interaction among the teachers, specialists, and administrators in the school system, and what is the impact of this on the student's problem?
- How does the larger community outside the school define and deal with the student and the family? Is this a difficult or hostile environment to which the family or student must make adaptations or adjustments?

In asking these and other questions focusing on the larger ecology of the student's difficulty with reading and learning, we are attempting to widen the lens of inquiry beyond the nature of the individual student. We are suggesting that there may be much to be learned from a closer look at the ecology of the student, and much to be gained from not blaming the victim in the labeling process.

At present, there is much controversy over the causes of problems with reading and learning. The theories about how and why a student becomes disabled in reading and learning are as prolific as the diverse terminology to describe the problem. Over the past several decades, we have seen such terms as word blindness, dyslexia, hyperlexia, minimal brain dysfunction, soft neurological signs, attention-deficit disorders, reading disabled, language impaired, and the term currently in vogue, learning disabled, all of which describe students who essentially are having difficulty in learning to read. In addition to much frustration and concern on the part of specialists, teachers, administrators, and parents, the one thing the students all seem to have in common, regardless of the label, is trouble with reading.

There is very little agreement or conclusive evidence in support of any single theory of causation. Neither neurologists, educators, nor psychologists have been able to substantiate any agreed-upon remedial treatment for the variety of disorders they have attempted to identify and label. Therefore, regardless of the theorized derivation or label for the problem, we will take the broad ecological view of looking at the multiple interacting systems of school, family, and community, for ways to help the student learn to read.

In time, there may be advances in brain research, biochemistry, or cognitive processes that will give us more detailed and conclusive information concerning the causes and cures for specific reading and learning problems of some students. Until that time, we believe we should act on what we presently know to be the observable and documented problems for the largest number of students. Recent reviews of research on disability

(Lipson & Wixson, 1986; Hynd & Hynd, 1984) have concluded that the number of students with actual biological problems is quite small compared with the large number of students diagnosed as having reading and learning disabilities. Other researchers (Coles, 1978; Vellutino, 1987) have stressed the ineffectiveness of remediation geared to specific perceptual defects or deficits.

We believe that the ecological approach developed in this book not only will help in understanding and teaching the growing number of students who are presently experiencing difficulty in reading and learning, but will also be preventative in reducing the number of students who might otherwise suffer future failure. Our approach has several added integrative and ecological benefits that we will detail in Chapter 8. It can

> reduce the fragmentation in the language curriculum
> reduce the isolation of professionals attempting to help the student
> prevent incongruity in the mainstream and remedial language curricula
> provide congruence between curriculum and evaluation
> connect with the wider ecology of the learner.

The ecological framework is also in agreement with recent statements made by neurologists Frank Duffy of Boston Children's Hospital and Richard Restak of Washington, D.C., author of two books on the brain. Duffy (1987) agreed with Restak in asserting that "there is a huge leap from discovering physical abnormalities in the brain to an explanation for educational underachievement." Duffy added a further complication. His findings from dyslexia research suggest a "rather comprehensive abnormality of entire portions of the brain." Thus the notion of specific treatments geared to the functioning of particular parts of the brain (auditory and visual perception, for instance) is suspect at best. We do not deal with biological factors in this book. Those interested in neurological/perceptual research are referred to Hynd and Hynd (1984), and Vellutino (1987).

It appears that, since a number of sensorimotor operations must be coordinated in the brain in order for a person to learn to read, attempts to remediate a problem with reading should be directed at using the whole brain. Thus we are committed to a focus on higher level thinking in our approach to teaching, with lower level subskills and sensorimotor functions attended to in the process. This provides a balanced reading program, which, according to Vellutino (1987), is the best type of remediation for dyslexia or reading disability.

Many years of research have gone into the development of this framework for learning, and many more years have been spent implementing the framework in various forms in a variety of schools. And it is the successes reported by specialists and teachers that have motivated us to write this book. Chapter 5 includes some of the actual applications and descriptions of the approach as used by specialists and teachers presently in the field.

Having witnessed the successes of these excellent, dedicated professionals, we feel that we have cause to celebrate in education today. There continue to be educators who are committed to their own professional growth, and who daily are transforming the educational system to the benefit of their students. Specialists and teachers in growing numbers are taking a broader, ecological view of language learning, and they are finding successful ways to meet the needs of all students regardless of their labels.

As educators ourselves, we have been very much a part of the traditional education scene: teaching and testing subskills of language; devising methods for grouping and separating students from their peers; writing individualized curricula that separate learners from learning, context from content, and content from skills. We have contributed to this fragmentation, so we feel very much a part of the educational system that we seek to change. As we join in this dialogue that has been going on for a long time, we hope that those who presently use a more ecological approach will help us to continue to broaden our vision and deepen our understanding.

Giroux and McLaren (1986) have challenged all of us in education to become "transformative intellectuals" who make knowledge meaningful, critical, and emancipatory in an ongoing struggle for democracy. They cite problems with the new reforms such as lockstep sequencing of materials; competency-based testing for teachers; teacher-proof, prepackaged curricula with management-type pedagogy; accountability schemes; cultural uniformity; and a narrow view of both teaching and learning. We hope that this book will contribute to a broader view, and that it will allow even more educators to become the transformative intellectuals we have already witnessed many others becoming.

Our approach in this book attempts to follow a systems plan for change, as outlined by Watzlawick, Weakland, and Fisch (1974). Their four-step process for meaningful, lasting change includes

1. A clear definition of the problem
2. An investigation of the solutions attempted (problematic solutions often maintain the problem)
3. A clear definition of the change to be achieved (a redefinition of learning and reading ability and disability)

4. A plan for change that is aimed at the attempted solutions and avoids the problem/solution paradox.

As with all attempts at change, this approach will need more thinking, experimenting, and dialogue from many more transformative intellectuals in the field. Only with this collaborative interaction in the continual field testing, revision, and refinement of both theory and practice will we as an educational community make great strides in reducing the number of students labeled as reading and learning disabled. We welcome the opportunity to join with other teachers, specialists, administrators, and researchers in a collaborative effort to understand more about the ecology of reading and learning disability.

Part I
AN ECOLOGICAL WAY
OF LOOKING

Since the mid-1950s, there has been a movement in a variety of fields toward a more ecological view: one that looks at the relationships between organisms and their environment, that is focused on interaction and interdependence, and that sees the whole as greater than the sum of its parts. In the disciplines related to language learning—particularly linguistics, sociolinguistics, education, and psychology—the ecological view has emerged to reshape the way we look at and define language, learning, and the learner. Figure I represents the point of view of the wider ecology of the learner.

Through an ecological lens, the language arts of reading, writing, listening, and speaking are viewed as interrelated and interdependent rather than as separate subjects or composites of skills and subskills to be taught and tested in isolation. Language is viewed as context dependent and learned more meaningfully in whole language activities. This focus on the whole of language is kept in place through an integration of content with skills and an emphasis on higher level thinking.

Likewise, students are viewed as context dependent within the ecology of the classroom, as are the teachers and specialists who shape the learning environment. Students are not viewed as separable from their classrooms, and specialists are not viewed in isolation from the classroom context. In an ecological view, teachers, students, and specialists are integrated into the mainstream classroom to encourage higher level learning for all students.

Taking current research from the fields related to language, we arrive at what we will call an ecological approach to language learning. In reading, for example, the transactions and interactions among the learner, the text, and the social context shape a larger meaning than the text alone. Building a classroom climate in which these relationships can develop is a major thrust of the ecological approach. In the writing processes, the meaning, function, and significance of the whole composition are much greater

FIGURE I.   Wide Ecology of the Learner

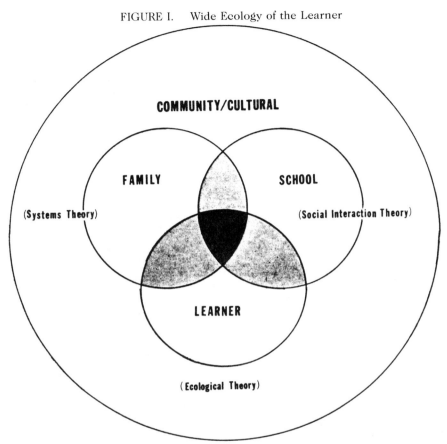

Helping the student to learn involves understanding the multiple interacting dynamics of the interrelated systems in the wider ecology of the learner.

than the sum of its surface features. Thus, the focus is away from subsystems of language and is instead on developing writing processes in interaction with peers as well as the teacher or specialist. Editing, like phonics, is kept in its proper place.

An ecological view of language learning focuses on social interaction variables, interdependencies, and social relationships that shape and give meaning to language learning. Language learning is studied in context by ethnographers and other field study researchers (including researcher/ teachers) rather than being analyzed as the results from decontextualized clinical experiments or tests. In the classroom the specialist and teacher view observation as more valuable than test results in understanding the student's language learning. The specialist and teacher are linked in a collaborative interaction to build a classroom ecology that fosters optimal development of the potential of all students. Together they affirm the value of whole language learning in lieu of the more difficult and abstract learning of decontextualized parts.

The learner is likewise viewed as an interactive and interdependent part of the various systems of school, family, and community. This more ecological view of the learner is evident in descriptive case studies based on contextual, observational data. It is also evident in studies like those included in this book, which go beyond cognition, perception, and biological functioning of students to the multiple interacting systems in which they are embedded: that is, their schools, their families, and their communities. An ecological view reminds us that students have families, family literacy shapes school literacy, and both families and schools are interdependent parts of the community.

To illustrate this view we present two in-depth, longitudinal case studies of middle-grade students who were labeled as learning disabled. Though names of people and places have been changed, the actual observations and stories of these students are nonfictional. The descriptions of their families, schools, and communities are true-life accounts of the problematic solutions that too often result from a more narrow, traditional approach to reading and learning disability.

There are several reasons that we are calling our approach to reading and learning disability an ecological approach. First, we focus on whole language activities and attempt to keep the analysis of parts in proper perspective. Various educators have termed this holistic, whole language, or wholistic—the term we tend to use. Second, we are concerned with the relationship of language to its ecological context. Herein we refer not only to the language text and its meaning context, but also to the larger context of the social/cultural environment that affects a student's language learning. The ecological approach collaboratively links the classroom teacher to the specialist to shape the classroom ecology, and in particular the classroom climate, as it shapes the learning or nonlearning of the student.

Third, we view the sociolinguistic relationships and functions of language use and users as integral to learning. Herein we include relationships of students, peers, teachers, specialists, and parents as well as their purposes and motivation for communication. Fourth, we see our approach as ecological because we attempt to include the wider ecology of the whole learner. To the extent that it is possible within our own limitations, we attempt to widen our lens to include the social, cognitive, and affective world of the student in the contexts of school, home, and community.

And finally, we see this approach as ecological because its purpose is to help specialists and teachers make connections with their own and each other's previous experiences, successes, and knowledge. Many aspects of this approach will only make more explicit what teachers and specialists have known intuitively or have already experimented with in part. We wish to share with those in the field who are already making connections, and provide a framework that will allow them to further integrate learning and link with each other as professionals. A network of professionals established through such connections is the best safeguard against a fragmented, bits-and-pieces approach to learning, which is so easy to fall into.

1
The Paradox
in Reading and Learning Disability:
Has the Solution
Become the Problem?

As teachers and reading and learning disability specialists, we have tended to focus on the immediately apparent reading and learning problems of individual students in our attempts to reduce the illiteracy and failure rates in our schools. Too often our vision has been restricted to solutions for these diagnosable surface level problems as we seek the efficient and effective solutions typical of our modern technological society. We have painstakingly analyzed errors in standardized tests and criterion-referenced tests, such as informal reading inventories; we have used intelligence tests, neurological assessment techniques, psychological evaluations, behavioral assessments, and medical examinations—all in the hope of precisely identifying the student's problem.

Our solutions have followed a similar course, leading us down the road to more and more quantitatively refined methods for identifying the specific problems and pathologies in the reading and learning disabled student. But are we helping more students with their reading and learning problems, or are we testing more now and profiting from it less? Have, in fact, the solutions become the problem?

Seymour Sarason suggests that it is our ways of looking and thinking that need assessment. "If the more things change the more they remain the same, it is because our ways of looking and thinking have not changed" (Sarason, 1971). We have tended to view narrowly students with reading and learning problems as deficit-ridden individuals isolated from their larger ecological contexts of classroom, school, family, and community. And along with this narrow and fragmented definition of the student's problem, we have accepted an equally narrow and fragmented definition of reading and learning, which parallels the test and subtest categories. This not only has maintained the original problem, but has caused additional problems as well.

5

In this chapter we will explore these problematic definitions and solutions that maintain the problem, and we will consider a more ecological and potentially useful way of thinking about students' reading and learning problems. We feel that this broader ecological view not only holds the promise of discovering more valid and useful solutions to reading and learning problems, but it also has the power to avoid the problem/solution paradox and provide a foundation for revitalizing and transforming the quality of life in the classroom.

For the many good, intuitive teachers and specialists who have always thought and taught this way, this approach will not seem so much new as it will be a reaffirmation of their basic beliefs and practice. Our hope is that we can provide theoretical support and additional ideas that will be useful for those educators who already see students and their learning problems in a more ecological way; and that we can present a way of looking, teaching, and evaluating that is exciting and challenging to others who presently have a different view.

DEFINITIONS

Definitions are powerful. As Thomas and Thomas (1928) remind us, "If men define situations as real, they are real in their consequences." A definition of a student as "disabled" may be a social prescription for failure due to a self-fulfilling prophecy. A definition of reading as subskill teaching may create a fragmented, trivialized curriculum with tests to match. Defining evaluation of reading and learning by profiles of performance on subskills in tests may have the consequence of segregating, stigmatizing, and labeling students, while it diminishes the scope, depth, and quality of education offered to the student.

The definition of reading and learning ability and disability that we use shapes and controls not only our teaching practices, but the curriculum and evaluation methods as well. If present teaching and curricular materials in the field are representative of our current definition, we appear to be operating under a definition of reading as fragmented subskill instruction. This definition was called into question by the International Reading Association (IRA) in 1978, the National Council of Teachers of English in 1977, and the Essentials of Education Consortium (comprising 27 national organizations) in 1981. Statements from IRA included:

There is no agreement as to what these subskills are.
There is evidence that mastery of these subskills does not necessarily lead to reading.
There is no agreement as to the hierarchy of these subskills.

Subskill teaching accompanied by the subskill testing common in standardized tests, criterion-referenced tests, and informal reading inventories supposes a definition of reading and teaching that is not supported in current research of linguists, cognitive psychologists, sociolinguists, and other language and education scholars. This fragmented approach supposes that subtests of isolated skills (for example, phonics, punctuation, auditory discrimination, syllabication, and such comprehension skills as finding the main idea) add up to the totality of reading. More recent research calls into question this notion of isolated skills teaching and testing as well as the whole notion of what reading is about. The new definition that is emerging views reading as a socio-psycholinguistic process: a social, constructive, strategic, transactional process rooted in social interaction and prior experiences, one that is dependent on meaningful purpose and context, and is orchestrated in a complex and individual way by each reader.

An Ecological Definition

Clearly, what is needed is an integrated, ecological definition of reading and learning. Mellon (1981) suggests that we err in thinking that development of language skills is merely a matter of more drills and practice, more memorization or more time spent with the latest reading kit or grammar workbook. He describes instead a definition put forth by linguists and cognitive psychologists: a complex network of unconscious knowledge within the mind that informs language uses—reading, writing, and speaking—and makes them possible. Language scholars tell us that five-year-old students come to school with innate language ability and tremendous potential as language learners. They have a large vocabulary, they can communicate for their own purposes, they have control of the language of their communities, and they can comprehend and construct meaning.

Research on the metacognitive aspects of reading and learning (A. Brown, 1982) has made us aware of the constructive, strategic, problem-solving aspects of the process. Through interactive reading protocols (students thinking aloud while they read), we have learned more about what the reader actually does and thinks while reading. And in this way we come closer to an understanding of the active mind of the individual student.

Social interaction research (Vygotsky, 1962) suggests that language learning is a social as well as a cognitive process. Language learning always has a context: neighborhood, community, school, classroom, home, clinic. And within that context are the social relationships that make language learning meaningful. Children do not learn to communicate in isolation—they learn from adults and peers in their environments. This social interaction theory adds a wider dimension to our definition by looking beyond the cognitive processes of the individual student to the interactions between that student and others who influence the learning and nonlearning of the student.

Ecological theory suggests that many factors work together and are interrelated in the learning process of the student and that learning to read involves orchestrating all of these aspects of meaning making. It suggests that we need to look beyond the level of the individual toward the wider focus on the total ecology or ecosystem of the student. An ecological focus goes beyond the linear cause-and-effect blaming of student, family, or school for the student's problems with reading and learning. Instead of placing blame, the search is for a deeper understanding of how all of the systems of school, family, and community work together in the learning or nonlearning of the student.

The implications that flow from the sort of definition we are describing suggest quite a different role for teachers than that imposed by basal reading workbooks, kits, and packaged programs. It suggests a role of facilitator, collaborator, and mediator rather than subskill instructor. It implies teaching that begins with whole language experiences, encourages the student's discovery of the system within language, and facilitates lifelong learning. It suggests a focus beyond tests and labels for the student: a focus that both encourages and necessitates the collaboration of parents, teachers, and specialists in a deeper understanding of the student's problems with meaning making. Defined in this way, language learning suggests a shift of thinking from notions of failures, incompetence, and disabilities to a need for more mediated learning or leading ahead toward the student's potential. In the following section we will explore the roots of this new definition and briefly describe some of the theory and research that we have found to be important in the development of our definition of reading and learning.

Roots of the New Definition

Cognitive/metacognitive roots

Cognitive research in the past decade on reading and learning has given us a picture of the rich variety of perceptual, constructive, reconstructive, and memory skills that are part of the reading process. Readers actively construct meaning with the help of the author's words but using their own schema. Rumelhart (1980) calls these units of stored and organized world knowledge the "building blocks of cognition," because schema theory assumes that comprehension proceeds through the interaction of schema and text.

Recent metacognitive research has attempted to apply this knowledge of cognitive processes to the study of the reader's own awareness of the learning process. A. Brown (1982) includes both knowledge of one's own thinking and learning, and self-regulatory mechanisms (self-monitoring, self-correcting, using meaning cues) in her description of metacognitive aspects of reading comprehension. Learning to learn about reading includes reflection on one's own cognitive processes in the acquisition, retention, and retrieval of information from the text, as well as the strategies one uses to accomplish the task of making meaning from the text. It is, in short, knowing what one is doing when reading.

What do readers do when reading? Cognitive and metacognitive research informs us that readers are activating their own schemata, becoming engaged with and transacting with the author and text, sustaining doubt long enough to allow inquiry, and a host of other active, meaning-construction mental processes involving the text, the task, the readers, and their strategies. A reading protocol study of three middle-grade boys labeled as learning disabled (Bartoli, 1983) found these students to be self-monitoring, making substitutions, revising, reading ahead, reasoning, using context clues, elaborating, and trying phonetic analysis. In short, they were doing all of the things that "good" readers are supposed to do.

Researchers using a Piagetian developmental model focus their research on these cognitive processes taking place within the mind of the individual reader. Psychological, linguistic, and neurological processes are explored clinically; and an attempt is made to isolate the various cognitive parts and pieces of the comprehension process for a fuller understanding of what one is doing while reading. This approach is typical of American cognitive psychological and educational research in general. The focus remains on the mental processes of the individual student removed from the contexts in which those processes were developed.

A more interactive and interactional view is taken by Vygotsky (1962, 1978) and Luria (1979), who have criticized this model of mind, learning, and reading because of its failure to capture the full range of human experience. They describe the individually oriented model as a static, linear, stage developmental idealization that does not reflect human nature, which they describe as dynamic, interactive, and transformational. What they maintain is missing from the cognitive models are the vital social interactions that mediate between learner, task, and text and that provide models for the strategy development of the reader.

Social interaction roots

Vygotsky's research suggests that the higher psychological processes (cognition, metacognition) can be acquired only through interaction with other human beings. Comprehension depends on social interaction to mediate in the creation of meaning. Thus the focus of research for Vygotsky is the socio-historical relationships that give shape to the cognitive development of the student.

Researchers and teachers using the social interaction model of reading explore the student's activity in the classroom, among peers, in the family, and in the community to understand language learning. The mental processes of thinking, learning, and reading are studied as part of the student's activity and environment because they would make incomplete sense if seen as separate from the whole student. These mental processes are both formed and studied in the student's social activities, and the researcher/teacher seeks to uncover the interactive relationships that influence the process of language development.

Vygotsky's fundamental hypothesis is that the higher mental functions are socially formed and culturally transmitted. He suggests that a student's cognitive development is shaped by this social and historical interaction to the extent that "if one changes the tools of thinking available to a student, his mind will have a radically different structure" (Vygotsky, 1978). It is through language and words that students learn to think and make meaning in their worlds. And since meaning is determined by social interaction in the student's own particular historical and social context—since words are "shaped, limited, or expanded through individual and collective experience"—language learning is defined as a profoundly social process.

Vygotsky's concept of the "zone of proximal development" is particularly important in defining the student's potential for language learning. He describes this zone as the distance between the actual development level, as determined by independent problem solving, and the level of potential development. The zone of proximal development includes those mental processes that are currently in a state of formation, and it was Vygotsky's position that the state of a student's mental development could be determined only by taking both the present development level and the zone of proximal development into account. Learning, in his view, must lead development.

Herein we see the dynamic, interactive nature of Vygotsky's theory. Rather than determining a student's development by static tests (yesterday's development), he proposes focusing on learning that is in advance of development. Both Vygotsky and Luria have aptly criticized reductionist research that concentrates on analyzing test instrument results, abstracts cognition from the social context in which it develops, and looks at "fossilized behavior" that is a product of a previous developmental process. Their challenge to teachers, specialists, and researchers is to move away from a registering science that creates stationary categories, ignores motives and meaning, and freezes potential through instruments and tests, and instead to move toward a science of understanding, intervention, and change.

P. Johnson (1985) likewise has criticized current explanations of reading and learning difficulty that focus on "the level of operations, devoid of context, goals, motives, or history." He has also spoken of the need to integrate the context of reading with mental operations: "Until we can integrate the depth of human feeling and thinking into our understanding of reading difficulties, we will have only a shadow of an explanation of the problem and ill-directed attempts at solutions" (1985).

Ecological systems roots

An ecological view of reading and learning disability looks beyond both the level of the individual student in isolation from context and the level of interactions within separate contexts, to the combined contexts or systems of school, family, and community in which the student functions—what we will refer to as the student's ecosystem. The goal is knowledge and understanding of the interdependence of these systems—to understand how they all fit and are connected, how they are interrelated and interactive in the ecology of the student.

During the 1960s and 1970s, there was an increased concern for and awareness of the relationship between physical and social environments in human development. Concern with environmental factors was not new, but the use of ecology in human development was. Using the field biology definition of ecology, the focus in this research shifted from the individual alone to the individual plus the environment and the reciprocal interactions between them.[1] Rather than negating or ignoring the dynamic character of human development with static categories, labels, and decontextualized data, these researchers insisted that understanding the system and its multiple interactions was equally important to understanding the individual.

Family systems research and the family therapy movement have paralleled the ecological movement. Haley's (1981) comparison of the "past science of man" (humans studied in isolation, focusing on the individual's nature) and systems theory (humans studied in the context of relationships they create and inhabit, focusing on systemic patterns) provides a good explanation of the value of a systems lens for understanding students' learning problems. He describes the systems lens shift away from assuming

---

[1]See Bronfenbrenner (1979); Hobbs (1978); Rhodes (1967); Bateson (1972); and Kuriloff (1973).

that the "cause" of a symptom (such as reading disability) resides within the student, toward a focus on the context or ecosystem of the student. Family systems thinkers define symptoms as responsive behavior to a particular context, suggesting that change cannot occur unless the context of a relationship in which the student lives also changes.

An ecological view of reading and learning would allow us to see beyond the linear thinking of the present ill-directed solutions based on shadowy explanations that blame the student (neurological dysfunction, perceptual deficit, heredity, environment), the family (single parent family, working mother, poor, black, Hispanic, poor attitude toward education), or the school (incompetent teachers, not enough of the basics, not enough special classes/teachers). It would also bring us closer to real human feelings, perceptions, and understanding of the student in context.

We need an ecological definition for reading and learning that avoids the fragmentation of language; of skills from real language events; of teachers, specialists, and parents from each other; and of students from their ecosystems. But in the best interests of students with learning problems, we have created decontextualized language programs, isolated both professions and professionals, and isolated and labeled students. We have separated students from their peers as we place them in special classes and high, middle, and low groupings within classes; and we have separated ourselves as professionals from each other and from the families of the students whom we wish to help. In short, we have separated and isolated ourselves from our best sources of deeper understanding.

In the following section we will take a closer look at the solutions that we have created, which, in fact, have maintained the problem of reading and learning disability. When "the more things change, the more they remain the same," we have an example of what systems theorists call first-order change (Watzlawick, Weakland & Fisch, 1974). This type of change essentially leaves the school system intact and preserves the status quo.

SOLUTIONS MAINTAINING THE PROBLEM

Clearly we have in reading and learning disability a first-order example of "more of the same," which has prevented a much needed transformation (second-order change) of the educational system. We change textbooks and workbooks, we change testing companies, we change labels for failing students and special classes, we change from whole word emphasis to phonics emphasis and back again, we add individual learning centers and computers—but essentially we are doing more of the same. We are continuing to fragment the teaching and testing of reading into isolated subskills whose definition and hierarchy have been questioned by the International Reading Association, the National Council of Teachers of English, the Essentials of Education Consortium, and the best of current research in language and learning.

Furthermore, we continue to group and label students according to how well they "master" these elusive subskills, and we continue to test the fragments we are teaching as if mastery of these pieces of language indicates competence in reading and learning. Our solution to the problem of improving education in reading and learning has indeed become the problem.

Three major problematic solutions to improving reading and learning deserve particular attention: testing as an evaluative solution; fragmented, subskill-oriented curricula as the accompanying pedagogical solution; and special remedial programs as organizational solutions to the problems (created by the first two "solutions").

Firm, Reliable Measures of Trivia

Subskill scores on standardized tests and criterion-referenced tests, such as informal reading inventories, basal end-of-unit tests, and minimal competency tests, have been offered as scientific, objective, egalitarian solutions for the ills of education. Yet such subtests have often wreaked disaster on the curriculum, fragmenting and trivializing it, and on the teachers and students by demoralizing and stigmatizing them.

We have in education a paradox: We have spent many decades and incredible sums "advancing" our reading curriculum to the point of triviality and fragmentation. In our sincere desire to advance, we have in fact gone backwards in terms of our teaching and testing practices—all in the name of science, equality, and objectivity. In 1975, Williams estimated that in an American school district of 10,000 students, nearly $150,000 was spent on standardized testing that was viewed by the teachers as irrelevant, by the administrators as less than useful, by researchers as unreliable for individual diagnosis, and by the students as frustrating and stigmatizing. Furthermore, our language curriculum is shaped by such testing, despite current research that points to the vital importance of a more integrated, whole language curriculum for optimal learning.

But beyond the fact that the solution has become the problem is the irony that the original problem was in fact misinterpreted—what was thought to be the problem was not the problem at all. Our students' basic skills, which standardized and minimal competency tests evaluate, have not been declining (even though we think these skills can be learned more efficiently through more integrated approaches). It is their higher level thinking that is in danger of extinction. The solution—more basic subskill testing and establishing minimums—is an absurd paradox.

The Fragmented Curriculum

The fragmented, subskills-oriented curriculum is a problem for several reasons, the most obvious of which is that it deprives students of opportunities to engage in higher level critical thinking, which they need for survival in a complex society. Instead, it substitutes preparation-for-the-test skills, which they do not need (or would not need were it not for the equally fragmented tests). A less obvious problem with a fragmented curriculum is that it fragments work tasks and separates action from introspection, while it negates individual responsibility, self-direction, and ownership. Instead of dynamic meaning-making transactions with texts, a fragmented subskills-oriented curriculum substitutes decontextualized parts and pieces of language, which may frustrate and bore the student. The reading task is made more difficult because words are abstracted and separated from the larger context that gives them meaning.

Many reading and learning disability programs are mechanistically individualized, denying the need for interactive meaning making with real texts and people. In addition, their prepackaged, prescribed procedures eliminate the need for self-direction and individual autonomy of thought and action, robbing both the student and the teacher. Critics such as Apple (1980) and Bart (1984) have described the way these standardized and individualized programs fragment the learning process, sort students, de-skill teachers, trivialize teacher autonomy, and isolate teachers to subordinate positions.

Teachers and specialists are too often relegated to a lower-echelon managerial role that precludes their judgment about student needs and abilities, and substitutes behavior control to keep the system running smoothly. Even the control exercised by the teacher is largely predetermined by the standardized curricular materials. Thus critics of current disability programs see the teacher becoming less a teacher and more a technician. Furthermore, since teachers' knowledge becomes irrelevant to meeting their daily work demands, such programs foster teacher de-professionalism, isolation, and alienation.

A further problem with the traditional subskill curriculum is the lack of a sound theoretical base on which to build a valid framework for language learning. This, of course, is a problem for all learners and teachers. The absence of a valid theoretical framework to support and improve language learning results in the problematic solutions of fragmentation and trivial pursuits, which we have just described.

The ecological approach builds on the critical experiences framework, which is supported by the knowledge and experience of 27 national organizations (see Chapter 5). Centering on experiences that are critical for language learning, this approach proposes that students will become more skillful learners by both using and studying language. When language is taught as a series of discrete subskills, it is decontextualized and removed from its ecology. But viewed as part of the larger ecology of language learning, such skills can be seen as subsystems that are inextricably related to their context.

A final problem with the traditional language curriculum is the incongruity between the classroom and remedial programs. This incongruity is a particular problem for those who are labeled as disabled. The learning task is further complicated by two separate, possibly conflicting (but certainly not interactive or mutually supportive) programs. Allington and Shake (1986) argue that remedial programs in reading have lost sight of the original goal of improving classroom reading performance.

Labels and Segregation

The third solution that has become part of the problem is the labeling and segregating of those students who do poorly in the tests and/or who resist the fragmented instruction of the classroom. Though the best research tells us that integrated whole language experiences are vital to growth as a reader and writer, we say through our actual practice of teaching and evaluation:

> Though you need whole language experiences, we will teach and test you on disconnected bits of language (thereby suggesting that the parts are more important than the whole). We will spend more time on these parts (spelling, phonics, punctuation) to prepare you for the tests, thereby robbing you of time for integrated language learning. Furthermore, if you fail the tests (and thereby signal your frustration with this fragmented way of teaching and testing), we will give you more of the same.

Or politically we say:

> Since we are a democratic country, we will educate all students equally. To do this we will test, track, and label so that quite differ

ent kinds of educational opportunities are open to some and not to others. Furthermore, our labels will tell us who cannot learn equally, so we will not frustrate them by expecting them to learn well.

Who is labeled unfit, disabled, or incompetent in our schools? Various researchers (see Hobbs, 1975, 1978; Cummins, 1986; Thomas, 1981; Mercer, 1973; and Rist, 1970) have viewed special education and disability labeling as a sorting process for regular education and society: an institutional practice for getting rid of those who do not fit society's norms for normal, fit, and competent. They suggest that we as a society have little tolerance for individuality, variability, and deviation from the norm of white, middle-class, Anglo-American. Thus they see labeling arising from and perpetuating the values of the cultural majority, protecting them from the anxiety of contact with those who do not fit the norms, and separating the "unfit" who pose a threat to the status quo or the equilibrium of the system.

The overrepresentation of minorities and lower-class students in special education as a result of tests that are biased in favor of mainstream cultural values and behavior has been well documented (see Mercer, 1973; Cummins, 1986; Rivers, 1975; Rowitz & Gunn, 1984). In a Riverside, California study, there were 300% more Mexican-Americans and 50% more blacks identified as mentally retarded as would be expected from their respective proportions in the community, but there were 40% fewer whites than would be expected. In the San Francisco schools, black students constituted only 28% of the student population, but 53% of those in mentally handicapped classes.

Researchers in the ethnographic tradition (notably Rist, 1970; McDermott, 1974; and Ogbu, 1980) have criticized the school and cultural systems for their caste-like grouping and labeling processes, which they feel maintain and perpetuate the reading problems of minority students. They suggest that students of lower social status suffer a stigmatization outside their own choice or will: that they do not come to school disadvantaged—rather, they leave that way.

Other critics describe labeling as social control that defines normality in terms of conformity. They say that the pseudo-medical and scientific flavor of such labels as learning disabled, hyperkinetic, or minimal brain dysfunction allows them to serve as justification for institutional management and control of students (Schrag & Divoky, 1975; Hobbs, 1975). As a result, they feel the rights of students to be slightly different or to exhibit nontypical behavior are rapidly disappearing.

One wonders if there is, in fact, a lesson to be learned from the labeled: Are they the messengers of the fallacy of our curriculum, the poverty of our definition of reading and learning, and the deficiency of our evaluation techniques?

A PLAN FOR CHANGE

The ecological definition of reading recognizes that language is innately scheduled within the mind of the student; views students as socially interactive, constructive, strategic, and dynamically embedded in their ecosystems; and establishes the role of the teacher as facilitator, mediator, and collaborator with students in their own learning. From the firmer foundation provided by this broader ecological definition, we can begin to build a plan for change of the second order, transformation type rather than the first-order, more-of-the-same variety.

The change to be achieved begins with a change in our way of thinking. We are accustomed to thinking of meaning in language as something inherent in texts: something that must be decoded out, precisely replicated, and dissected for examination. This static, mechanistic view contrasts sharply with the dynamic social interactional view of meaning making in our new definition. In the new view, meaning results from the reader's transactions with the text and the context. It is a social process occurring in interaction with the author, wherein the student "learns to mean" in interaction with others in the environment. The words "come alive in the process of human intercourse" (Rosenblatt, 1980; Halliday, 1978).

Along with a static, fragmented definition of language as a product to be packaged and delivered, we have accepted a view of the student as an isolated, individual mechanism with interchangeable parts occasionally in need of repair by our efficient production line. Our view of reading and learning disability essentially blames the victim. For too long we have espoused this behavioristic medical model in education, assuming that disabled readers have defective parts whose deficits can be diagnosed scientifically and repaired mechanically.

Parents have been sold the same bill of goods. Hence the mobiles over the cribs, over the changing table, over the bassinet, and hanging from the ceiling to stimulate the baby. Also the packaged phonics kits for 18-month-olds and the racks of preschool skills workbooks polluting department stores across the nation. As parents we are told that what is important to our children's learning is artificial stimulation, quality time, progressive day care, and academically accelerated nursery schools, rather than the personal, interactive, mediating, and meaningful relationships we can build with our children.

If there is an illiteracy problem in our nation, and if more students are becoming disabled readers and learners, it may be a sign that separating child from parent, teacher from student, specialist from teacher, and student from student is not a successful approach. Learning and meaning making demand social interaction. They demand leading students ahead through personal mediation in a meaningful context. They demand caring human beings who personally interact with students to encourage their growth toward their potential. That vital human resource cannot be replaced by standardized test teaching, subskills workbooks, computers and cassette tapes, programmed learning kits, individualized learning centers, special disability classes, academically oriented day care centers, or intellectually stimulating nursery schools.

Part of the problem (and the reason things have not changed) is our way of looking at individuals as the source of the problem—as the site of pathology or deprivation—rather than in the contexts of their ecology. We are not accustomed or trained to look at the interacting systems of school, family, and culture for the source of our problems. Thus we are caught in a game without end, the paradox of our solutions becoming the problem, a stuck system that lacks the power for transformation to second-order change.

Sarason hopefully reminds us that "if at least part of the problem has been a consequence of the ways we have been thinking, one is not justified in concluding that we are dealing with a hopeless situation" (1971). We as teachers, specialists, and parents have been led to think that there is a better substitute for our personal talking and reading with our students. We have been duped into spending money and precious time on workbooks, kits, skills exercises, and machines (technology's answer), to the neglect of the personal human interaction and collaborative search for meaning that are fundamental to reading and learning. Our schools have been led to believe that there is a technological substitute for good, wholistic teaching and for the perceptive, sensitive observations of concerned teachers and specialists in evaluation of the student's learning.

It is possible, however, to define reading and language learning in an ecological way, just as it is possible to relate to our fellow human beings in a more ecological way. One can imagine, for instance, an individualized education program (IEP), developed through the collaborative efforts of the teacher, specialist, parent, and student, that integrates skills and content in whole language experiences and is orchestrated through the combined efforts of both the school and the family. The IEP would include those powerful experiences that allow the student to think divergently and creatively, to process a wide variety of information, to create meaningful texts, to discover and use strategies for reading, and to share ideas with others. The student would read self-selected books, write on self-selected topics, talk with others about books, ideas, and each other's writing topics, share and expand experiences, and respond individually to texts, but would still be linked to the community of learners in the class. Thus, the learning program would be based on a more integrated, ecological definition of reading and learning.

An ecological approach to reading and learning disability can lift us out of the futility and frustration of the problem/solution paradox. In the following chapters we will further describe the ecological systems approach to reading and learning disability. We begin Chapter 2 by further defining and tracing the history of the ecological view. We then describe the various aspects of ecological theory and research that are most significant for our approach to reading and learning disability. In Chapter 3, we explore the interrelationships of the systems of school, family, and community in reading and learning disability. Two longitudinal case study examples illustrate these important dynamics in each of the various systems of the student's ecology.

2

An Ecological Systems View

The new ecological way of looking at language ability and disability can perhaps best be illustrated by comparing this view with the more narrow view common in our traditional school systems. As we have illustrated in Chapter 1, this reductionist and fragmented view leads to a subskill approach to reading, to isolation of teachers and specialists, to fossilized labels that freeze potential, to separation of parents from schools, and to a false separation of cognition from social interaction, motivation, and feelings. And ultimately this narrow view leads to the paradox of the solutions becoming the problem. Language, learning, and people are removed from meaningful context—from their larger ecological whole. The result is isolation and fragmentation throughout all systems, instead of the integration and unity of word and world that is vital for the meaning making of the student.

A further problem results from the narrow view. Our perceptions are shaped by our way of looking, and a fragmented view not only reduces our capacity for deeper understanding of the student, but it limits the way that we view that student's potential and ability. As the case studies to follow will illustrate, the perceptions of school personnel were a powerful influence on the labeling process of both students. These perceptions were the result of the school system's way of looking—not of uncaring professionals. The very fact that these students became tragedies of the system despite the best intentions of concerned teachers, specialists, and principals illustrates the power of perceptions as shaped by a narrow, fragmented view.

The important question is, What would happen if we took the larger ecological systems view? And, of course, What exactly do we mean by an ecological view?

THE EMERGENCE OF THE ECOLOGICAL SYSTEMS VIEW

Systems theory emerged in the 1950s and 1960s along with ecological theory as an alternative to the individually oriented theories typical of twentieth-century psychology. But Freudian and Piagetian theories maintained the lead in research focusing on individual psychosis and cognitive development, and educational research focused similarly on individual intellectual achievement. Our twentieth-century focus on the individual in the social and psychological sciences and education has, until the past several decades, caused us to neglect the dynamic interactive relationships between individuals and the various contexts in which they are embedded.

Education followed the lead of the social sciences in basing its theories on individual achievement, intelligence, personality characteristics, and cognitive capacity. We began thinking about human ecology, with its focus on the interrelationships between humans and the environment, and the importance of the environment in human development 30 years ago. That was paralleled by the development of the family therapy movement, which focused on the relationships within the family as they contributed to human development. Even so, the focus on individual cognition and behavior still dominates the research field.

During the 1960s and 1970s there was an increased concern about and awareness of the relationship between physical and social environments in human development. Concern about environmental factors was not new, but the idea of ecology in human development was. Using the field biology definition of ecology, the focus in this research shifted from the individual alone to the individual plus the environment and the reciprocal interactions between them. Causes of emotional disturbance, for instance, were attributed to complex and differential interactions within and among biological, psychological, and social phenomena. Ecologically oriented psychologists like Bronfenbrenner (1979), Hobbs (1978), and Rhodes (1967) sought knowledge of the way a person was functioning in the "maintenance of progressive equilibrium" or to balance the system. Rather than negating the dynamic character of developmental processes with static categories, labels, and data stripped of context, they maintained that understanding the system and its multiple interactions was equally important to understanding the individual.

Systems thinkers saw the student as an integral, interactive part of larger systems (family, school, community/culture) and believed the student's actions could not be fully understood apart from those contexts. A person was less an independent island, and more an interactive part of dynamic systems that helped shape development and learning. Both ecological theory and systems theory looked beyond the individual in isolation to the individual as a part of larger systems that both interact with and give shape to the developing human being.

Haley (1981) compared this shift in scientific thought with that of the seventeenth-century scientific world, when the physical laws of the universe (for example, the sun revolving around the earth) were questioned.

There were many who rejected such a radical break with traditional belief and science, and many who continued to consider Copernicus quite mad and blasphemous. The Church feared that its God-centered universe was being questioned, and few scientists were enthusiastic about abandoning their lifelong knowledge base.

So it was (and is) with the shift from linear cause-and-effect, quantitatively precise, elegantly staged laboratory experiments. Few researchers relished the attack on their lifelong beliefs and practices, and few wanted to open the contextual, ecological Pandora's box that threw out control, predictability, quantification, and "pure" research. And even after 30 years of research confirming the vital importance of the ecological context in all human development and behavior, there are those who insist that "Copernican" ecologists and systems researchers are renegades. P. Johnson noted in 1985 that *Reading Research Quarterly* had yet to publish an ecological case study approach to reading problems.

But, as Haley (1981) recounted, physical scientists of the seventeenth century eventually had to agree that the abundant evidence proved that the earth did, in fact, revolve around the sun rather than the other way around. So he saw a parallel shift coming in basic beliefs about the understanding of humanity. More people are coming to see the student as a part of multiple interacting systems. They are resisting the reductionist notions of cause-and-effect linear development, just as they are resisting the dualistic tendency to separate students' cognition from their equally important motivation, perception, and feelings. This more wholistic research direction avoids fragmenting the student into parts and pieces that have no meaning—that are stripped of their integration in both the student and the context. Vygotsky's social interaction research follows in this same direction, focusing on meaning in context and the broader view of the student's ecosystem. The student's meaning making in language is seen as dynamically interactive in the school system and family system from which it stems.

Lessons from Bateson's Group

The Batesonian systems theory (toward which we lean) differs from early systems theory in several significant ways. Early systems theory situated persons in the context of multiple interacting systems, and thus was a fuller view of human beings than are the dominant context-stripping theories focusing on the individual (Freudian and Piagetian psychology, for instance). But it had some serious flaws that still allowed a cause-and-effect, linear kind of thinking, and it was not based on a dynamic view of evolution. Bateson's group, which included Jackson, Haley, Satir, Watzlawick, Weakland, Beavin, and Fisch, sought to go beyond these limitations by taking an interactional view of human communication.

Early systems theory used the cybernetic machine model to illustrate the equilibrium maintaining functioning of systems. An analogy to this model is the home thermostat, which functions to maintain a certain steady state through controlling the fluctuating temperature in the house. It is an error-activated model which controls deviation from the norm. This model allowed a view that went beyond the individual to the operation of the system as it functioned to maintain equilibrium or homeostasis. But it still permitted the mechanical linear thinking of blaming the parents or the family, for instance, for the student's problem or symptom rather than understanding the interactive process. Furthermore, the steady state of homeostasis (illustrated by the thermostat function of error-activated correction of the heat level) was thought to be the desired state for the family; it was the goal toward which family therapists strove.

Bateson's group embraced a more complex model that took into consideration new discoveries in both physical and biological sciences. A new challenge to the second law of thermodynamics viewed deviance from the norm as an alternate "natural" state along with equilibrium or homeostasis. Deviation could be viewed as a positive element in change and an equally "natural" state. In biological science newer evolutionary research was rejecting the idea of a steady, gradual, upward progression and was viewing the evolutionary process as one of radical transformations or shifts and recursive loops. New forms were found to arise in radical shifts—a kind of punctuated equilibrium—rather than in slow, steady, gradual upward progressions. This suggested to systems thinkers a new view of deviation. It could be a positive sign of preparation for a new growth stage. The research also brought a new view of homeostasis as not always the desired end point. Status quo maintenance could actually prevent needed change.

This, of course, is the significant point for our understanding of systems dynamics in reading and learning disability and for a deeper meaning to "the more things change, the more they remain the same." This transformation direction parallels Vygotsky's focus away from "yesterday's development" and "fossilized" tests of current behavior toward an assessment of the unrealized potential of the student.

To these changes in early systems theory Bateson added his aversion to three "villains":

1. Linear thinking—which assumes cause and effect and ends up placing blame;
2. Dualism—which artificially separates cognition from affect and emotions;

3. Chopping up the ecology—which allows for fragmentation (parts studied separately from the whole) and meaningless research.

It is clear that these villains are alive and well in our traditional education system.

Gregory Bateson's (1972) example of the double-binding message perceived by the schizophrenic reveals yet another interdependent and interactional adaptation. Bateson observed the interaction between hospitalized patients and their mothers, and found that otherwise improved patients would suffer a relapse of schizophrenia following family visits. Looking more closely at the process, he found that the mother would react coldly to the patient, yet give a contradictory verbal message that demanded a loving response from the patient. The patient was thus caught in a double bind—feeling rejected by the nonverbal coldness, yet verbally admonished to be more loving. The patient was (nonverbally) damned if he was more loving and (verbally) damned if he wasn't. Bateson and his associates suggested that this type of double-binding communication process was integral in the development of schizophrenia.

How does this relate to reading and learning disability? These widely divergent examples illustrate the ecological processes of adaptation and adjustment (or maladjustment) of organisms within an ecosystem. All living organisms are interrelated and interdependent, they exist in interactive ecosystems, and they can only partially be understood (and more often misunderstood) outside of their ecological contexts. Thus, if we are to understand the complexities of students' learning, it is important that we look at the interactive and interrelated systems of the school, family, and community. In this way, we will not (1) unwittingly unbalance the system even more or (2) contribute to a dysfunctional status-quo-maintaining equilibrium. Our many problematic solutions are testimony to our facility in this process.

Lessons from the Reading/Learning Disabled

In 1950, Gates stated that it was unfortunate that there was an increase in the number of reading specialists, because that might signal a corresponding increase in the population of students who would be so labeled. Preston (1950) made a similar prediction, and in fact the populations of students labeled as reading/learning disabled have dramatically increased over the past several decades. Many interrelated factors contributed to this increase, of course, beyond a simple increase in the number of specialists. But the fact that reading and learning disability was defined as a problem inherent in the student and remediable only through techniques owned by the specialist was not insignificant.

Consider the repercussions of only this in the case of Sunny, whom you will meet in Chapter 3. Her teachers assumed that she was disabled and thus maintained rather low expectations for her. Both her teachers and her parents felt that they were not equipped to deal adequately with her problem, so they tended to leave it in the hands of the specialist. The specialist, overrun with many such seemingly unsolvable problems, tried unsuccessfully to get more help from the parents and the teachers (who felt they were not trained to deal with the problem). Amidst these interactions, the relationships among the specialist, parents, teachers, and student became tense and strained. The specialist experienced more burnout, the student's expectations for herself dropped to match those of her teachers, the parents appeared more ineffectual as they became more frustrated, and the school continued to define the family as incompetent and uninterested. The way the problem was defined and the specialized solution were powerful dynamics in this student's ecosystem.

In any ecosystem there is no simple cause-and-effect relationship. All parts of the system are interrelated and interdependent. If we try to look at school and family systems in an ecological way as we attempt to understand more about reading and learning disability, some broader areas of interest take on a new light and suggest potential avenues for more effective remediation and prevention of reading and learning problems.

APPLICATION OF THE NEW VIEW

Since the environment in which the student is labeled is the school, we will take a closer look at the various subsystems of that system. We know from previous research that the language arts curriculum has suffered from fragmentation and trivialization. We know that there is an increase in the isolation of skills from their meaningful contexts, the isolation of labeled students from their peers, and the isolation of professionals in the school from each other. And we know that when a student is labeled as learning or reading disabled, there is a dramatic increase in this fragmentation and isolation.

Major social forces have shaped the evaluative system of the school, and these same forces operate to keep the status quo of the school system, particularly with respect to who is labeled as competent and incompetent. When these evaluative and diagnostic tools shape the future of students in immeasurable and irreversible ways, it is important to take a closer look at the process by which these tools came into being and the societal forces that keep them in operation.

Any professional in education can give ample testimony to the over-abundant uses and misuses of tests. Pressures from the accountability movement, along with the parental press for excellence, drive school systems to teach to the tests, thus reducing and further fragmenting the curriculum and instruction. When we add to this the low reliability and the invalidity of these measures, we get a glimpse of the multiple dynamics of yet another part of the student's ecosystem as it interacts with learning.

The research implications and parallels for study of both family and school systems that flow from this ecological systems theory will be illustrated in Chapter 3 through the study of two students with reading problems. The case study examples are the result of three years of observation in the contexts of the home, school, and community of two students between the ages of nine and twelve years, labeled as learning disabled (Bartoli, 1986b). These cases illustrate the way perceptions were shaped by a narrow, fragmented view—the school and community system's way of looking—and the resultant loss of potential of both students. They also illustrate the fragmentation and isolation that pervade all systems in the ecology of each student, underscoring the vital need for a broader, integrative approach to reading and learning disability. Our approach to the study of these students considers the following: the school/family parallels in the definition of the problem, the research focus, the process or functioning of the problem, the aim or goal of research, and the implications for remediation.

Definition of the Problem

In our ecological systems (ecosystems) approach, the family system is defined as an interactive whole, the sum of which is greater than the individual parts. The student is defined as an integral part of the organized family system, which has its own rules and functioning. The student affects and is affected by the family system in a reciprocal manner. Relationships are maintained in accordance with family rules, and behavior is a function of those dynamic relationships. The student's problem is also defined in relation to these important family dynamics. This view rejects defining the family as a collection of individual roles, just as it rejects the notion of individual pathology independent of the system.

The school system likewise is seen as a dynamic interactive system in which the student is an interconnected part. In the school, the student is seen as an interactive part of the classroom system and the larger school culture. Behavior is a function of the social relationships and communication within and among the subsystems (for example, classroom, specialist, administration) of the school. Language learning in the school system is defined as a broader meaning-making activity embedded in the curriculum, rejecting the notion of reading as a collection of isolated subskills (much as the family systems theory rejects fragmenting the family into a set of isolated roles).

Language learning is understood as beginning in the family system in meaningful interaction with parents and other family members. This interactional base of communication is carried into the school system, where learning includes the social interaction within that system as well as the interrelationships between the family and school systems. The student develops and learns not in discrete, progressive stages, but rather in recursive loops punctuated by leaps to new levels of development. It is not a steady, linear ascension. A student may appear to be "stuck" at one level before making the shift to a new transformation (the leap to automaticity in reading, for example).

Rather than viewing reading below grade level as a deficiency in the student, an ecosystem approach might define the student as in transition to a new level. This deviation from the norm could be a signal of difficulty in the school or family system, or a need for mediation with social relationships within the school or family system or between the two systems. What might have been termed deviance in an individual paradigm could be viewed positively in a systems paradigm as a signal of needed change.

Overall, the problem of the student's reading difficulty is defined as one that is contextually bound, dependent on social interaction within the system, and embedded in the wider ecology of the student. The systems focus in both family and school systems is on the larger system as a whole and on the interactions between systems in the ecology of the student. Unlike a fragmented view, which dissects parts and pieces of the student and strips the context from the more meaningful whole, a systems focus takes a broad view of human behavior in its multiple interactive contexts.

Research Focus and Goal of Research

The ecosystem approach, following Bateson's and Vygotsky's theories, rejects separating cognition from affect—thinking from feeling. So the narrow traditional focus on the individual student out of context is changed in both family and school systems research. Instead the focus in both systems is on social interactive processes and systems interrelationships that are a part of the problem. Communication patterns, social relationships, and nonverbal behavior are considered to add a fuller understanding of the dynamics of all systems as they relate to the student and the reading problem.

The typical goal of traditional research is prediction, control, quantitative reliability, and universal, context-free laws. Systems theory instead seeks an understanding of the problem as it functions in the contexts of the multiple systems in which it is embedded. Only with this kind of ecologically valid understanding and information can meaningful intervention strategies be planned, according to systems researchers. Herein is the parallel between ethnographic or other observational/descriptive field study research in the school and family systems research in the home: Both seek contextually grounded understanding of the social interactive processes that define and maintain the problem of the student. The ultimate goal is knowledge and understanding of how all the circuits fit together in the system—a fuller understanding of the ecology of the student so that more meaningful intervention strategies can be developed.

Functioning of the Student and Implications for Remediation

Ecosystems theory directs research toward a better understanding of process and functioning of the student in the family and school systems. Behavior is always viewed in context, in relation to the wider ecology, rather than separated into isolated categories (such as I.Q., which Vygotsky refers to as yesterday's fossilized development, or self-concept—one of Bateson's special aversions). In this way, the functioning problem can be understood as a process of accommodation to a particular context, and linear cause and effect or blame placing can be avoided.

The remediation implications that flow from systems research and theory are quite different from traditional remediation of reading problems, which uses fragmented subskill teaching and segregation into remedial reading classes. Instead, in systems theory the focus for remediation is on change in the system and transformation of the student. The school implications, for instance, might involve changing the nature of the teacher/student relationship, changing from a fragmented subskill curriculum to a more wholistic curriculum, or changing the definition of the student from "deficient" or "disabled" to "in transition" (shifting to a new stage of development) or "in need of mediation."

ROOTS OF THE ECOLOGICAL VIEW: A SUMMARY

In schools, clinics, classrooms, and communities educators and therapists are becoming increasingly dissatisfied with a narrow, linear, fragmented view of human beings. They are seeking a meaningful alternative to the medical or machine model of human behavior, which treats the human being as a defective machine in need of repair by mechanical means. This narrow, reductionist model has restricted our thinking, our practice, and our research for too long.

Over the past several decades, there has been an interdisciplinary movement toward a more wholistic, complex model of human behavior and development. This model takes into account the multitude of interrelationships and interactions with the surrounding ecology that are crucial to a meaningful understanding of human behavior. It is from the research and theory building of various fields—ecological psychology, educational ethnography, family systems theory, social psychology, sociolinguistics, and the wholistic movement in education—that the ecosystems approach that we are developing takes its roots.

The three charts that follow attempt to summarize and integrate the viewpoints of these various fields to present a clearer picture of parallels in thought and implications for a deeper understanding of students' reading and learning disability. Chart 1 contrasts the research approach and assumptions of the traditional view with those of the more wholistic ecological systems view of disability. Chart 2 lists ecological systems principles for understanding reading and learning disability in both family and school systems. Chart 3 contrasts the ecological and traditional ways of looking at schooling and learning.

CHART 1.   Research Approaches: Contrasting Ecological and Traditional Views

Ecological Systems View	Traditional View
Focus on the whole system—the wider ecology	Focus on parts—the individual apart from the ecosystem
Symptom = problem/imbalance in ecosystem	Symptom = problem in the person
Research aim = knowledge of person's functioning within the ecosystem	Research aim = decontextualized knowledge of person's behavior and functioning
Person studied in natural context— little manipulation by researcher	Person or animal studied in controlled context regulated by researcher
Search for how all circuits in system fit and are connected (Bateson's "wisdom")	Search for causes of individual behavior (may end in blaming the victim)
Research question = What is happening? (How)	Research question = What is the cause? (Why)
Problems viewed as systemic: Problem may be solution	Problems viewed as isolable and individual: Causality as linear
Disability viewed in context of social/ historical interaction	Disability lies within the individual
Respect for singularity, individuality, and deviation from norm	Seeks predictability and universal laws or stages of development
Deviation may be signal of positive change or growth	Deviation often viewed negatively as deficit or abnormality
Growth and development viewed as recursive and transformational	Growth and development seen as following predictable stages
Results often indicate needed change and transformation	Results tend to maintain social/ cultural status quo

CHART 2.   Using the Ecological View to Understand Reading/Learning Disability

Family System	School System
Definitions:	
Family system's parts are interactive and interrelated	Reading/learning problem must be viewed in context
Family *not* a collection of roles to be separately analyzed	Language arts *not* a collection of subskills to be separately taught and tested
Functioning of the student:	
Inadequate parenting does not necessarily *cause* student's problem	"Deficits" do not necessarily *cause* reading problems
Literacy:	
Literacy begins and continues in interaction with parents and family	School literacy flows out of family literacy, requiring the interaction of the two systems
Problems:	
Symptom in family member may be warning sign of family relationship problem	Learning problem may be sign of problem in curriculum or management
Problem may be interactional in response to family system dynamics	Learning problem may stem from the reactive environment rather than residing in the child

Language learning: Progress is not linear but recursive. The integration of skills is more important than the accumulation of isolated subskills.

Focus of research: Directed at total field of problem and at the process that creates deviance rather than at individual deviance. Looks at the social relationships and interactions between systems.

Goal: Knowledge of the interdependence of systems and understanding of how the systems work for a future science of intervention.

CHART 3.   Two Ways of Looking at Schooling and Learning

Ecological View	*Traditional View*
Teaching = orchestrating the learning environment (to enable learning to happen)	*Teaching* = techniques and control of learning (follow prescribed steps)
Students = adapting, interactive, interdependent parts of an ecosystem	*Students* = Independent repositories of skills and competencies
Education/learning = growth toward potential as critical thinker	*Education/learning* = display of what is taught and "mastery" of subskills
Curriculum = integration of skills, subjects, concepts, and communication across the curriculum	*Curriculum* = separate subjects and separation of skills and content, and skills from each other
Researcher = practitioner seeking understanding of questions from within the setting	*Researcher* = expert from outside of setting seeking objective data
Evaluation = observation and description of student in process of learning	*Evaluation* = results from tests
Model of learning = spiral (learning is recursive, integrative, and transformational)	*Model of learning* = linear and accumulative (learning is stage developmental)

3
Sunny and James: Ecological Case Studies

Traditional case studies of students labeled as reading or learning disabled present data concerning the student's intellectual, biological, and affective development derived from tests and clinical methods. In contrast, the ecological case studies of Sunny and James in this chapter view the student in natural contexts, present perspectives and observations of the people in those contexts, and attempt to present a more wholistic view of the student in the interrelated contexts of school, family, and community. The data were collected using ethnographic observation and interviews (Spradley, 1979, 1980) in addition to dialogue journals, reading protocols, and student's narratives (see Chapter 11). Transcriptions of informal interviews attempt to be faithful to the actual conversational speech of the participants. Such colloquialisms as "gonna" and "nothin'" denote not impoverished grammar but rather common informal speech patterns.

The school, family, and community systems were all found to be significant in the process by which Sunny and James came to be labeled as learning disabled. Thus their case studies will be presented through a description of these three major systems in their ecology. Sunny was observed over a period of three years in her elementary learning disability (LD) classroom, and James was observed in both his LD classroom and the middle school to which he was transferred in sixth grade. Historical and current data were collected from the community and homes of both students as well. As their stories unfold, the reader can see not only the wealth of information that is available from a careful look at the ecology of a student, but also the multitude of misperceptions that result from a more narrow view.

THE SCHOOL SYSTEM

Sunny is a girl who somehow was missed or overlooked when mandated testing was due, whose I.Q. dropped twenty points during her four years of special learning disability training, who was observed but still allowed to daydream and sometimes do nothing all day in school since first grade, and whom counselors overlooked because she was not a behavior problem—she just sat in school and did nothing. This is the story of a student for whom teacher and principal expectations included:

> I hope a miracle happens, because otherwise it's just not gonna go.
> Now I know where bag ladies come from.
> She's gonna find ways to be successful other than in school—she'll probably get pregnant and quit school.
> She's like her mother—not working with a full deck.
> She's like her father—one of the slowest students I ever had.

James' story is one of a boy whose first grade teacher thought "had a lot of brain power," but whose second grade teacher used special education material for him. He is a boy whom one teacher found to be a charmer and with whom another established a good relationship, but whom another teacher found intolerable in the classroom, and whom still another recommended for SED (socially and emotionally disturbed) placement. It is the story of a boy whose reading level was measured in second grade to be 2.6, but whose reading progress was reported at the end of sixth grade to be "growth" from low-second to mid-third-grade and 1.5 in word recognition. And it is the story of a boy whose teachers refrained from challenging him because they wanted to "ensure success" and who, like Sunny, appeared to live down to everyone's lowest expectations for his potential.

Fragmentation I: Grouping and Tracking

In Sunny and James' school system, tracking and ability grouping were important not only with respect to the division of students into different classes (and groups within those classes), but also in determining the nature of the curriculum in individual classrooms, teacher expectations for students, and eventually student expectations for themselves. In the elementary school, students were first separated into reading groups within each classroom, some classrooms having as many as five groups. When James was diagnosed as having difficulty in even the lowest reading group, he was sent to a remedial reading resource room several times a week. And when both he and Sunny were thought to be in need of more help than the remedial reading teacher could provide, the teacher referred them for LD placement in a separate, self-contained classroom.

At the middle school level, there were five sections ranging from the high to the low ability groups. "Ability" was determined by standardized test scores and the previous teacher's recommendation (which was often based on the student's previous reading group placement). According to the middle school LD teacher, students who have been previously identified as LD end up in the lowest track, described by one of James' middle school teachers as follows:

> This low group is really a problem because some of them have no home, you know, whatsoever . . . I mean, I can't believe that they're in sixth grade . . . you can see it in the math scores. . . . They're just very low—this is just a very low group. I'm talking about the LDs and generally speaking in the class. The class is about the same every year as far as this section.

Another middle school teacher said she would "naturally not expect as much of the low section," and a third teacher said he goes "much slower with the lower section" and tries to "guarantee success," whereas he "challenges" the upper groups.

James' drop in math from 6.0 at the beginning of his sixth grade year to 5.7 at the end of the year was explained by his LD teacher as the result of his low track placement.

> I think he had a lot more ability than most of the kids in his class. And I think what they were doing were the things that he already knew how to do. So there wasn't a real growth there.

But she explained that the LD students are placed in the lowest track supposedly because they could not "survive" in the upper tracks. She thought James should be in an average section for math; but because of the school's inflexible scheduling with respect to tracks, low track students are in low tracks for all subjects.

> I don't like it, because none of them belong there. . . . It's unfortunate. It has to be at this point. . . . When we put them in an average section, things move and there's an awful lot of reading involved. They just could not keep up.
>
> Until a lot of things change, as far as teachers' attitudes, teachers' willingness to understand and teach students in a different manner—then work sheets and reading and answering questions—they're probably gonna have to be placed in the low section to survive.

A previous junior high teacher described the low track there. She said the tracks "freeze" at this level and there is no mobility for students. She described the students as follows:

> These are low ability kids . . . terminal high school . . . red neck kids, kids who have no interest in education. They hate school. They tend, for the most part, to be uncooperative. . . . Now there are some very nice low level kids, but they are in an incredible minority. These are the kids with social problems. These are the kids—I hate to stereotype, but I can walk into a group of kids and not know any of them, and I can tell you who the low level kids are by looking at them.

The students who were in the low section were further described as "dirty and scuzzy," and as "living in economically depressed situations," with parents who were factory workers with very few goals. Furthermore, according to this teacher, the low level students' parents were never seen at Back-to-School Night.

A former high school teacher said of the low section students that they felt like failures, they knew they were stupid, and they were not motivated. She described their parents as tired factory workers who did not know how to help the students and who never came into the school. Several other teachers cited incidents where students in the low sections referred to themselves as dumb and stupid, and a principal recalled being told by some low section students that they could not be expected to know some material he was presenting (he was covering a class for a teacher) because they were in the slow group.

Though the separation of students into reading groups, tracks, or sections stigmatizes and demoralizes them, as is evident from the above teacher and student perceptions, an even further stigmatization seems to result from the separation of students into learning disability classrooms. They are isolated even more from their mainstream peers, they are further divided within the LD classroom, and they often regard themselves as stupid and incompetent.

The self-contained LD classroom removes students from their mainstream peers except for those few classes in which they are diagnosed as able to keep up with their peers (if the mainstream teacher can schedule them). Learning disability students complain that their mainstream peers jeer at them and call them names (sped, sped-ed, dumb, retard), and that their brothers and sisters do the same. The removal from the mainstream appears to accentuate whatever atypical behavior the student might have initially exhibited in school, and it appears to elicit stigmatization from "normal" (nonlabeled) peers and siblings.

James' sixth grade teacher commented that James "radiates toward bad apples"—a tendency that might have been learned in his previous two years in the LD classroom, which had its fair share of "bad apples" with respect to disruptive behavior. Membership in the class club was dependent on doing "good deeds" like punching someone out; the past year's bidder for class leadership greeted the teacher with, "Are you ready for my bad boy trouble?" on the first day of school.

Some LD-labeled students seem to have made use of the separate classification to excuse themselves from work and/or appropriate behavior in school. They appear to have mastered what has variously been called "the art of being stupid" (Peck, 1971) or "learned helplessness" (Dweck, 1976) with regard to their learning ability, absolving themselves of any control over their own progress in learning. Some have used the LD label as an excuse for misconduct. One student whose disruptive and obnoxious behavior continually interrupted class work commented, "You can't do anything to me—I'm learning disabled." Similar comments came from James' low track group in sixth grade: "Oh, we're in the low group—we can't answer that." And "Well, I'm in the low group, you know. What do you expect?"

Sunny and James' LD classroom was separated by movable dividers, a row of individual cubicles, and several individual learning centers. The desks were spaced along the walls and windows and separated by the dividers and cubicles. The students had many separations between them to encourage their individual work and to discourage social interaction, a reflection of both the administrative demand for order and control with these problem students, and the philosophy of individualized learning inherent in many LD classrooms.

Fragmentation II:
Misperceptions from the Narrow View

One of Sunny's teachers said, "They picked her out when she was in kindergarten . . . [because] you can tell." Her first principal said, "I can spot them when they're in kindergarten"; the spotting appears to be connected to a combination of student and family factors that school personnel view as characteristic of the LD student. Student factors included Sunny's inability to remember the names of letters and numbers, her inability to keep up with the rest of the group, both socially and academically ("inappropriate social interaction" and not completing assigned work in class or at home), and the opinion of school personnel that she was very disabled or slow and "doesn't have much [mentally] to work with."

The family factors cited most often as typical of the LD student by the school include little stimulation from the home, little support for education and the school (parents never come in for conferences, PTA, or Back-to-School Night), and a family history of academic and social problems. In Sunny's case, her father was described as "one of the lowest students I ever had in all my years of teaching," and her grandparents were described as "always beaten down—nothing ever went well for them." It was further noted that the grandparents also never visited the school for conferences or PTA meetings: "And there again you see there was just no interest in [Sunny's father] in school."

School personnel felt that it was "rare for a kid to break out of such a family pattern," and that it would take a miracle to make things go well for her.

> Over the years I've noticed that, when parents have difficulties in school, their kids will come along and have quite often the same kinds of problems. I've seen this many, many times. Now sometimes one will slip through and for some reason will do very well with school and go on and be successful in life. But I think that's very rare.

Sunny was described as coming from a family where "Mom and Dad didn't do well in school, and they had a child, and because there's not much push for learning in the home, then the kid comes to school and we find the same problem exists." It was further assumed that Sunny's parents did not finish high school and were very low academically.

> So Sunny has come from this kind of background. There is very little stimulation as far as learning is concerned in the home. Sunny came to school and was very low academically too. . . . There wasn't anybody at home to really help her with some difficult things, because I'm sure now Sunny knows as much about some academic areas as her parents. So there's very little help that she'll get at home.

The reality beyond the school's misperceptions about Sunny and her family was quite a different picture, as can be seen in the family system section to follow. And though she was thought to be very low academically (like her father), and she was considered to be "not working with too much" (like her mother who was regarded as "not working with a full deck" and presumed to have been in special education), Sunny's Wechsler Intelligence Scale for Children–Revised (WISC–R) intelligence test scores were average (93–96) in first grade. After her second year in first grade, however, when her teacher reported she was still on a readiness level, Sunny was placed in the LD classroom, where her teacher said she was "stuck at a first grade level the whole time (two years) she was with me."

She was reported to daydream a lot from first grade on, sometimes doing nothing all day in school; and she continued to be in the lowest reading group in her second (grades three to five) LD classroom, where her teacher assumed she was just marking time until she could quit school. The low intelligence expectations voiced for Sunny appeared to have been met by fourth grade: Her I.Q. score dropped to 78, which could qualify her for EMR (educable mentally retarded) placement.

James was assumed by school personnel to be typical of the black community of the town: low income, single-parent family, working mother, "unstructured" family life, and parents who did not have the time, interest, or energy to read to their children. James' first grade teachers felt the spread was so great between the more "deprived" students and those who were not, that they decided to homogeneously group the students to "better serve their needs" and to "help the students feel better about themselves." Somehow this did not work for James, and he had to repeat first grade. Although the permanent records list a 2.6 reading level at the end of that second year, James was assumed to be below the bottom reading group in second grade (the second grade teacher and remedial reading teacher said they had to use special education material with James since nothing else was low enough).

In part, this placement may have come from the assumptions of the school system. James' first grade teacher said that the district automatically puts students in remedial reading when they repeat first grade. Additionally, as one black parent informed us, when students are transferred from the school James began in (the school with the largest black population in the town), they are often routinely placed in remedial reading, as were her children though they were excellent readers.

By third grade James was considered such a disturbance in the classroom that the teacher recommended him for SED placement and used her own detailed journal of his "disturbing" behavior as evidence. James' sixth grade teacher had a similar view of his behavior. He said James had a "potential of being very violent . . . I have to watch him all the time because I'm afraid he might break out into a fight with other kids. Very explosive." He further described James as a "very low student—he's probably reading on a second grade level and his attention span is about one minute." Interestingly, James' previous teacher in fifth grade considered him to be close to grade level in reading and a bright boy. And his LD teacher at the middle school described him as a "very good student . . . very intelligent when he *wants* to be."

The negative expectations for James seem to be related to the school perceptions about James' family and environment. The above-mentioned sixth grade teacher said of James' low group:

> There's a pattern [in the low group]. Usually your discipline prob-lems run with broken homes, divorces—things like that. . . . Per-haps this might have gone back to an accident or something like that . . . the home, or not having a father, or you know he lives with his mother but he has no father. You know, there's more behind this than . . . you know.

Other teachers, specialists, and counselors commented on James' home as well, implying the futility of making a difference in school. One reading specialist said that James was like 75 percent of the students in remedial reading: They have emotional problems relating to their homes and fami-lies (divorce, boyfriends, beatings, insecure conditions, poor attitudes toward education). He felt that both the remedial reading room and the LD classroom were a haven for such students: "You can quote me on this—the LD room is a dumping ground for kids that we don't know what to do with."

It was also assumed that James' mother was not too invested in him. The middle school LD teacher said, "The feeling I get from him, mom doesn't want to be bothered." James told her that his mother watches TV all the time, and when he asks her a question she says, "That's a dumb question. Why are you asking me that?" The counselor (who had never met James' mother) thought his problems stemmed from his home envi-ronment, that he had not had limits set at home, and that his mother was not willing to work out his problems except through the use of physical punishment. She felt that "you have to have a family that is willing to work on problems," and thus James has no basis to work on them.

This same counselor described James as defensive about authority, lacking in motivation, defiant in behavior and walk (she noted that he had a Mohawk hairdo for a while), and deliberately trying to get attention. She cited an incident that she described as a "power play" in which James' English class went to the library to learn reference skills and his teacher told him to go instead to the LD room to work on paragraph skills (at the 1.5 to 2.5 grade level). It was assumed that library reference skills would be "too difficult and frustrating" for James. When he tried to be included with his class and would not leave the library until the English teacher came to remove him, it was interpreted as a power play for attention. Incidentally, the counselor asked at one point during the interview if James' mother's last name was the same as James'.

Fragmentation III: The Fragmented Curriculum

The curriculum of Sunny's first LD classroom was described by the teacher as

> much as you would do with kindergarten students: directionality, classification skills, listening activities, sound and letter identification . . . we spent a very long time on just beginning consonant sounds.

This LD teacher felt Sunny needed a "phonetically pure" program and more skill work at the readiness level. But she said that if she had it to do over again, "I might have pushed more sight vocabulary on more of a drill basis—you know, drill, drill, drill, drill, drill." She would still include phonics skill work, however, since "on this level the kids are too young to give up on phonics: I still firmly believe they need that, and they need it a lot."

The curriculum in Sunny's second LD classroom reflected a continuation of the isolated subskill approach accompanied by much individualized skill work. Sunny was assigned three drill sheets, a letter finding activity (sorting rubber letters from a box to spell the words), and writing words five times each for her weekly list of ten spelling words. She was given phonics skills workbooks to drill her on letter and sound identification, and factual recall questions to drill her on comprehension.

Sunny was never observed choosing or reading a book on her own in her second LD classroom, and her previous LD teacher said that to her knowledge Sunny never read books either in school or at home. Her grandmother said that she never saw Sunny bring books home either. The only work she saw from school was ditto sheets. When Sunny was observed at home, her homework consisted of isolated word exercises, matching pictures with words, adding endings (s, ed, ing) to her spelling words, and two pages from a test booklet of factual questions on a story that Sunny said she never read. She had no book or story to accompany the questions, and she said she never had books to go with the questions. Her mother later refuted this, saying that Sunny probably just forgot the book or was not permitted to bring it home due to past book losses.

Analysis of Sunny's reading protocols (see Chapter 11) revealed the result of her "phonetically pure" training. Her most frequently employed strategy was phonetic analysis. After a substitution (which was as often nonmeaningful as meaningful), Sunny's next move was phonetic analysis, one letter at a time. When asked how she was figuring out a word, Sunny said she was "tryin' to sound it out." When asked what else she was thinking about when she read, she said, "I don't think about nothin'—I clear my mind out and read." Her definition of what counts for reading appeared to be restricted to the identification of letters and sounds. Higher level thinking was put on hold.

James experienced the same fragmented curriculum. It was assumed that, since he was placed in remedial reading and later in the LD classroom, he must need more work on the subskills of language. Thus whole language learning, reading and communicating in meaningful contexts, self-selected reading and writing, and comprehension questions that went beyond the literal, factual level were as inaccessible to him as the library reference skills.

James' kindergarten teacher described the "night and day" difference between the curriculum in her present school (mostly white middle class) and Carver, James' first school (many black, poor, and "disadvantaged"). Whereas she now has some students reading before first grade, she said she was "not into that" with the Carver students because they were not "capable" and were "not ready for it." Since James' subsequent placements were homogeneously grouped—first grade grouping, second and third grade bottom reading groups, remedial reading, LD classroom—he continued to be regarded as "not ready" for reading and thus was continually subjected to subskill training. The only break from this occurred in his fifth grade LD classroom, wherein the teacher placed him at a fourth grade reading level. But this was reversed by the sixth grade LD teacher, who had him working on a 1.5 to 2.2 grade level.

The middle school principal commented that he had some problems with the tracking system: "My problem is in some of the offerings—the curriculum that's offered to the lower track just doesn't compare." The sixth grade teachers described James' low track curriculum as follows:

> [In math] we go much, much slower in James' section. They're finishing up basic division of whole numbers. The other groups went through that earlier, they finished, and they've moved into reading problems and decimals. . . . I gear the material down.
>
> [In social studies] we try to gear to the level of the student. Sometimes I find I am a little above their heads. . . . I'm just basically trying to get them to know that there are states, you know, without going beyond.

[In science] there's a lot of difference [between the tracks], not only in testing but in questions and answers and everything. . . . They're just very low—this is just a very low group.

These teachers said that they would "naturally expect more" from the high track students, but they want to "almost guarantee a kind of success" with the low ability students. They keep homework—especially reading—to a minimum because they "don't want to overload the kid. . . . The kids who are higher ability take a more difficult kind of problem—more of a challenging type of thing. But with a lower ability kid you want to try and make sure there is some kind of success."

But guaranteeing success for James appears to have had the net effect of lowering his competence in math and freezing his potential at the second grade level in reading. Or perhaps he has decided to live down to everyone's expectations.

THE FAMILY SYSTEM

Sunny's family story is one of a family judged by the school and community as typical of poor white factory workers: no interest or ability in helping their students with school work, no support for the school or for education in general, and a family history of failure and illiteracy. But it is also the story of a family for whom education was so important that the mother had tutors come to her home while she was pregnant so she could later return to school to graduate. It is the story of a family wherein both sets of grandparents supported that education and helped with child care to make it possible. And it is the unhappy story of a father who feels the painful inadequacy of his own "special" education, while the mother senses the futility of her dreams of going on to college.

James' story also traces the social process of mislabeling and misperceptions stemming from a narrow view. It is the story of a boy presumed to be part of the "disadvantaged" black community and locked into a no-exit cycle of failure due to this environment, although, like his mother before him, he has spent his life in white middle-class neighborhoods. It is the story of a family for whom education and reading are so high a priority that severe pressure has sometimes been placed on family members to achieve academically (one teacher suggested that James' aunt's death—a possible suicide—was related to her father's pressure on her). Yet it is also the story of a family assumed by the school to be unsupportive of education and unlikely to benefit from homework contracts because of the family's unconcern.

Fragmentation I:
Labeling Effects from the Narrow View

Sunny's mother worries about pushing her too much academically because of the "block in her brain" that the school diagnosed as the reason for Sunny's LD placement.

> I don't push for it [better school work], cause, the fact that she has trouble anyways. And I think to push for it would make it maybe, you know, block her even more as far as doin' what she can do.

Thus little is expected at home from Sunny, just as little is expected at school, because of the narrow view that the problem with her learning is in her head. The mother not only accepts this fragmented, reductionist view of her daughter's potential; but she accepts as well the lowered expectations that have made it a self-fulfilling prophecy.

> I think if they expected any more [in school] they would totally lose her altogether. She's at a point that she can only do so much and have to constantly be helped even to do that—if they tried for more, I don't think she'd get anything out of it.

So the stage is set for Sunny's continued daydreaming in school, for her continued failure, and for the self-defeating expectation that it would take a miracle for her to learn to read.

In contrast with the family and school opinion of Sunny, the feeling of both systems about her brother is that he could do the school work, but he just does not want to do it. He is assumed to be capable, whereas Sunny is assumed to be disabled. But her brother is also far behind in reading and has been in danger of permanent suspension from school. Both parents have given up on pushing him for better school work because, "there's no point pushin' him because the more you push, the worse he'll—he backs away from it."

The school assumes that this family is caught in a vicious failure cycle because they are poor, illiterate, disadvantaged, unmotivated factory workers who have no interest in education. Paradoxically, it appears that their concern for their students' learning and their unquestioning adoption of the school's narrow view of their students is part of what keeps the cycle operating. The students get the message from both home and school that not much is expected of them, that they can get away with doing very little at home and at school, and that perhaps they are too dumb to do anything else. So we end up with the story of ungrounded misperceptions, false assumptions, cultural bias, and unsuccessful education that culminates in the tragic loss of human potential.

The interaction of James' family with the school resulted in similar miscommunication and misperception. It was rare for James' teachers to talk with his mother. Most made their assumptions on the basis of their view of the black community, their view of single-parent families and working mothers, and James' previous school history, which recorded his remedial and LD treatment. Even when teachers did meet with James' mother, they did not say what they really thought. His mother reported feeling frustrated that they offered no suggestions at a middle school team conference, yet the teachers reported that they thought their suggestions would not be carried out—so they said very little and were "surprised" that she even came.

The effect of the school's LD label on James' family is evident in the ridicule he describes from his brother, cousins, and grandfather. James has often complained about his brother, who calls him "stupid" and "sped ed," and he says that his grandfather calls him "dumb." His grandfather said that anyone with "even half a brain" can teach himself to read, so he assumes that James must be lazy.

No one in James' family appears to be aware of the limitations of the label, grouping, and subsequent curriculum that James has been exposed to in school. His mother says that she wants him to go on to college, and his grandfather says there should be no reason why black parents cannot demand that their children be placed in college preparatory sections. But these hopes and expectations have never been communicated to the school system, which has continued to slot James for anything but an academically successful future.

Additionally, the grouping and tracking accompanying James' labels of reading and learning disability have resulted in bringing out his worst behavior. Both the LD classroom and the low track at the middle school were described by teachers as "dumping grounds" for behavior problems, and several observations record James following the leader in misbehavior. James' middle school teachers likewise reported that he seemed to team up with the "bad apples" in the class.

Fragmentation II: Misperceptions and the "Real" Family

It was assumed by Sunny's principal that her mother had been in special education and that she had never finished school after she became pregnant. It was assumed that Sunny's father probably did not finish school either because he was such a slow student, and he was variously described as "greasy, grimy, toothless" and a "cartoon character." The image painted was of a rather shiftless parent, who probably spent most of his time in front of the television ignoring his children. He was assumed to be laid off from work most of the time, and he was thought to be of no value in helping with his children's learning since he did not value education.

When the school psychologist looked up Sunny's permanent record file, she was visibly surprised to see that both parents had, in fact, graduated from high school. Sunny's teachers would no doubt have been equally surprised to learn that for the previous 15 years her father had held a responsible, full-time job; and that her mother (described as "spacy, disorganized" and "not working with a full deck") was in a supervisory position at the factory where she had worked for the previous 11 years.

What does the real family look like? Sunny's father explained that when his wife was pregnant with their first child, she had tutors come to the house because "she had a real interest in school" and "she was good at it." After the baby was born, he said that both his parents and his wife's parents shared the child care so that his wife could finish school, and he talked about how proud he was of her when she graduated from high school.

His experience had not been so successful. He said his parents helped him with homework, "kept on him" about getting it done, and encouraged him to finish school; but he was placed in a special education class in junior high school, from which he eventually graduated in a separate ceremony apart from the rest of the students. He described with regret and discouragement the wish that he had "paid more attention" in school, the excluded feelings that he had at graduation, and his classmates' sense that they were just being pushed through even though they were far behind their peers in academic work.

The sense of failure and incompetence from his own educational experience comes through in his relationship with his wife and with Sunny. During an interview at his home, he shared his embarrassment at having to ask his wife for help with reading and math; he also said, "I feel awful" about not being able to help Sunny with math.

> She comes with some of her math. Sometimes I don't know. Then she'll sneak off and do it with the calculator. But then I have to fall back on it too myself. So I, you know—you just try to do the best you can. Mary [her mother] checks it in the mornin'.

The contrast between the school picture of Sunny's grandparents and her father's description is particularly striking. Sunny's father described his parents as trying to motivate him to study more—to try to make something of his life.

They kept on me about doin' my work—gettin' it done, my home-work especially. They was always on me to do that. They wanted me to get through school—do what I could. . . . My dad used to help me out at the kitchen table a lot. Sometimes my mother would help me with spelling words. If I had homework they'd sit me down at the kitchen table, no TV or nothin', and help me with it.

The school principal described them as follows:

They were hard working folks—had to struggle for everything that they had. I know learning didn't come easy to them either. Neither [Sunny's father's] mom nor dad had finished school, so here again you see they raised their children in a background that wasn't very supportive of education.

He added that they never came to meetings or conferences, "and here again you see there was just no interest in [Sunny's father] in school."

When one of James' teachers was describing her curriculum material (which "re-teaches phonics"), she said the story in the book was about a poor black family in a ghetto-type area, and that this was really James' type of story—"he really identified with it." Like the rest of the school personnel, she was not aware that neither James nor his mother ever lived in the black sections of the town.

It was assumed by the school that there was little control or supervision for James, particularly since the mother worked an alternating shift (2 PM to 11 PM one week, and 7 AM to 3 PM the next week). They seemed unaware of the strict control that James' grandfather exercised over his family. James' grandmother said her husband would sometimes force James to sit and read the newspaper to him orally, or he would restrict James to his room for several hours to read alone.

School personnel seemed to have a less than favorable opinion of James' mother coming to the school in order to paddle James when necessary. Rather than crediting her attempts to discipline, one principal interpreted James' mother's request to paddle James herself as a reduction of his options in controlling James, and a counselor considered the paddling a refusal of the parent to work out problems.

Black families in the town were generally assumed by the school and the white middle-class community to be unsupportive of the school and education in general, and James' teachers from kindergarten to sixth grade suggested that this assumption held true for James. Comments like "little stimulation, economically deprived, broken home, no father, un-structured family life, working mother, too tired to read to student, doesn't care, emotional and social problems, no long-range goals, doesn't come in to school" were repeated in many conversations and interviews with teachers, specialists, and administrators. The underlying assumption was that James' family's values were significantly different from the school's values. But the real family unknown to the school presents quite a different picture. James' mother said of her expectations for James and her other son:

> I expect them to go through school, go to college. . . . But I don't want them to be pushed through like some of them are, you know, instead of sayin', if you're a good athlete they'll give you any grade just to be able to get you out there to play football.

At the end of James' sixth grade year (in the low track of the middle school), his mother commented enthusiastically about his report card:

> When I saw his report card this year I was really pleased—he had a real great report card. Even my dad commented on it. I think—I mean I'm just hopin'—but I think this next school year he's gonna do just as good.

Unfortunately, however, she was unaware of the relative value of the grades James received. His good grades in reading were still based on second grade material; and his competence in math actually went down, according to his LD teacher, because no new concepts were introduced in his low section. Additionally, James' continued placement in both LD and the low track will never prepare him for either the college preparatory courses in high school or the college career she so wants for her son.

THE COMMUNITY SYSTEM

The small eastern town in which both Sunny and James live is very much a conservative, traditional, white middle-class town with only a small black population and no cohesive ethnic groups. In this community James' black, rather middle-class family is as isolated and fragmented from the mainstream social groups as is Sunny's poor white family. It would be just as unusual to see James' family at an informal social gathering in the town, at Back-to-School Night, at a PTA meeting, or on a parent advisory board as it would be to see Sunny's family there. The town appears to be stratified along both economic and racial lines. There seems to be somewhat of an exception, however, for upper-middle-class blacks who move in from another area.

The school system, particularly with respect to the grouping and tracking practices as well as teacher expectations, appears to be a microcosm of the community. Lower-class and black students are frequently found in the lower tracks. It is very rare to find either a poor white or a black student from the community in the top sections in the school; but it is not unusual to find them in remedial reading classes and LD classes. This same situation has been found to exist in many other studies of schooling (see Mercer, 1973; Cummins, 1986; Rist, 1970; Rivers, 1975; Ogbu, 1980; McDermott, 1974; Hobbs, 1975, 1978; and Bart, 1984). It points out the very real need to move from our homogeneously grouped practices to heterogeneous groups that permit the development of the potential of all students—not only the economically advantaged members of the cultural majority.

PARALLELS, INTERRELATIONSHIPS, AND CONCLUSIONS

What are the significant parallels in these two ecological case studies? What can we see from this broader way of looking at students' reading and learning problems, other than the multifaceted, complex nature of the problem? And what can we learn from this way of looking that may be helpful for meaningful prevention and intervention strategies?

First, it appears that a narrow view of the student and the problem has prevented our looking at the student apart from cultural biases and values. Too often in education we have adopted the traditional, fragmented, quantifiable, reductionist view of both the student and the problem of reading/learning disability. This has led to misperceptions, socially stratified labeling and grouping, and the frozen potential of the student. The misperceptions of Sunny and James and their families serve as two examples. Only parts and pieces of the students and their families were viewed by the school system; the school, in return, was viewed equally narrowly by the families. As the system presently operates, neither family would ever feel comfortable with more interaction with the school system. Yet it is only with more collaborative interaction between the two systems that the situation will improve.

Perhaps the only valid way of looking at the student is with a willing suspension of disbelief: a view that is open to surprise, to more potential than has been displayed or assumed, to the possibility of growth and learning through mediation. This way of looking prevents writing students off; it prevents the failure cycle as described by McDermott (1974) and Rist (1970)—the self-fulfilling prophecy of failure in school common among many minority groups and those labeled as "disadvantaged." By focusing on understanding rather than grouping or labeling, on communication rather than categorizing, and on dialogue rather than dissection, we may achieve a broad enough view to provide a base for trust, cooperation, and collaboration.

Second, from these case studies we can see that the narrow view led to the labeling, grouping and tracking practices that in effect have frozen the potential of both students at (or below) the second grade level. This is what Vygotsky has referred to as fossilizing human behavior and potential: the static test scores of yesterday's development prevent us from focusing on tomorrow's potential. And furthermore, they result in placement in static groups and tracks such as Sunny and James' remedial reading class, low reading group, LD classroom, and low ability section, which chart a course of continued failure to reach potential.

Deviation from the norm need not be regarded as a deficiency or a reason for separation of the student from peers. Our new definition suggests that learning does not progress in a neat, stage development ascension. A student may appear to be "stuck" at one level before making the shift to a new transformation in learning. Reading below grade level may be interpreted as a transitional stage, a signal of difficulty in the school or family system, or a signal for needed social interaction or communication between the school and family systems. In short, what might be termed deviance or deficiency in the narrow view might instead be a positive sign of change or transformation.

And third, we can see from the case studies the result of the narrowly conceived language curriculum with its fragmented definition of reading and learning. Both Sunny and James were fed steady diets of parts and pieces of language removed from meaningful context. They were continually schooled on the subskills of language to the neglect of whole language learning that integrates skills with content. They had six years of spelling, phonics, and answering main idea questions; but they were only rarely observed reading a book of their choice, writing to extend and develop their own thoughts, or developing higher level critical thinking to approach new learning. So we have two more examples of the paradox of the solution becoming the problem—victims of a system operating under a narrowly conceived framework that leads to fragmentation, stigmatization, and fossilization of potential.

But what if we take the larger ecological view and embrace a more wholistic framework? What if we expect more and write off less? What if we work toward more problem solving, collaboration, and the integration of people and language to reduce fragmentation and isolation? What if we try a networking approach: teacher partners, staff review process, specialists teaming with teachers as collaborators and orchestrators of learning?

The clear implication from these case studies, and from many other studies as well, is that we need to take a broader, ecological view of the student, the problem of reading/learning disability, our definition of language learning, and the curriculum and evaluation that flow from this view. The cases of Sunny and James illustrate what would happen if we knew more, and they suggest the need to remain open in our expectations and evaluations of students' potential. There is a world of information that we may never have complete access to, though we try our best to use more wholistic ways of understanding the student's world view, and though we try to make the family/school connection that can lead to better communication and collaboration. So, at the least, we must recognize the possibility that there may be much that we do not know that might cause our perceptions of the student to be quite different. We must, in short, maintain a willing suspension of disbelief.

Part II of this book will describe and illustrate a more ecologically valid, wholistic, integrated curriculum that embraces the definition of reading and learning that we have introduced in Chapter 1, and the view of both the student and disability that we have explored in Chapter 2. But before turning to the integrated, wholistic curriculum and teaching practices, we will present a broad overview of the ecological approach as it would look in the school system.

Chapter 4 presents an ideal situation in which both the theory and practice of the school system are congruent with ecological theory as we have described it: a situation in which all participants take the broader ecological view and a school system in which both administration and faculty develop together an ecologically valid curriculum. This is the ideal—it is not common practice. But it has been implemented in part in some school districts. Actual classroom examples from one such school district will follow in Chapter 5.

To make meaningful strides toward real solutions rather than problematic or paradoxical ones, we need a way of both looking and understanding that avoids fragmentation and simplistic, reductionistic interpretations. An ecological systems approach allows us to be researcher/teachers in our own classrooms. As teachers and specialists we are encouraged to observe and collect data from the student's ecology, and then to analyze and interpret the data with a view toward how all the circuits fit and are interrelated. We can be continually instructed by this type of ongoing evaluation of learning as we continue to build a more optimal learning climate in our classrooms. This is a view that recognizes that the interconnected whole is greater than the sum of its isolated parts, and it is a view that focuses on tomorrow's potential.

Herein lies the congruence of the ecological systems approach to reading and learning disability. It is the recognition that fragmented pieces apart from the whole ecology can never yield complete, significant, or meaningful answers. It is the recognition that there is a higher order of significance and meaning to be found in the whole of language and in the whole of the student's ecology.

4

A View of the Future

The case studies of Sunny and James serve to illustrate one of our central themes: that the origin of reading and learning disability is not in cognition or neurology alone. There was fragmentation throughout the ecologies of these students that erected formidable barriers for them in learning to read. Fragmentation was particularly evident in the curriculum to which both students were exposed, not only in terms of separating skills from content, and language from context and meaning, but also in segregating the classroom curriculum from the remedial/disability curriculum. The pervasiveness of fragmentation throughout these ecosystems points to another of our central themes: the need for a more integrated, ecological approach to language learning.

The lack of congruence between the remedial curriculum provided for Sunny and James and their classroom curriculum erected yet another barrier in meaning making. It is cognitively complex enough for the student to try to make meaning in the mainstream classroom using an isolated subskill approach that strips language learning of meaning and purpose for the student. But when this is accompanied by a further isolation of more and different forms of the same sort of fragmented learning in the remedial classroom, the student has a double burden in making sense of language. The other sources of fragmentation—the standardized tests that follow (and lead) the curriculum, the separation of labeled students from their nonlabeled peers, the separation of specialists from teachers in the classroom, the separation of the home and school, the separation of district, state, and national testing practices from sound, defensible learning theory and practice of the school—all point to the need for a more ecologically valid approach to students' reading and learning. It is these sources of fragmentation that are the real problem for which we must continue to seek meaningful solutions.

TOWARD A SOLUTION

Before further delineating the problem/solution paradox as evidenced in our teaching and evaluation methods and the response of the ecological approach to each of these, let us take a glimpse of the future as suggested by this new ecological way of looking at reading and learning disability. We will paint with just a broad stroke the way the approach would look if it made use of the resources from both the school and family systems and drew from research on social interaction, ecological systems, and wholistic language theory.

We will attempt to answer the question of how all aspects of our approach work together to provide a balanced ecosystem that operates in support of deeper understanding, further development, and strengthening of the potential of each student, while also promoting growth and strengthening of the teachers, specialists, and parents involved in the process. Part II of the book will then detail the curricular and pedagogical aspects of the approach.

The ecological view of students' language learning is based on both a process orientation and a collaboration of systems. As a process orientation it avoids linear cause-and-effect blame placing by looking to the dynamic social interactional processes at work in language learning—not at static products such as test scores. As a collaborative interaction of people from different systems, it draws both information and resources from all parts of the student's ecosystem. To illustrate this collaborative process orientation, let us imagine the ecological response to a student with reading difficulty. This would replace the decontextualized clinical testing by a specialist, which results in a prescriptive professional report that rarely relates to actual classroom behavior as observed by the teacher and rarely is translatable to actual classroom teaching.

In the school system, the ecological approach would draw on the strength of collaboration of specialists and other staff with the teacher. They would come into the classroom to observe, document their observations, meet with the teacher as a colleague, and together work toward a better understanding of the student's difficulty. The parents might be invited to share in this collaborative effort to more fully understand the problem; they would be treated with the same degree of collegial respect as that between the teacher and other school personnel. The staff would respect the vital role of the parents as educators, just as the specialist respects the vital role of the teacher in the classroom. Together they would arrive at an ecologically valid IEP for the student (who might also be included in the planning), simultaneously promoting trust, communication, growth, collaboration, ownership, and learning.

The staff would take a broader ecological view of language learning across the curriculum, and the program would embrace whole language learning, peer interaction, integration of skills with content, integration of the student into the community of learners, and integration of reading strategies and skills into a unified, efficient system of language learning. This approach would strengthen and make full use of the total resources of teachers, specialists, other staff, and peers. It would further the growth and understanding of everyone involved in the process, and it would provide the best chance for simultaneous improvement of peer learning in the classroom and sibling learning in the family. The wholistic, observation-based evaluation methods would be congruent with the ecological definition of language learning across the curriculum, so there would be a balanced, democratic approach to improving the quality of life both in and out of school.

The ecological view avoids assigning blame—it asserts that no one produced the problem reader or learner—and it suggests exploring the student's process of learning to find the significant dynamics in the various systems that seem to work against learning. It demands a collaborative effort of teacher, specialist, other staff, parents, and student to promote growth and learning; and it avoids the pitfall of causing an additional iatrogenic disability wherein the solution becomes the problem. This vision suggests that the joy of teaching and learning can fill the ecology of the classroom and the home; that teachers, specialists, students, and parents can work cooperatively toward that end; and that we may witness fewer reading problems as a result.

A NEW ROLE FOR THE SPECIALIST

The specialist's role in an ecological approach to language learning is defined as collaborator, teacher/leader, and resource colleague for the classroom teacher. The specialist not only has the key role of providing congruence between the regular classroom curriculum and the remedial program, but also is in the best position to demonstrate and orchestrate a movement toward a more wholistic, integrated approach to language learning in all classrooms.

As collaborator with and colleague of the classroom teacher the specialist would come into the classroom at the request of a teacher who was concerned about the progress of a student. The teacher would first observe and describe the student in a wholistic, respectful, nonjudgmental way (Carini, 1982). The description would focus on the student's behavior in a variety of learning activities and in a variety of groups and situations in the classroom. Ideally the teacher would observe and describe the student involved in each of the critical experiences (see Chapter 5). The teacher would essentially be writing to the specialist as a colleague, saying, "Here is what I am seeing in my classroom."

The specialist also observes the student and documents the larger context of the classroom, with a focus on the behavior of the student in that classroom ecology. Again the description is nonjudgmental, respectful, and focused on the physical, social, cognitive, and affective behavior of the whole student in a variety of critical learning tasks and contexts. The specialist in addition looks at the congruence of the classroom curriculum and teaching methods with whole, integrated language learning. The framework for this analysis is the critical experiences that provide the basis for congruent, integrated language learning across the curriculum.

After both the teacher and specialist have completed their observations of the student, they meet together as colleagues to problem solve. In arriving at an answer to "What is the problem?" they interact in a respectful, collegial, validating manner, using each other as resources in the extension of their own professional learning and growth. Together they arrive at suggested strategies based on the critical experiences, and they begin what will be a continuing professional dialogue on the growth of the student toward competence in language learning. The observations and dialogue will continue as needed in the progress of that particular student.

As teacher/leader the specialist is in an ideal role not only to contribute to the improvement of the learning environment of the individual student, but also to strengthen and improve the entire classroom climate. Rather than attempting to deal with a student alone for several hours a week in a pull-out program, for instance, the specialist can make a contribution to the entire 25 hours that student is in the classroom, as well as connect to the wider ecology of the student. From the beginning, students can engage in higher level thinking (evaluating and interpreting whole, meaningful texts, drawing on prior knowledge and predicting, expressing and writing their own ideas) in the classroom, while learning the lower level subskills in the process. And this can all be accomplished within their own peer-group community of learners.

The role of leader or teacher of teachers evolves as specialists respond respectfully to the problems of teachers, as they strengthen teachers' abilities to be reflective of their own practice, and as they support teachers in building a more theory-based, integrated curriculum. As specialists build strong, trusting, supportive relationships with teachers, they will be able to lead forward or strengthen the already evolving ecological classroom practice.

As resource colleague for the classroom teacher, the specialist can contribute to improving the quality of life both in and out of the classroom. As the teacher and specialist plan together for the strengthening of the classroom learning environment to meet the needs of the student who is having difficulty, the specialist will share resources and help to gather new ones for that particular classroom and student. Specialists may contact other school resource personnel (librarians, for instance) to find more resources to upgrade a classroom library or a collection of books for a thematic unit. They may draw on the resources of other faculty members who have worked on a similar unit, or they may go to the public library, the community, or the state department of education to find more resources for the whole classroom and/or the individual student.

As resource colleague in the larger ecology of the student, the specialist might make arrangements for a parent to come into the classroom to observe the student, just as the teacher and specialist observed the student. The parent might then meet with the teacher and/or specialist to explore ideas and make suggestions. A meeting might also be arranged that included the student along with the parent, to allow student help in shaping their own strategies for improved learning. Ownership is a powerful motivator in learning.

In addition to making links between the home and the school, the specialist might make connections with other professionals both within and outside of the school. Guidance counselors, principals, tutors, psychologists, and other specialists who may have already worked with the student might be consulted for their suggestions; and referrals might be made for the student to meet with one or the other of these professionals for additional help. Of utmost importance in the orchestration of the program for the student is the continual communication among all members of the student's ecosystem and the coordination of efforts in a congruent direction. The specialist role is vital in keeping the ecosystem of the student open and productively interactive in a progression toward improved learning. This includes keeping communication lines open and removing barriers to learning as they arise.

A NEW WAY OF TEACHING

The new definition of reading as social, constructive, strategic, integrative, and transactional suggests a teacher role of facilitator, mediator, and collaborator rather than subskill instructor. Yet what teachers are too often forced into, partly because of the poverty of our definition of reading as subskill competence, is a role of "watchdogs of trivia, the monitors of kits and prepackaged programs" (Myers, 1981). What has occurred in the school system is the tragedy of trivialization of language arts education. Teachers have been trained to teach to the tests and to focus on subskills of language to the neglect of the deeper comprehension processing that is vital to meaningful reading. If higher level thinking is taught at all, it is generally reserved for the gifted, the advanced, or the "top" reading group students. So we have created differential education in a supposedly democratic system: Only the select learn to learn. The new way of teaching begins with higher level thinking for all students and teaches lower level skills in the process.

What we are referring to as a new way of teaching will not be new to most good, intuitive teachers who have always taught this way. Rather, we are proposing a freeing of teachers from the restrictions of trivial pursuits lodged in fragmented, subskill curriculum materials: an opening of the door to the meaningful, interactive mediation with whole language experiences that could otherwise occur in the classroom. Mellon (1981) describes this as "an investment in human beings teaching human beings . . . in a fellowship of service that lifts the spirit and uniquely unlocks and draws forth and brings to full flowering the myriad skills of language." We are not short of resources and models for this not-so-new way of teaching—there are many good, intuitive teachers and specialists whose art, wisdom, and sensitivity continue to lead students ahead toward their own potential.

Rachael Carson (1956) captures the spirit of this type of teaching when she describes keeping alive the student's inborn sense of wonder and excitement—"that clear-eyed vision, that true instinct for what is beautiful and awe-inspiring." To keep this alive, she tells us, the student needs "the companionship of at least one adult who can share it, rediscovering with him the joy, excitement and mystery of the world we live in." And it is this sense of wonder, so indestructible that it would last throughout a lifetime, that is "an unfailing antidote against the boredom and disenchantments of later years, the sterile preoccupation with things that are artificial, the alienation from the sources of our strength."

The quality of life in classrooms suffers not only from the lack of this sense of wonder, excitement, and mystery; but it suffers also from its replacement with technology's answer to education. This technological and mechanistic model espouses efficient manipulation of the environment and the student; a static, fragmented definition of language as a product to be packaged and delivered; a view of meaning in language as something inherent only in texts, something that must be decoded, precisely replicated, and dissected for examination; a view of the student as an isolated individual with interchangeable parts occasionally in need of repair by our efficient production line; and a view of reading disability that often blames the victim, suggesting that disabled readers have defective parts that can be scientifically diagnosed and mechanically repaired.

Teaching Higher Level Thinking

Once freed from the constraints of mechanistic subskill monitoring, the teacher can return to the role of interactive mediator and collaborator with the student, a role that leads the student ahead toward what Vygotsky (1962) calls the zone of proximal development. Learning, in his view, must lead development; and the zone of proximal development defines those functions that are currently in a state of formation: "What the student can do in co-operation today [with an adult or more capable peer] he can do alone tomorrow. Therefore the only good kind of instruction is that which marches ahead of development and leads it."

In Vygotsky's social interactional model, the student engages in meaningful interaction with teacher or peer, and through this interaction inner language unfolds. There is a dynamic relationship between the student's biology and culture as mental processes develop through individual social relationships. Progression through the zone of proximal development is a complex, dialectical, social process characterized by periodicity, recursiveness, unevenness, and transformation. No static universal stages can represent this dynamic relationship, which is unique to the ecology of each student.

If teachers embrace this definition of language learning as an active, social, constructive, transactional process, their teaching will be more active and interactive. This dynamic interactional process stands in sharp contrast to the view of comprehension teaching as asking questions that have one right answer—as workbook pages, basal reader questions, or tests and quizzes that engage only memory and lower level thinking skills. Vygotsky's model allows the teacher to model metacognitive learning and to enable the students to interact with each other, raise questions that make use of their prior knowledge, and develop their cognitive awareness—to learn to learn.

One example of this process is the heterogeneous, large group discussion of a text, in which the teacher models the strategies of drawing on prior knowledge, of predicting textual events, of questioning, arguing with, and interpreting the text, and encourages the students to do likewise. As they engage in transactions with the text, the teacher, and classmates, the students learn what it means to be active processors of the world and the word. Furthermore, they become aware of their own strategies and purposes as they become aware of what the teacher is doing.

Durkin (1979) and Goodlad (1984) found in their studies of classrooms that there is little of this sort of comprehension going on. Instead they saw students answering questions of factual recall, rarely in a real transaction with the text, the teacher, or other peers, and losing their right to interpret, question, and dissent. One wonders how long a democracy can survive without the skill to question the text. Are we teaching students to be slaves to the dominant view—the one right answer—the trivial pursuit?

Widening the Lens

The role of the teacher needs to be strengthened as a decision maker, curriculum designer, and problem solver, rather than merely the implementer of someone else's materials and ideas. To achieve this goal there needs to be a reconceptualization of the role of the specialist and administrator as colleagues of and collaborators with the teacher in the classroom. A teacher who is concerned about a student's learning may discuss this with the specialist and principal, invite them to the classroom to further observe the student in the context where the student appears to be having difficulty, and then meet to collaboratively discuss both the problem and possible solutions.

Taking an even broader ecological role, the teacher and specialist or administrator might invite the parents and the student to be part of the decision-making process, interviewing them and encouraging their analyses of the problem and their suggestions for change. Not only does this ecological approach allow for a fuller, more valid diagnosis of the problem and open the doors to a variety of intervention strategies; but it eliminates the isolation of and miscommunication among teachers, specialists, parents, administrators, and students. It is a collegial problem-solving approach that uses all the resources from both the school and family systems—the social interactional process of communication and understanding so vital to the student's capacity to learn both in and out of school.

The vital need for such ecological understanding was made clear in the case studies of Sunny and James. The misconceptions and biased perceptions of the school personnel concerning the families of these two students were found to be powerful dynamics in the disability labeling process of the students. Negative expectations shaped the educational course of these students, one of whom was assumed to be caught in a hopeless cycle of failure, and the other of whom was presumed to be a product of culture/environmental disadvantage. One teacher said of Sunny, "Now I know where bag ladies come from." And an administrator said, "She'll probably end up pregnant and quit school like her mother did, and the cycle will start all over again." So little was expected of this student that at age 11 she was still reading on the first grade level, and her I.Q. scores had dropped from 98 in grade one to 78 in grade four.

Byers and Byers (1972) describe the importance of full human communication—the process taking place between and among people by which those people relate to each other. The function of communication is to implement, maintain, or change those human relationships; but students can learn no more from their adult world than the members of that world will share with them. Students will remain incompetent with language, they say, if the adults in their ecosystem do not provide enough full human communication and meaningful social interaction: "The student's capacity to learn from a teacher would be impaired, and the capacity to relate subject matter (factual information) to the lives of people, would be limited."

Both Halliday (1974, 1978) and Britton (1970) stress the importance of this social interactional process as the student learns to make meaning both in life and in language, interacting with the adults in *her* ecology. Halliday (1974) tells us that "the student's task is to construct the system of meaning that represents his own model of social reality. This process takes place inside his own head. It is a cognitive process but it takes place in the context of social interaction." Britton describes the continuation of the student's "zest to explore" from family to school, suggesting that learning, growing, and living seem "alternative names for the same process."

THE ECOLOGICAL APPROACH
TO READING ABILITY AND DISABILITY

The ecological approach, rooted in collaborative social interaction and a whole language curriculum, has the advantage of being congruent, contextual, global, and integrative. It allows for a fuller understanding of the process of language learning, while it encourages the maximum in growth and development of the student. It encourages and expects responsibility, competence, communication, and cooperation not only from the student but also from all of the significant adult educators in the ecology of the student: teachers, parents, specialists, and administrators. The same collaborative helping process is at work throughout the ecosystem.

In the relationship between the teacher and the specialist or administrator, the process involves a global evaluation of the context of the student in diagnosis, and it requires collaboration for intervention, a leading ahead and strengthening of the teacher, and continued professional growth. In the relationship of the school personnel with the parent, the process involves a broader understanding of the ecology of the student and arriving at solutions together. And in the relationship of all of these adults with the student, the process involves a further understanding of the student's unique perspective for a more ecologically valid understanding of the problem and a more collaboratively shared solution.

Throughout the ecology of the student there would be evidence of respectful collaboration, cooperative social interaction, the expectation of potential that lies just ahead of present behavior, and a continual leading ahead through mediation and modeling. In the relationship of the teacher with the student, the leading ahead and modeling would be observable during interactive writing conferences, strategy demonstrations, and whole, heterogeneous class discussions of meaningful topics. There is no failure, incompetence, or disability in such an approach—only a need for more mediation and leading ahead.

The crucible in which higher cognitive skills develop includes both the family, where the student begins, and the school, wherein the student continues language learning in social interaction with teachers and peers in an environment that is open to the student's potential. Rather than a steady, linear progression, the picture that emerges is more uneven, sporadic, and recursive, as the developing student interacts with a changing environment, at times seeming to regress but eventually leaping to automaticity in reading. Freire (1980) describes the pedagogical contribution to this process as an authentic dialogue between the teacher and the learner: the use of dialogue to synthesize (mediate) the educator's knowledge and the learner's knowing, ultimately leading to the awareness of learners of their right and capacity as human beings to transform reality.

> Becoming literate means far more than learning to decode the written representation of a sound system. It is truly an act of knowing, through which a person is able to look critically at the culture which has shaped him, and to move toward reflection and positive action upon his world.

Herein we have the essence of the power of an ecological approach rooted in a social interactional view of language arts and family literacy: interactive meaning making that can both inform and transform the lives of people and their worlds.

BEYOND TRIVIAL PURSUITS

We are not dealing with a trivial process when we speak of language learning in the sense of meaning making or of Halliday's learning to mean.

We are dealing with what gives shape, depth, and meaning to life—what makes it worth living. And this brings us full circle to the problems with which we began: the problems of meaninglessness, fragmentation, alienation, boredom, isolation, and despair, which too often appear to be replacing the natural zest for learning and the drive to explore with which a student begins life and learning.

Sarason and Doris (1979), in their discussion of iatrogenic disability, suggest that incompetence is actually produced by the school system: A considerable part of the problem "derives from the way in which we have devised our educational system." And indeed it does seem that too often our solutions have become our problems in language education. Until recently we have been hindered by an inadequate theory of learning to read—a static, mechanistic, stage development theory that narrowly focuses on individual deficits and decontextualized, unintegrated subskills. But Sarason (1971) also reminds us that if part of the problem stems from our way of thinking, there is hope for change. He suggests that our narrow focus on the individual student may prevent us from seeing the regularities and structure of the school system as well as the interdependence of systems, societies, and members, which might yield significant data for a science of intervention. Archer (1984), critiquing atomistic empiricism, agrees.

> In the twentieth century the greatest stumbling-block to the explanation
> of educational achievement (or non-achievement) was the assumption
> that the factors responsible were the properties of the individual pupil.

An ecological approach to reading and learning ability and disability can provide us with a new way of looking, teaching, and evaluating that lifts us out of the quagmire of the problem/solution paradox. This approach promises the best opportunity for continued growth and development of the student, the parent, and the professional. It returns us to the original Late Latin definition of the word *competence*: a "striving together (for something)" from *com* (with, together) and *petere* (to seek). Our present day word *compete* has the identical root word derivation, so perhaps this is one of the real basics we should be getting back to in reading: a definition of language learning that is more cooperatively structured and collaboratively oriented than our individually competitive and socially stratified society reflects.

Part II
AN ECOLOGICAL WAY
OF TEACHING

In this section of the book we link the ecological way of looking at students and language disability to an ecological view of teaching and language learning. Taking this broader view of students as integrally embedded in their own ecosystems, including their school, family, and community systems, we move to the integration of their language learning with a critical experiences framework (see Figure II).

The critical experiences framework, *A Pennsylvania Comprehensive Reading/Communication Arts Plan* (Botel, 1981a), has been built over the past two decades in concert with the philosophy of 27 national organizations concerned with educating children. The framework, founded on current research in language learning, was first commissioned and published by the State of Pennsylvania in 1977. It has been implemented in numerous public and private schools both in and out of the state since that time. From that experience and the steadily growing research supporting more integrative education, the State of Pennsylvania commissioned an updated version of the framework (*PCRP II*, Lytle & Botel, 1988).

We view the critical experiences framework as ecological because it integrates content material with skills across the curriculum, because it is rooted in whole language learning in meaningful contexts, and because it focuses on integrating all students into the classroom community of learners rather than fragmenting them into special groups or classes. With a view of the student as innately capable, a framework built on a curriculum created by the teacher and owned by the student, and a plan that links the specialist with the teacher as collaborator in the learning of the student, this approach has the potential not only to help those who are currently experiencing difficulty in reading, but also to prevent many from developing learning problems in the future.

Rather than fragmenting content from skills, cognition from affect, or students from peers, this framework seeks to connect all of the critical

FIGURE II.   Ecology of Classroom Learning

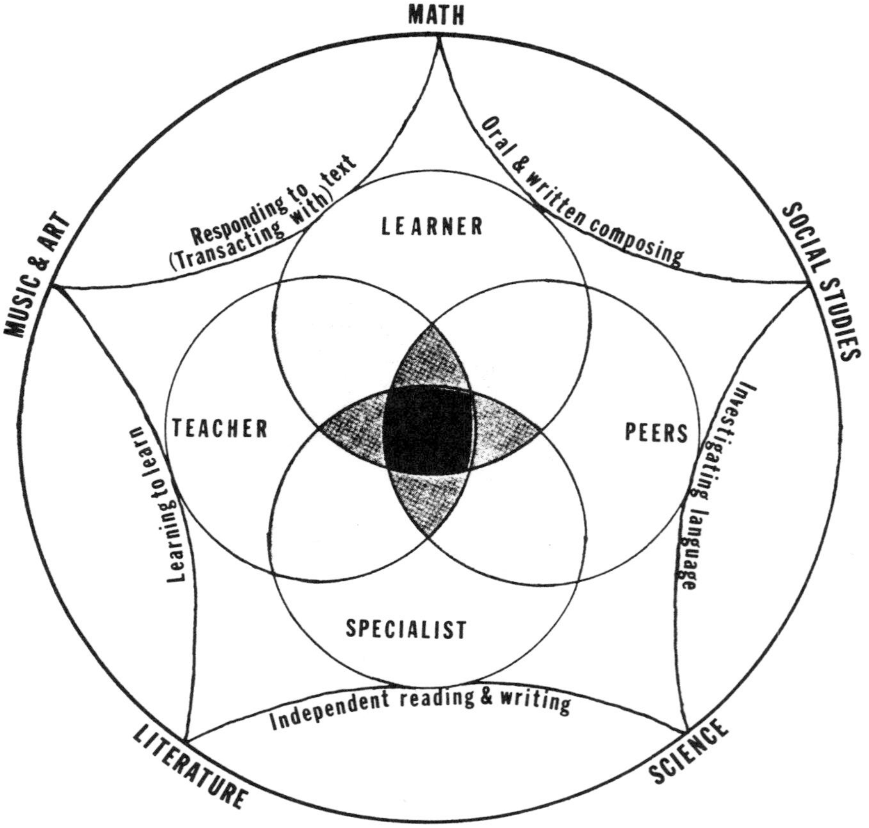

Student learning in the classroom is an interactive process in which teachers and specialists collaboratively foster the critical experiences which help students learn subject matter in the classroom community.

experiences necessary for optimal learning into an integrated plan. The experience of the student (prior knowledge and background experiences) is linked to the classroom experience (the experience of the community of learners). The student's cognitive experiences (strategies) are linked both to content and concepts across the curriculum and to the personal meaning making (affective experiences) of the student. And the experience of the teacher is joined with that of the specialist in a collaborative approach to meet the needs of all students in the classroom.

The critical experiences framework begins with higher level thinking for all students, acknowledging the wealth of language ability with which all students begin their formal education. Students are viewed as unique in their individual learning pace, style, and background; but they are also viewed as capable of full participation in the mainstream classroom. Reading, writing, listening, and speaking are linked with content material in every classroom across the curriculum so that language learning is both meaningful and continuous. Skills are thought of as processes that must be integrated with content learning, not taught as discrete or separable from whole language learning in context.

Many good, intuitive teachers and specialists will not see this approach as new but rather as a way of orchestrating many of the practices that they have previously found to be successful in helping students to learn. These professionals have always known that the individual is more than the sum of various parts, just as language learning is more than the sum of separate subskills. They have always known that cognition cannot be separated from affect, just as language learning cannot be separated from meaningful context. And they have always known that higher level concepts and critical thinking must be taught to every student in a democratic society.

What we have attempted to do in this part of the book is to integrate this wealth of current and past knowledge and practice into a unified curriculum plan that will allow all students to be accommodated in the mainstream with the help of collaborating specialists. We also include a fuller description of the role of the specialist as collaborator and orchestrator of the approach with the classroom teacher. The activities and teaching methods presented should be thought of as suggestions and idea generators rather than prescribed, unalterable techniques. We presume that experienced, creative teachers and specialists will create their own unique adaptations, revisions, alterations, and additions to the examples we present.

Chapter 5 introduces the critical experiences of *A Pennsylvania Comprehensive Reading/Communication Arts Plan* (PCRP), a theory-based and methodological framework for teaching reading, writing, listening, and speaking across the curriculum. As this book goes to press, PCRP II is in the final stage of development. Some of the fine points of definition, theory, and conceptualization have been changed from PCRP I, including the way some of the critical experiences are phrased. At this writing, the critical experience originally called Self-selected and Sustained Silent Reading (SSR) has been changed to Independent Reading and Writing. A fifth critical experience, Learning to Learn, has also been added; it is actually a part of all the other critical experiences. And Responding to Text is being changed to Transacting with Text. We have attempted in our description of the framework to include many of the newer refinements, but we have not altered the original PCRP I terms as used in some of the examples of actual classroom practice. We hope that this inconsistency will not confuse the reader. For additional clarification, we have used the alternate PCRP I terms in the descriptions in Chapter 5.

To illustrate the framework, we present in Chapter 5 a sample school day for a second and a fifth grade classroom and a thematic unit plan for a fourth grade classroom. The thematic unit was prepared and taught at a public elementary school as part of a Literacy Network Seminar (Botel & Seaver, 1985). The framework is further exemplified in Chapters 6 and 7 by showing how a teacher might accommodate James, one of the case study students presented in this book. Finally, Chapter 8 discusses the issues of grouping and management in the classroom, collaboration of specialists and teachers, and the family world view.

One of the more obvious ways to integrate the curriculum is the use of thematic units. It is possible to think of six, six-week units per year in a total thematic approach. Thematic units allow for the integration of various subjects such as social studies, science, literature, music, and art under unifying concepts and themes. Thus reading, writing, listening, and speaking are integrated across the curriculum and centered on unifying themes.

Teachers and specialists using this approach must have the thematic unit totally planned beforehand, including a congruent evaluation plan. It is not possible to just follow the textbook and use end-of-unit tests. Instead, teachers and specialists create their own curriculum for learning, supported by the critical experiences framework. The collaboration of these professionals is particularly important in the planning, organizing, and teaching of thematic units since they are quite time consuming to plan. In addition, teachers, specialists, and students all benefit greatly from the pooling of resources, ideas, and energy of collaborating professionals.

The thematic unit presented at the end of Chapter 5 was prepared collaboratively by a classroom teacher, a reading specialist, and a learning disability teacher. The unit is included exactly as it was planned and taught at the Shippensburg Area School District during the winter of 1987. The congruent evaluation plan and a sample student portfolio from the unit are included in Chapter 11. District planning is necessary for providing the time necessary for the creation of thematic units. In this district the planning time was built into a Literacy Network Seminar arranged by the district with the University of Pennsylvania. Other possibilities include inservice workshops and scheduled planning periods for specialists and teachers to collaborate.

All experienced educators are eclectic, drawing good ideas for their practice from a variety of sources, adapting them to the needs of their students, and refining them with their own expertise and art. There are several dangers to be avoided in this openness to new ideas and methods, however. One is the danger of accepting techniques that are not firmly rooted in an ecologically valid theory of learning. This would only lead to increased fragmentation, isolation, and a reduction in the quality of education. A second danger involves ideas for practice that essentially rob teachers, specialists, and students of ownership of the curriculum—those that treat teachers and specialists as technicians relegated to carrying out someone else's prescribed programs. This would be a grave disservice to the many excellent and creative professionals presently in the field. A third danger is accepting methods that either limit the potential of the student to develop higher level critical thinking or foster less than optimal expectations for the learning of all students. This would lead to the sad loss of potential for human beings who might otherwise have developed into contributing members of a democratic society.

Many excellent teachers and specialists have devised other ways of providing ecologically valid learning experiences for their students, and we have included some of these actual classroom practices in Chapter 5. Regardless of the specific activity, method, or technique, when educators continue to strive toward more integrated reading, writing, speaking, and listening in the classroom for every student, they are building more ecologically valid learning experiences. And when they strive to integrate content with skills as well as students with peers and teachers with specialists, they are increasing the possiblity that the growing number of students labeled as reading and learning disabled will be reduced.

5

An Ecological Framework for Teaching Reading, Writing, Listening, and Speaking Across the Curriculum

The Essentials of Education Consortium, a group of leaders of 27 national educational organizations, called for greater integration between the teaching of content of each subject and the language learning skills of reading, writing, listening, and speaking. This strongly worded clarion call, entitled *The Essentials Approach: Rethinking the Curriculum for the 80's* (Mercier, 1981), was in response to the Consortium's general distress over the fact that for years we had been traveling in the opposite direction. Skills had been taught as if they were another content, divisible into so-called discrete, measurable subskills such as main ideas and details in comprehension, and spelling patterns and affixes in decoding and encoding. The belief was that if students mastered these particles, they would somehow become better readers or writers. More than that, it was believed that such skill would transfer to the reading of literature, social studies, and other subjects. In the view of the Essentials Consortium, this is an exercise in wishful thinking.

Skillful learning is, in fact, the complex orchestration of knowledge and strategy by individuals to accomplish their own purposes (Bussis & Chittenden, 1987). Such skillfulness is honed by experiences in which the learner, in interaction with others in the context, engages in successive approximations of the task to be learned. Gibson and Levin (1975) have reported the cognitive principle for becoming skillful: "When teaching a complex task [such as reading and writing] it is preferable to start training on the task itself, or a close approximation to it, rather than giving training on each component skill and then integrating them." They note that during and after experiencing the task itself, the teacher should follow a differentiation model, guiding students to a consideration of the parts and their interrelationships. Furthermore, in a classroom there is a social aspect to skill development: Skillful learning develops in a social context, a

71

community of learners with a common cause. Let us look for a moment at these dimensions of skillful learning: knowledge, strategy, and social context.

1. *Knowledge*: At every level teachers and specialists can draw out the prior knowledge and personal experiences of their students through such means as discussion, questioning, and brainstorming. No knowledge is entirely new to a classroom of learners, and the shared knowledge of the classroom community is always greater than that of an individual alone.

2. *Strategy*: Strategies are mental and linguistic tools for processing information from texts. Students must learn how to retrieve their own relevant prior experience and knowledge, to look for pattern and structure in their subjects, to question what they read, to predict what is coming up in the text from clues and personal knowledge, to summarize, and to know what to do with difficult passages. These strategies are learned while acquiring information. Cognitive psychology explains the concept of skillful learning as the interplay of knowledge and strategy from the perspective of schema theory (Rumelhart, 1980). Schemata are complexes of concepts and dynamic thinking processes with which human beings make sense of their experiences.

3. *Social context*: Sociolinguistics provides the theoretical basis for a social interactional theory of the language processes. Comprehending, composing, and communicating with others are more than events in the brain. These processes involve social communities—sociocultural, school, and family—each of which shapes thought. When students comprehend texts, they are trying to understand and interpret what others are saying or writing. When they compose texts there is an audience in mind. When communicating with others there are listeners and speakers. The teacher or specialist who models a strategy or who facilitates understanding in a class discussion is providing the social interactional scaffolding that supports further learning. The interactions and interrelationships between the student, teacher, specialist, and peers in these social contexts are a central part of the meaning-making process.

The implication of this transactional and interactional view of skillful learning is that reading, writing, and oral communication are learned by using these language processes purposefully to acquire knowledge rather than by studying aspects of these processes as if they were prerequisite foundational building blocks. Students learn to read best by reading something of significance to them, they learn to write best by writing something of significance to them, and they learn to communicate best by talking with others about something of significance to themselves.

While using language purposefully in meaningful interaction with others in the social context is the central part of becoming skillful or competent as a learner, it is also possible to include the study of certain aspects of language in the process. Linguistic features such as sound/ spelling patterns, syntax, and vocabulary choice can be studied more meaningfully while in the process of using language than when they are treated separately from significant context as preconditions for using language. Likewise, aspects of content, including relationships, interpretation, and concepts, can be studied more meaningfully while in the process of using language. Linguistic features and aspects of content can be differentiated either during or after experiencing the text as a whole (see Critical Experience 4).

A methodological framework for teaching students to become skillful in using these language processes is proposed in *A Pennsylvania Comprehensive Reading/Communication Arts Plan* (Botel, 1981a). This PCRP framework consists of four experiences that are critical to becoming skillful in using oral and written language to learn. The critical experiences, described in the following section, enable all students (including those labeled as reading or learning disabled) at any grade level and in every subject to become skillful learners. A fifth critical experience is presently being added to PCRP II, along with other refinements and enlargements of the original PCRP framework. We have included this fifth experience and some of the other changes in the descriptions.

THE CRITICAL EXPERIENCES

Critical Experience 1:
Responding to Text

Responding to Text is defined as interacting with and responding orally, in writing, or through the arts to texts that students read, hear, or view. In a well-rounded program, teachers and specialists find a variety of ways to encourage students to respond to texts from four different perspectives (Purves, 1981): personal and affective (How do I feel?), descriptive and analytic (What does it say?), interpretive (What does it mean?), and evaluative (How good is it?).

While there are many commonalities in interacting with and responding to all texts, we differentiate between response to literary texts and response to informational texts, because of some significant differences in function and purpose. The purpose of literary texts (defined as imaginative, fictional, dramatic, lyric, or poetic) is often persuasive: They may instruct, recommend, demand, advocate, argue, or judge (Mellon, 1981). Though informational texts may also seek to persuade, their purpose is frequently to inform. They often record, report, define, explain, compare, characterize, analyze, generalize, reason, or theorize.

Given the nature of literary texts, many theorists regard response to them as an aesthetic and lived through experience. Rosenblatt (1980) describes the experience of a student's response to a poem as follows: "That child has not been passively listening to words. He had been travelling that road, had glimpsed places familiar and distant. . . . The poetic experience had for him a certain kind of reality. He had lived through that journey." This description of literary response illustrates that meaning is not in the text alone, but is a function of a reciprocal transaction between the reader and the text. And this view suggests that there are many possible interpretations of the text. It can be contrasted with the typical lessons in basal readers, where the meaning is regarded as being entirely in the text and where response is thought to comprise questions that call for one correct answer.

Informational texts, on the other hand, call for what Rosenblatt labels a more "efferent" reading. There is less of a personal or emotional association with the text, and the student's attention is focused primarily on what is to be retained after reading. In Chapter 6 we present activities for responding to both literature (literary text) and a science text (informational).

The following general and specific strategies represent some of the major ways of helping students to comprehend texts. In planning a lesson it is helpful to keep several things in mind:

1. Are the texts literary or informational?
2. Which activities should be used before, during, and after experiencing the text?
3. Is there a balance between written and oral responses?
4. Which activities are appropriate for primary, middle, and secondary levels?

Table 5.1 provides information to answer these questions. The table is not meant to be limiting, however, and Sapir reminds us that all tables "leak." In planning lessons, one should look for a varied set of experiences from lesson to lesson. Creative teachers and specialists will see many other ways to use these strategies and adapt them to other levels.

STRATEGIES TO HELP STUDENTS COMPREHEND TEXTS

1. Drawing on personal knowledge and prior experience
   - Have students respond to the question, What do you know about . . . ?
   - *Doing a reflection*: Write for five minutes about a concept that is key to the text to be read and share ideas with classmates.
   - *Brainstorming*: Take a problem related to a theme in the text and propose ways of solving the problem.

2. Predicting
   - Use *text clues* such as titles, heading, pictures, and opening paragraphs to predict some event or content in the text.

3. Questioning
   - Think of questions suggested by the title or headings.
   - Think about what question the author tried to answer in writing a particular paragraph or segment.
   - Write as many questions as possible suggested by the opening paragraph.
   - Write five multiple choice questions on some segment of the book.
   - Think of questions a lawyer would ask one of the characters.

4. Summarizing
   - Tell the story in the students' own words.
   - Tell the story from the point of view of one of the other characters in the story.
   - Make an outline of the main ideas and supporting details.
   - Make a map or chart of the key ideas and supporting details.
   - Write an abstract of a selection.

5. Sharing
   - Tell what stood out or what was worth sharing.

6. Acting
   - *Echo reading.* After reading an entire poem or story to the class one or more times, the teacher reads it line by line. First she reads a line, then students echo it, etc.
   - *Choral reading.* Plan together an oral interpretation of a selection.
   - *Oral reading.* Students choose a segment of a selection and practice reading until they are ready to present a fluent oral interpretation. Before reading it to a small group or partner, they tell why they chose the segment.

TABLE 5.1. Comprehension Strategy Planning Chart

	Which Texts		When Used			Mode of Response		Grade Level		
	Literary	Informational	Before	During	After	Written	Oral	Primary	Middle	Secondary
Strategy 1. Drawing on personal knowledge and prior experience										
What do you already know about . . . ?	X	X	X	X		X	X	X	X	X
Doing a reflection	X	X	X	X	X	X	X	X	X	X
Brainstorming	X	X	X	X	X	X	X	X	X	X
Strategy 2. Predicting										
Using text clues such as titles, headings, charts	X	X	X	X		X	X	X	X	X
Strategy 3. Questioning										
What questions are suggested by the title or headings?	X	X	X	X		X	X	X	X	X
What question was the author trying to answer in writing this paragraph or segment?		X		X	X	X	X	X	X	X
Write as many questions as you can think of suggested by the opening paragraph	X	X	X			X			X	X
Multiple choice questions		X			X	X		X	X	
What questions would a lawyer ask one of the characters?	X			X	X	X	X	X	X	

Strategy 4. Summarizing									
Storytelling	X	X					X	X	X
Point of view	X	X					X	X	X
Outlining		X	X		X	X		X	X
Mapping		X	X	X	X	X	X	X	X
Abstracting		X	X	X	X	X	X	X	X
Strategy 5. Sharing									
Tell what stood out or what is worth sharing	X	X	X	X	X	X	X	X	X
Strategy 6. Acting									
Echo reading	X	X		X	X	X	X	X	
Choral reading	X	X		X	X	X	X	X	
Oral reading	X	X		X	X	X	X	X	X
Doing a book-in-hand theater	X		X	X	X	X	X	X	X
Improvising	X		X	X	X	X	X	X	X
Role playing	X		X	X	X	X	X	X	X
Panel discussion	X		X	X	X	X	X	X	X
Doing poetry	X		X	X	X	X	X	X	X
Strategy 7. Reporting									
Writing a news story	X	X		X	X	X	X	X	X
Writing a book review	X	X			X	X	X	X	X
Writing an editorial	X				X	X		X	X
Writing a letter to the editor	X				X	X		X	X
Strategy 8. Making Things									
Illustrations	X	X				X	X	X	X
Collages	X	X				X	X	X	X
Dioramas	X	X				X	X		
Strategy 9. Doing a think-aloud	X	X	X	X	X	X	X	X	X
Strategy 10. Keeping an academic journal	X	X	X	X	X	X	X	X	X

- *Doing a book-in-hand theater.* Given a story or play with considerable dialogue, students join a small group, including a narrator who
  reads the connected prose. Decide with group members who plays
  each part. Plan an interpretation of the segment and after some
  practice read it aloud into a tape recorder until all are satisfied with
  their versions.
- *Improvising.* With a small group, plan an informal dramatization of
  a story or segment or act it out impromptu. Don't read from a script.
  Discuss with members of the group possible interpretations of the
  story.
- *Role playing.* Work in groups of two or three, taking the parts of
  characters in the selection and improvising what they might say to
  each other about some event in the book.
- *Panel discussion.* Pretend to be characters in a selection being
  interviewed by a host or moderator (like Donahue or MacNeil and
  Lehrer) about the characters' actions and motivation.
- *Doing poetry.* In a small group, read the poem aloud together and
  talk about how to interpret it chorally. Plan where to use solo and
  group voices, louder and softer voices, boy and girl voices, etc. Add
  pantomine or movements such as swaying or dancing and sound
  effects such as clapping and tapping the interpretation.

7. Reporting
   - Write an account of the story as if reporting it as a news story,
     keeping in mind the six *wh* questions: who, what happened, when,
     where, why, how.
   - Write a book review, responding from these four points of view: (1)
     Tell how the book affected the reader; (2) describe enough of what
     happened but don't give away the key events; (3) explain the values
     and purposes of the author or characters; (4) tell how important or
     worthy the book is and why.
   - Write an editorial on some issue in the story.
   - Write a letter to the editor on some issue in the story.

8. Making things
   - *Illustrations.* Draw pictures for the cover of a story or book or
     illustrate key scenes from the story or book.
   - *Collages.* Work with a small group to make pictures of the key
     characters by drawing, using newspaper or magazine cutouts, and
     bits of colored paper. Make scenery the same way. Put it all together
     on a big sheet of paper and paste it down. After talking it over, write

down what was learned about the characters while making the collage.

- *Dioramas.* Construct a three-dimensional representation of some significant event in the story.

9. Doing a think-aloud
   - Using a poem or somewhat difficult paragraph in a story, article, or book, read a line, several related lines, or a paragraph. After each segment, describe the thoughts it evoked as it was being read.

10. Keeping an academic journal
    - Write in an academic journal daily responses to the texts or self-selected books being read, noting what stood out, why it did, and its significance.

Critical Experience 2: Oral and Written Composing

It would be hard to find anyone who would not agree that a main goal of education is to have our students use oral and written language effectively to communicate, to learn, to get things done, and to discover their own creativity. Unfortunately, we subvert this goal when we postpone or minimize speaking and writing in favor of drilling students on the subskills of grammar, spelling, and punctuation, so that someday they will have the required skills to communicate. As in the case of transacting with text, we have things backward when we put the greater emphasis on having students learn the parts of language rather than actually having them use language to comprehend and communicate.

The critical experience of composing involves the student in making choices of topics and modes of expression—personal, literary, and informational—and in planning drafts, revising, editing, and publishing or presenting their compositions to particular audiences. The teacher's role is to find a variety of ways to encourage students to talk about their own ideas and write their own stories and poems. In this way students may better explore, discover, reflect on, and as a result deepen their awareness of what they know, what they are learning, and what they can imagine.

In Critical Experience 1, Responding to Texts, talking and writing are fundamental modes of response. By talking and writing about texts, students are able to more deeply process the content being read or heard. Such oral and written response is typically a one-stage process. But the composing process is different, particularly for writing original pieces.

Donald Murray of the University of New Hampshire has pointed out that most writers have similar experiences when working on a piece of writing. An adapted version of his recursive activities in writing involves the following experiences (Seaver & Botel, 1987).

THE INTERACTIVE WRITING PROCESS

1. Prewriting
   - *Collect.* The writer collects an abundant inventory of specific, accurate information through observing, interviewing, remembering, reading.
   - *Connect.* The writer plays with relationships between pieces of information.
   - *Rehearse.* Through conferencing with the teacher or peers, or rehearsing in the mind or on paper, the writer establishes leads, titles, partial drafts.

2. Writing
   - *Draft.* The writer writes a first draft as fast as possible to find out what the student knows or does not know, what works and what does not work, so the positive aspects about the piece of writing can be extended and reinforced.

3. Rewriting
   - *Develop.* The writer usually has to add information to bring out the potential meaning of the draft. Often the draft has to be restructured.
   - *Clarify.* The writer anticipates and answers the readers' questions. The writer cuts and polishes to produce the illusion of easy writing, which means easy reading.
   - *Edit.* The writer goes over the piece word-by-word, line-by-line, often reading aloud, to make sure that each word, each punctuation mark, and each space between words contributes to the effectiveness of the piece of writing. The writer "repairs" any break with the customs of spelling and language.

These aspects of the composing process are not rigid, linear steps to insist on; rather they are dimensions of a recursive process. Each dimension of the process involves strategic planning: choosing the topic, collecting and organizing information, writing drafts, or editing. The process has a social as well as a strategic perspective because in authentic writing and speaking, writers or speakers are aware of their audiences. These may include the teacher, classmates, oneself, family, authors, prospective employers. Writers or speakers often benefit from conferring with peers and teachers at various points of work in progress. This social interaction with partners, small groups, teacher, or specialist helps students extend their thinking, refine their ideas, and draw more fully on their personal experience and knowledge.

The writing workshop

To build composing into the curriculum a writing workshop should be scheduled for at least 30 to 40 minutes several times a week at every grade level (K–12) as a part of the language arts block or English course. Students should have writing folders or portfolios to hold dated samples of their writing in progress (including drafts) and completed writing. Stapled to the inside front cover of the portfolio might be a page for listing "Topics I know a lot about." This list can be started by having pairs of students tell each other what those topics are. They then write them down and number them in the order of greatest interest, knowledge, and expertise. Students should regularly expand the list.

The topics would come from the students' own experiences in or outside of school, from their imaginations, or from response to ideas from texts or thematic units they are studying. Students in middle and secondary grades might be prompted to write topics by having a list of types of writing in their portfolios or posted in the room, such as the following:

Personal writing—diaries, book logs, dialogue journals, academic journals, letters or notes
Imaginative writing—short stories, novels, poems, plays, songs
Informational writing—reports, letters to the editor, letters of inquiry, biographies, autobiographies, book reviews, interviews

During the writing workshop the students work on a piece of writing; regular conferences with the teacher and peers are held, thus providing for considerable oral composing. Teachers should demonstrate the dimensions of the writing processes by thinking aloud about what they are working on or have written. Using a fishbowl technique, the teacher can also demonstrate the collaboration process, which encourages the students to reflect on, expand, and refine their own work. The teachers or peers confer with the student-authors by having them read their work aloud, commenting on their writing in progress, restating what they heard or read, asking for more information, and making suggestions.

As students write and compose orally, they tend to draw on their experience with texts they have read, heard, and seen as well as their own life experiences. Just as in the case of learning to speak, improvement comes with using language. Each time they work through the processes of speaking and writing they are practicing successive approximations of what is evolving into mature writing. While students work through the writing processes, teachers should be alert for opportunities to help them individually or collectively in facilitating their writing in each dimension of the process. (Further aspects of competence in spelling and usage will be discussed under Critical Experience 4.)

Story taking and invented spelling

Brian Sutton-Smith (1982) has studied students' storytelling development by asking them to tell their own stories over a period of time. He found that if the teacher expresses delight at the stories, students want to tell more stories, and the stories get better. Furthermore he reports that the experience encourages them to write their own stories (see more on students' narratives in Chapter 11).

But how can students in kindergarten or first grade and disabled older students write journals or do process writing if they cannot spell correctly? The answer is, let them invent spellings. Teachers should encourage students to write their words as best they can (see Chomsky, 1979). Students can read aloud what they have written, and the teacher can write standard spelling above the invented spelling. As students continue writing about their own topics, mature through developmental spelling stages (Beers & Beers, 1981), and respond to phonics and spelling instruction (see Critical Experience 4, Investigating Language), they will continue to improve in their ability to spell correctly. Both Chomsky and Clay (1979) have documented the benefits of allowing students to go through this phase of the natural language-learning process. They affirm that the invented spellings form an excellent base for later reading and writing.

Critical Experience 3:
Independent Reading and Writing

Robert Frost once said he did not want to analyze authors, but to enjoy them. He thought that criticism comes with age, but youth should first build up a friendship with reading and writing. Nothing teachers do is as likely to foster such friendship as opportunities to choose books, to have time in class to read them, and to respond to them in one's own way. Reading widely and continually is the prime way persons develop knowledge. C. S. Lewis once remarked that by reading widely he could be "1000 men and still be myself." When students have read widely, they bring that prior experience and knowledge to all new learning situations.

Sustained silent reading

Through a series of lectures, Lyman Hunt of the University of Vermont developed a rather remarkable way of fostering independent reading, using a management plan called SSR (sustained silent reading). Here is an adaptation of his plan.

Step 1. Develop a classroom library of appealing paperbacks and periodicals.

Step 2. At the beginning of some of the SSR periods of 20 to 30 minutes, read aloud or comment on one of the books or part of a book, thus selling the book to the class.

Step 3. Each student selects a book.

Step 4. Everyone reads, including the teacher. A sign is posted on the door saying "SSR in progress. Please do not interrupt."

Step 5. At the end of SSR, invite some students who want to share something from their reading to do so. The teacher might ask them, "What stood out for you?"

Daniel Fader (1976) tested this plan in a major experiment with teenaged boys who read books of their own choice and wrote about topics of their own choice. The experimental group improved significantly over the control group, not only in reading and writing but also in their attitude about themselves, school, and books. Another kind of indirect evidence further supports independent reading and writing. Students who become early readers are typically surrounded by books at home, see others reading, and peruse books themselves in a kind of "pretend" reading that soon becomes real reading. Further indirect evidence about the significance of wide independent reading comes from New Zealand, a country with one of the highest literacy rates in the world. There, students from the earliest grades take a self-selected book home with them every day.

Record keeping should be minimal. Here also, students may be given a choice of method. Two popular systems are book cards, on which students write brief comments on what stood out for them, and book journals, which allow them to write more about the books that interest them.

What seems to matter in independent reading and writing is that students make choices, and follow their own pace without interference in the way in which they make sense of the experiences.

Sustained talking and sustained writing

A variation to use on some occasions, which generates talk and writing about books, adds sustained talking and sustained writing to the plan. Here's how it works. Students pair up at the end of SSR to do nonstop talking to their partners about any book they have read or are reading. Partners have three to four minutes to talk nonstop to their buddies (that means half of the students are talking simultaneously, so they need to practice talking in a loud whisper to keep the sound level under control). After one of each pair has had the allotted time, a signal is given to stop and switch. When both partners have finished, they are told to write down everything they said to their partners in a period of sustained writing. Because they are writing about books they have chosen, read, and talked about in their own way, sustained writing results in a greater flow of writing than almost any other writing experience.

Personal journal writing

Under Responding to Text, academic journal writing was seen as a strategy for more deeply comprehending the text. Rather than focusing on content, personal journals focus on self-selected topics of personal interest to the student. To foster writing fluency and ease, many teachers plan a brief period of five to ten minutes per day for students to write in their personal journals. These journals are private even from the teacher unless the student invites the teacher or particular classmates to read an entry. These writings can often produce ideas that may be developed in later process writing, but ordinarily they are not revised and, of course, they are not graded. The value of journal writing is that it puts the students in the reflective mode of thinking and gives them more practice in writing. All they need to do is let the ideas flow. A variation of this is the dialogue journal in which the student and teacher or specialist engage in an extended written dialogue (Kreeft, 1984).

Critical Experience 4: Investigating Language

We have created in the field of language arts education an artificial separation between using language and studying language, not unlike the same duality that Bateson described. Though most teachers and specialists are aware of the vital connection between language subsystems and their larger context, the prescriptive materials from which they must teach too often separate the subsystems from their ecology. In addition, the separation of language arts into separate subjects such as English and reading, with divisions within them—phonics, spelling, composition, punctuation, capitalization, handwriting, vocabulary, grammar, creative (and noncreative?) writing, literature—has created the illusion that reading is a subject to be studied rather than an interactive process.

We appear to have two opposing camps: the whole language proponents, who insist on a focus on meaning, with language studied only in natural context, and the phonics/language skills proponents, who insist that students have a firm knowledge of the subsystems of language before attempting to make meaning in whole texts. One group seems to propose using language to learn it, and the other group seems to suggest studying language to learn it better. In real classroom practice, of course, it is more a question of balance between using language and studying language. Most good teachers and specialists are aware of the importance of both using and studying language in their efforts to help students become skillful learners.

So the issue is not really whole language versus phonics, or meaning making versus decoding. This artificial dichotomy misses all that we know about the functions and forms of language. It is rather a question of achieving a balance between meaning making in whole texts and seeing how language works—between using language and studying language.

The approach that we take in investigating language patterns allows teachers and specialists to achieve a balance by combining experiencing language with studying it. The first three critical experiences put prime emphasis on language events during which students use language to become skillful in comprehending texts, composing texts, and communicating orally. But while engaged in these whole language events, teachers opportunistically direct and guide students to describe, analyze, synthesize, interpret, problem-solve, and evaluate the texts they are working on.

More specifically, when students respond to texts they discuss, write about, and enact the texts. By doing so they come to see the relationships among main ideas, details, and sequences; the nature of inference; the structure of different types of texts; how context affects the meaning of words; and graphophonic (letter/sound) and syntactic patterns. And when working through the writing processes, students become aware of their purposes and audiences; of the need to spell, punctuate, and follow the rules of standard written English; of word and sentence options available to them; and of resources like dictionaries and thesauruses to help them make fine point decisions. Thus, while the uses of whole language are at the center of the event, attention is focused continually on knowing relationships of the elements, features, and aspects of language. This is what we mean by teaching higher level thinking while at the same time teaching the basic skills.

But many teachers and specialists believe that in addition to such opportunistic ways of teaching about language, there is a need for more deliberate, direct, and sequential instruction about the linguistic systems of language if students are to learn to decode, spell, and conform to the rules of standard English. In response to that perceived need two things are needed: a unified paradigm for investigating language and a logical sequence for teaching phonics, spelling, grammar, and usage as interrelated skills.

The fact that this is an integrated approach represents one major difference from typical approaches that treat each of these skill areas as separate. There are two major additional differences between the approach to be suggested and conventional methods. First, linguistic features and patterns of written language are initially experienced in a whole text rather than through studying a series of isolated elements or decontextualized rules. Second, patterns are presented in inductive exercises, which allow students to investigate or search for patterns, often engaging in what Bruner (1973) calls combinatorial play, rather than simply being told the rules and practicing them in multiple choice exercises.

A unified paradigm for investigating language and a logical sequence for teaching skills

We present an integrative paradigm developed by Botel and Seaver (1986) as a model for unifying the investigation of language. By contrast, much of traditional phonics is taught on the graphophonic level, rarely dealing with the other subsystems of language. Language study is often removed from meaningful content and made more abstract and difficult for the student, and it frequently lacks the fuller development students need to build experience on.

In the integrative paradigm students first experience the text as a whole piece of language. They begin with meaning making in a whole connected text that is chosen or developed to include the language pattern to be studied. This allows us to show that using and studying language are vitally interrelated: that language learning is essentially meaning making, but that it is also beautifully systemic. The subsystems of language are thus analyzed in the following sequence: textual, semantic, syntactic, and graphophonic. In Chapter 7 James is gaining experience using a chant with the *ee/ea/e* spelling pattern. He first experiences the chant as a whole, beginning with the largest subsystem of language—the textual. On this level James listens to the text and interprets it, he echo and choral reads it in concert with his peers, and he reads it interpretively with a partner to get a sense of the whole piece of language.

The next level of study is the semantic or meaning subsystem. The deletion of words in the text by the teacher and the reconstruction of the text by the student (termed "cloze" activities by specialists) allows the student to look at context and predictability as a way of determining what words would make sense. Here James and his partner take the role of detective and find the clues to reconstruct the meaning of the poem. The missing words are examples of words using the *ee/ea/e* spelling pattern.

The syntactic or structural subsystem of language is next investigated. For this level we take carefully selected words, mostly from the text, which when combined and recombined yield a large number of different sentences. Nouns, noun phrases, verb phrases, and adverbs are chosen in James' example, and the partners are to reconstruct sentences with correct capitalization and punctuation.

The final subsystem of language to be studied in this paradigm is the graphophonic or sound/letter level. Word elements such as consonant and vowel patterns of words that appeared in context are combined and recombined to produce many words. In our example the students are asked to make long-*e* words by joining letters from consonant/vowel/consonant/silent-*e* lists. As James is asked to write these words or find them in the poem, he is getting practice in constructing words using the *ee/ea/e* spelling pattern. He may then be able to induce the general spelling rule under the direction of the teacher. We view this paradigm as ecological because it begins with and preserves the whole text while still allowing for analysis of the interrelated subsystems.

In the integrated day to follow and in Chapter 7 we present a model for designing a sequence of units for investigating language at several interrelated levels—graphophonic, syntactic, and semantic. While engaged in these investigations, students simultaneously learn to decode, spell, understand sentences, and gain control of the conventions of writing: capitalization, punctuation, and usage. All of these interrelated skills are taught in a whole language context.

Critical Experience 5: Learning to Learn

Critical Experience 5 is concerned with helping students monitor their own ability to comprehend and therefore to become more self-reliant and flexible thinkers. Monitoring has two related aspects:

1. awareness of one's own prior knowledge and experience;
2. control of one's own processes or strategies so that the appropriate ones can be retrieved for specific texts and purposes.

Awareness means the ability to reflect on one's thinking, while strategies for control require deliberate planning, checking, and evaluating. Good students do these things automatically, but weaker students may have a more narrow range of strategies or integrate them less efficiently during the reading process.

Learning to learn probably ought not be separated from the other four critical experiences. In each of the others, students were instructed in strategies for comprehending, composing, and communicating. What is required is that students not only engage in the strategies recommended, but that time be spent having them consciously reflect on the strategies and discuss how the strategies might be employed in their studies and integrated into a unified approach to making meaning from texts.

For example, in Critical Experience 1, students learn through speculative talking and writing to brainstorm prior knowledge of a subject, predict, describe and analyze, question, summarize, interpret, and evaluate. By discussing how they deal with material that they do not understand, how these strategies helped them learn, and how strategies might be used to learn in other assignments, they will be learning how to learn.

In Critical Experience 2, Oral and Written Composing, students work through such processes as choosing topics, writing drafts, revising, editing, and proofreading. These processes by their nature involve conscious reflection and strategizing. Here too, students would do well to discuss their styles of writing, how they get "unstuck" when writer's block is at work, and how collaborating or conferencing with a peer helps.

Following Critical Experience 3, Independent Reading and Writing, students can discuss the effect on their learning of being able to self-select books and to respond to them in ways of their own choosing. And following Critical Experience 4, Investigating Language, students should reflect on how peer collaboration, and combining and recombining linguistic elements into words and sentences helped them learn to decode, spell, and capitalize and punctuate sentences.

It might be well to list and post key strategies to reflect on and think aloud about. For example, in Responding to Texts, the following list might be developed.

COMPREHENSION STRATEGIES:
ACADEMIC DETECTIVE WORK

1. I am aware of my purpose when I read.
2. Before I start reading I ask: What do I know about the subject?

3. While reading literature, I predict meaning from the title and opening paragraphs, and continue to predict events in the text.
4. While reading social studies and science texts, I predict meaning from titles, overview and summary paragraphs, and other text clues.
5. I make up questions about key ideas in texts before, during, and after reading.
6. I identify and investigate key words.
7. I try to get to the main ideas or gists of reading through retelling, summarizing, paraphrasing, and outlining.
8. I review what I have learned from a social studies or science text by reflecting on, rehearsing, and interpreting key ideas in the text, and by evaluating the key ideas.
9. I review what I have learned from a literary text by responding to it personally; by retelling parts of the story; by describing the characters, the problems they face, the actions, and the language and tone of the author; by interpreting the text; and by evaluating it.
10. I make up tests like the ones I am going to take.

SAMPLE INTEGRATED DAYS: A SECOND AND A FIFTH GRADE TEACHER IMPLEMENT THE CRITICAL EXPERIENCES

Portraits of a day in a second grade and in a fifth grade will detail how the critical experiences are planned and managed by two teachers (Botel, 1981b). Of course, many quite different styles of classrooms would have provided equally good examples.

A Day in a Second Grade

Mrs. Kelley's objectives for her class this day include:

1. Broadening their experience with literature by reading to them, providing time for self-selection and sustained silent reading;
2. Encouraging their responses to literature through talking, writing, and further reading;
3. Extending their systematic investigation of sound/letter patterns, using literature as a base and then specifically focusing on the long-*o* sound and its common variant spellings; through problem-solving and mastery approaches;
4. Broadening and deepening their understanding of the concepts of

energy and cause and effect by having them observe the effect of a rainstorm on a terraced lawn;

5. Extending their systematic investigation of the structure of arithmetic and the mastery of the basic facts of computation through problem solving;

6. Encouraging collaboration in the above problem-solving explorations.

Two specialist teachers work with Mrs. Kelley's class on the same day. The physical education teacher's objective is to broaden the students' knowledge of games by having them modify the rules of a familiar game and try them out. The music teacher's objective is to help the students interpret a piece of literature as a performance through music, body sounds, and movement.

Responding to literature (9–9:45)

After opening exercises, Mrs. Kelley reads *Amelia Bedelia* by Peggy Parish to her entire class. Amelia Bedelia is a servant who misinterprets the instructions of her mistress resulting from the double meanings of expressions like "put out the light," "dress the chickens," and "measure the rice." This day students are encouraged to interrupt the reading by asking questions, and Mrs. Kelley stops several times during the first reading to ask, "What do you think Amelia Bedelia is going to do next?" After the story is heard several times Mrs. Kelley asks the class, "What stands out for you in the story?" and "What questions would you ask of Amelia Bedelia?" This leads to a number of sensitive and perceptive questions and observations. Mrs. Kelley then tells the class that *Amelia Bedelia* will now become part of the class library, where they will have access to it.

Sustained silent reading, sustained talking and listening, sustained writing (9:45–10:30)

Because they are studying about energy in science, Mrs. Kelley tells the students a little about five new science books for their science unit, which she is adding to the classroom library. Then everyone, including Mrs. Kelley, engages in a 15-minute sustained silent reading period. At the end of the session, students are told to find a partner and tell each other about the books they are reading. Each gets three minutes to talk nonstop. Then they are given ten minutes to write about their books in their journals. Finally they read aloud to their partners what they have written.

Mrs. Kelley tells them they may want to work further on their compositions during choice time tomorrow.

Physical education: testing new rules (10:45–11:15)

Miss Johnson, the physical education teacher, has helped the class develop a set of rules for playing a circle game. Today they try out their new game and discuss how well it worked.

Investigating language (11:30–12)

When they return from recess Mrs. Kelley introduces a unit that will unfold over several days. Mrs. Kelley announces the sound for the day, the long-*o* sound, which, she explains, has several spellings. Examples are listed on the chalkboard: hope, soap, go, and low. She tells them she will read a chant to them that has lots of words with the long-*o* sound and its different spellings. The chant is called *The Oh, Oh, O Scary Dream Poem* by JoAnn Seaver:

THE OH, OH, O SCARY DREAM POEM

We go down a rope, we go down a pole,
we go down a hole as black as coal
so low, low, low.
Here's old Mr. Jones and a pile of bones,
Jones, alone, and a pile of bones.
Oh, no, no, no!
Up the pole, up the rope,
if we're quick there is hope.
We will go, go, go!
But the pole and the rope
are as slippery as soap.
It is slow, slow, slow!
With a poke I awoke.
Just a dream—a bad joke.
I'm at home. That's the poem.

The students follow along and then echo read (the teacher reads a line, they chant the same line, and so on). Finally, they do a choral reading after working out together a three-group plan for expressive interpretation and response to the chant. Students then practice reading the chant aloud in pairs.

Mrs. Kelley gives them a sentence-making page, which they cut into rectangles resulting in eight cards to slide around. The page is shown in Figure 5.1.

Students work in groups of four to collaborate in the investigation of how many sentences can be made using any combination of some or all of the cards. They keep a record of the sentences generated in their journals, and Mrs. Kelley reminds them to capitalize the sentences and add punctuation as she circulates to guide their exploration.

On the following day, after the class tries another choral reading of *The Oh, Oh, O Scary Dream Poem*, Mrs. Kelley will call their attention to the word-making chart on the board (see Figure 5.2).

They will be instructed to see how many different words they can make by combining the elements from two or more lists. They work from left to right. Mrs. Kelley guides the class in finding two examples of each pattern, which she records in a chart on the chalkboard (see Figure 5.3). The students work in pairs to expand a similar chart run from a ditto master, as Mrs. Kelley circulates.

Mrs. Kelley plans to continue developing awareness and mastery of the long-*o* sound and its variant spellings. She is planning to read aloud a camp song, *The Good Ship Canteloupe*, the next day, which she will write on the chart paper. She will point out that many of its words have the long-*o* sound and its several main spellings. Students will follow along as she

FIGURE 5.1. A Sentence-making Page

Mr. Jones		go goes going
is are was were		vote votes voting
we us		slow
hope hopes hoping		soap
for		Joan

FIGURE 5.2.   A Word-making Chart

Consonants	Vowel Spellings	Consonants	Silent-e
b	a		
d			
c	oa	l	
g	ow	m	e
r		n	
l		p	
n		s	
r		t	
s			
t			
v			

reads and then do echo and choral reading much as they did with *The Oh, Oh, O Scary Dream Poem* chant earlier. In pairs, or small groups, the students will practice the chants, sentence making, and word making.

Finally, after several days of exploration and when she thinks her class is ready, Mrs. Kelley will use a checkout test she developed to determine their mastery of the spelling and reading of words that have the common spelling of the *o* sound. In spelling, the students study some phrases and sentences and then write them as they are dictated, like "a load of soap" and "I hope you will go slow." In reading, they take a functional "maze" test with items like "She hurt her nose on the <u>slow</u> <u>rope</u> <u>go</u>."

FIGURE 5.3.   Two Examples of Each Sound Pattern

	Spellings of long-o sound		
oCe	oa	ow	o
bone	boat	bow	go
rose	soap	low	

Science: observing erosion (1-1:40)

After lunch Mrs. Kelley continues class study of an extended thematic unit on conservation. She takes the class on a nature walk to observe the erosion of a recently seeded incline on a lawn near the school. She elicits from the students that it was caused by a rainstorm the previous day. They discuss the energy of the falling rain and the greater energy resulting from the rain collecting and running downhill.

Music: linking the chant with music (1:40-2:25)

When they return from the nature walk, Mrs. Kelley tells the class that she had shared the lesson on the long-*o* sound with the music teacher, Mr. Hightower, and that he had written a tune for *The Oh, Oh, O Scary Dream Poem* from the morning lesson. Mr. Hightower plays the tune on his guitar several times, inviting the students to join in whenever they want to. Then he guides the class in creating body sounds (clapping, finger snapping, and thigh slapping) and movement to accompany the music.

Investigating math patterns in computation (2:25-3:30)

Mrs. Kelley then introduces a math problem. She gives each pair of students a red and a blue piece of construction paper and five beans. "How many ways can these five beans be put onto the two pieces of paper?" One student suggests that you could put one on the red and that would leave four for the blue. She asks them all to do that and to keep a record of this situation in a chart like the one she writes on the board (see Figure 5.4).

Another student says, "If you put three in the red box, you will have two left to put in the blue box." Everyone put counters on the sheets as

FIGURE 5.4.   Setting Up a Counting Chart

Red	Blue
1	4

FIGURE 5.5.   Recording Number Combinations

Red	Blue
1	4
3	2
0	5
2	3
4	1
5	0

indicated and that fact is recorded in their charts (see Figure 5.5). This continues until the students can find no more combinations. (There are six, using the whole numbers 0, 1, 2, 3, 4, 5.)

"Is there any other helpful way you could arrange the numbers in the left column?" Mrs. Kelley asks. One student notes that you can rewrite the chart starting with zero on the left side, followed by 1, 2, 3, 4, 5. "What would happen to the numbers on the right side?" They determine that the numbers would be 5, 4, 3, 2, 1, 0. "Two nice patterns," she says.

Mrs. Kelley then asks them to write in their journals all the combinations to the following related problems:

$$\underline{\quad} + \underline{\quad} = 6 \qquad \underline{\quad} + \underline{\quad} = 8$$
$$\underline{\quad} + \underline{\quad} = 6 \qquad \underline{\quad} + \underline{\quad} = 8$$
$$\underline{\quad} + \underline{\quad} = 6 \qquad \underline{\quad} + \underline{\quad} = 8$$
$$\downarrow \qquad\qquad\qquad \downarrow$$

She asks them to collaborate in groups of four to work on the problems. Vigorous discussion ensues as children manipulate counters and talk about how many ways they could make the math sentences true.

On the following day Mrs. Kelley will put a record of the findings of the investigations on the board with the help of the class. She will then present the following record of their investigations and ask them to think about how many combinations there would be if they did the experiment with 11 counters. They will be asked, "Can you do this problem without counters by just looking at the patterns in this table?" (See Figure 5.6.)

After some deliberation, discussion with peers, and clues given by the teacher some students are likely to know that the answer is 12, because

FIGURE 5.6.   How Many Combinations Will There Be?

If the number is	there are _____ combinations
5	6
6	7
8	9
11	?

"there is one more combination than the number" or "add one to the left-hand number to get the right-hand number."

Composing number stories

Also on the following day Mrs. Kelley will balance today's emphasis on the structure of arithmetic with the linking of these patterns to the real world through the construction of story examples. The students will be asked to work in teams to think of a story about going to the zoo that has the idea of $2 + 3 = 5$ in it and to write it in their journals. Mrs. Kelley will write several stories on the board, and the class will discuss them as examples of the number sentence.

"Two girls met three boys in the zoo. They were five friends."

"There were two monkeys in one cage and three in the next cage. Five monkeys in all."

Groups of four will then work on their own stories and come together to share them with the whole class. Mrs. Kelley will write their compositions on the board as they are dictated.

Homework assignment

Mrs. Kelley notes the homework assignment on the board and asks the students to copy it in their journals. They discuss the importance of each part of the assignment briefly.

FOR HOMEWORK

1. Read a library book at least 15 minutes.
2. Share your sentence-making and word-making games with your family.

3. See if anyone in your family can tell you what _____ + _____ = 5 means. Help them.

Analysis of the day's experiences

The Essentials of Education Consortium identified seven intellectual processes that characterize modern constructive theories of learning: comprehending, symbol making, communicating, expressing oneself, problem solving, logical reasoning, and learning general concepts. We can use these processes as a heuristic or analytic method for characterizing the day's experiences.

Comprehending: Students were encouraged to ask questions, tell what stood out for them in a story, read books of their choice, reconstruct their comprehension of their books both orally and in writing, work out a choral interpretation of chants, determine what combinations of letter patterns made sense as words, observe erosion and link its cause to rain, and use a chart to record their findings in an experiment.

Symbol making: Students were asked to notice how the same words might have double meanings, how vowel sounds are represented by several letter patterns, how capitalization and punctuation signal a written sentence, how numerals and a table can represent a counting experiment, and how body sounds can be used to interpret a poem.

Communicating: Students listened, spoke, interacted, read, wrote, charted, shared, and acted out.

Expressing oneself: Students constructed both orally and in writing their own versions of the books they had chosen, and constructed a choral and body-sound interpretation of the chant.

Problem solving: Students participated in the planning of speech ensembles for interpreting the chant; developed and shared hypotheses and strategies for exploring and recording the arrangements of words and letter patterns to produce sentences and words; planned, used, and evaluated new rules for a game; and explored the problem: How many ways can five objects be divided into two piles?

Logical reasoning: Students explored the logic of Amelia Bedelia as she interpreted double-meaning expressions; the logic of representing sounds in a regular way, as well as the ways of determining a procedure for finding all possible sentences and words by arranging and rearranging the element cards; and the logic of the order of counting numbers.

Learning general concepts: Students broadened and deepened their understanding of multiple meanings, the alphabetic representation of speech sounds, blending, what a sentence is, what a word is, the meaning of erosion, and the deconstruction of a number into pairs whose sum is that number.

A Day in a Fifth Grade

Mr. Matteo's objectives for his class this day include:

1. Broadening their social studies experiences by continuing to read to them *Farewell to Manzanar*, a biographical novel;
2. Providing them with time for self-selection and sustained silent reading, including a choice of materials that relates to the thematic unit in social studies based on their novel;
3. Exploring and defining their special assignments for the unit;
4. Expanding their grasp of *Farewell to Manzanar* through drawing political cartoons (with the help of the art teacher);
5. Teaching them to use question-making strategies for reading and studying textbooks;
6. Extending their systematic investigation of the structure of arithmetic through problem solving.

Social studies: linking a unit
with the production of a newspaper (9–10:40)

Mr. Matteo beings the day by reading aloud the final chapter in *Farewell to Manzanar* by Jeanne Wakatsuki Houston and James D. Houston. This moving biography is an account of the internment of Japanese Americans in American detention camps during the second world war by two people who lived through the experience. At the end of the reading, Mr. Matteo asks the students to think of something in the story that is worth sharing with a member of their family and to write it down in their journals. Given an opportunity to share their journal entries, several children read theirs aloud.

He then tells the class that what they experienced in hearing and discussing the book will be the basis for a unit on the newspaper, which, he says, will take about a week to do. On the chalkboard, Mr. Matteo has written the following:

ORGANIZING AND PRODUCING A NEWSPAPER

1. Reporters
2. Analysts
3. Editors

4. Headline Writers
5. Artists and Cartoonists
6. Advertising Staff
7. Production Staff

The students all have copies of the local newspaper, and together they locate the sections written or done by each of the persons who hold the various positions on the staff. Mr. Matteo makes a special point of the letters to the editor section, which is written by the readers of the newspaper.

Students indicate preferences for the various jobs, and Mr. Matteo suggests producing a newspaper with a one-week deadline. He clarifies the understanding that everything in this edition of the newspaper, except the ads, must relate to what they learned from experiencing *Farewell to Manzanar*.

Groups are assigned, accommodating their preferences wherever possible, and students are instructed to brainstorm ideas about their job assignments.

They are to choose a reporter in each group to inform the class of what they are planning to do, and to pose questions they need help with. Mr. Matteo joins each group as they deliberate, guiding them as needed. When they come together as a whole class, the reporters inform the class of each group's progress and problems. Interesting things come out of this sharing such as: the usefulness of visiting the local newspaper and interviewing people employed there; the fact that the librarian, Mr. Tanaka, is Japanese American and might be able to provide some more information on the detention camps; the need to talk to the principal about making a typewriter and mimeograph machine available. Mr. Matteo tells them to let the ideas percolate until tomorrow, and he suggests that after story time each morning the rest of the morning will be spent working on the newspaper. After the morning recess Miss Arnold, the art teacher, will work with them until lunch time on aspects of cartooning in a newspaper.

Art: political cartoons (11:10-12)

Following recess Miss Arnold works with the class to show them how to do political cartooning. They discuss the many examples she has brought in and brainstorm ideas for cartoons appropriate to *Farewell to Manzanar*. Students are given materials to produce a political cartoon, and Mr. Matteo and Miss Arnold stop by to admire the students' ideas and make suggestions. Just before lunch, some of the students place their cartoons on the chalk trays so that they can be seen by all.

Sustained silent reading (1-1:30)

The afternoon begins with a visit from the librarian, Mr. Tanaka, with whom Mr. Matteo consulted earlier. He has provided the class with a number of books and newspapers, on various immigrant groups that came to this country, and on people who experienced detention and concentration camps in other countries. Mr. Tanaka takes several minutes to introduce these books. A 20-minute period of self-selection and sustained silent reading follows.

Reading, writing, and studying science (1:30-2:20)

Mr. Matteo tells the class that he wants to help them learn some new strategies for reading, writing, and studying their science textbooks as well as other writings about science. The science material to be studied is a brief article, of which they are given copies, called "Housing Problems of Bluebirds." He explains that before actually reading the article in the conventional way they are going to work on three strategies that are often helpful.

On the chalkboard he has written the three strategies, which involve the students asking their own questions of the text.

1. What questions can you think of from the title?
2. Read the first and last paragraphs. What new questions can you add?
3. Turn the headings into questions.

The class is divided into random groups of four and students are instructed to try these strategies and to write the questions in their journals. Mr. Matteo circulates among the groups and after 15 minutes calls for sharing the questions generated. Then he tells them to listen to him read the article aloud, keeping their questions in mind since they will be asked to answer them after they hear the article. After the reading, students write answers to their own questions in their journals. They are told they may reread the selection and that they may do their work with a friend. Afterwards, Mr. Matteo has the class discuss how to use the question-making study strategies when doing assignments in their science textbooks.

Investigating computational patterns (2:30-3:15)

During the stretch break Mr. Matteo has placed cross-number puzzles on the chalkboard (see Figure 5.7). Groups of four are asked to tackle the

FIGURE 5.7. Investigating Computational Patterns with Cross-number Puzzles

What is going on here?

2	4	6
3	6	9
5	10	15

Will it work with any other numbers?

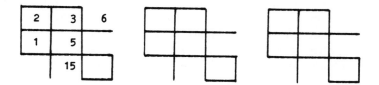

Will it work with multiplication?

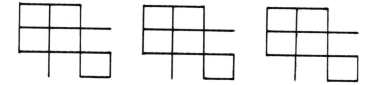

2	3	6
1	5	
	15	

Will it work with a 2 × 3 grid? Others?

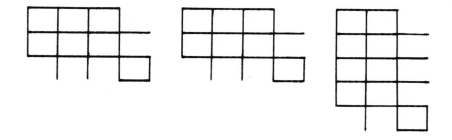

problems, keeping in mind *why* the cross-number puzzles work the way they do.

Mr. Matteo circulates to help groups as needed. After the exploration, several of the groups have realized that the reason the cross number puzzles work for addition and multiplication is because of the "any order" rule, that is, in addition and multiplication it does not matter in which order you add the addends or multiply the factors. Two children go to the board to show how that works. Mr. Matteo asks the class to explore for extra credit whether the cross number puzzles work for subtraction and division.

Mr. Matteo introduces the following story problem from the math textbook as a homework assignment:

> There's a sale on shirts for $2.00 and pants for $3.00. The limit is three of each to a customer. How many different purchases are possible? How much does each possible purchase cost? Hint: Consider keeping a record of purchases in a chart. One possible chart is suggested in Figure 5.8.

Tomorrow Mr. Matteo will ask the class to discuss their strategies and conclusions. He will then ask the class to examine and report on the patterns found in their charts. He will want them to be aware of the several horizontal, vertical, and diagonal patterns. One especially interesting pattern will be emphasized: Some of the purchases are unique, that is, only one combination of shirts and pants have that purchase price. For some purchase prices there is more than one combination of shirts and pants.

For additional homework, Mr. Matteo reminds the class of the extra credit assignment in math and tells them to study and clip sections of the newspaper that represent their specialization for the class newspaper project based on *Farewell to Manzanar*.

FIGURE 5.8.   Keeping a Record of Purchases

		Shirts ($2.00)				
		0	1	2		
	0	$0	$2			
Pants ($3.00)	1	$3	$5			
	2					

AN INTEGRATED THEMATIC UNIT

The following unit was prepared and taught by Ron Gilson, a fourth grade teacher; Grace Miller, a reading specialist; and Dona Weiland, a learning disability teacher in the Nancy Grayson Elementary School in Shippensburg, Pennsylvania. This teacher and specialist team collaborated in the planning, teaching, and evaluating processes. Their goals were to integrate reading, writing, listening, and speaking into the curriculum; to integrate various subjects into a thematic unit; to integrate all students (including those labeled as disabled) into the classroom community of learners; to collaborate as professionals both in and out of the classroom, particularly concerning students who might have difficulty with learning; and to provide an evaluation plan that was congruent with their wholistic, ecological approach. We present this unit as written by them.

Curricular Aims

The unit *Fossils and Dinosaurs* is an attempt to teach reading, writing, science, and oral communication through a holistic approach. In this approach, all areas of the curriculum are integrated. The fragmentation of skills and the isolation of subject matter, which are all too common in today's schools, are eliminated. Hence, learning becomes more global, more attuned to the real world. Students are encouraged *how* to learn, and are not restrained within the limiting boundaries of *what* to learn.

In the implementation of this holistic unit, students are to be directly involved with the critical experiences of learning—(1) responding to literature, (2) self-selected reading (SSR), (3) composing, and (4) investigating and mastering language patterns.

Each day, students must be actively engaged in each of the critical experiences. The management scheme is either teacher-led whole class, teacher working with small task-oriented heterogeneous groups, or students on their own. Students are not grouped according to reading ability. Heterogeneous grouping promotes more effective use of instructional time, higher teacher expectations, and increased student self-esteem. The opposite is often true with traditional three-group reading arrangements.

It is our hope that this unit will encourage each student to become actively involved in the writing, reading, and learning process. We hope our students enjoy this process and realize that reading and writing skills open up a world of new knowledge, power, and pleasure. The facts our students learn concerning fossils and dinosaurs are of secondary importance—a by-product of higher level learning experiences.

Ten-Day Lesson Plans

DAY 1

1. *Introduction to fossils*: Make a chart entitled "What We Know About Fossils." List all responses, right or wrong. Keep chart for future reference.
2. *Oral reading from literature*: Read *A New True Book—Fossils*.
3. *Responding to literature and composing*:
   • Compare new knowledge to previous knowledge. Use the charts for reference.
   • Have small heterogeneous groups of three students list accurate vs. inaccurate concepts from our charts.
   • Have each student prepare a list of questions to ask Dr. Drexler, a resource professor from S.U., who will be coming to the classroom for a presentation tomorrow. Put these questions in student folders entitled "Fossils and Dinosaurs."
4. *SSR*: Have students select a book from our fossil collection for a 20-minute SSR period.
5. *Book sharing*: Have pairs of students share their book.

DAY 2

1. *Presentation on fossils*: Dr. Drexler.
2. *Question and answer session*: Using questions students prepared yesterday for Dr. Drexler.
3. *Word wall*: Made of fossil-related terms to be used for spelling and language activities, as well as for reference when composing.
4. *Composing*: Have students write in their folders about Dr. Drexler's visit—What stood out for you? Did you learn anything new?
5. *SSR*.
6. *Book sharing*.
7. *Additional activities*.

DAY 3

1. *Oral reading from literature*: "Story of a Stone." This fantasy develops the concept of the earth's age and how fossils help us learn about the past.

2. *Responding to literature*: Dramatize sections of the story.
3. *Make fossil molds*: Using plaster of Paris and small seashells, each student will follow oral and written directions for completion.
4. *Composing*: After discussing sequence and time relationship words, each student will compose a paragraph telling how we made our fossils. These will be added to the "Fossils and Dinosaurs" folder.
5. *SSR and book sharing*.
6. *Additional activities*.

DAY 4

1. *Responding to literature*: Illustrate and retell "Story of a Stone."
2. *Make fossil casts*: Using plaster of Paris, students will follow oral and written directions.
3. *Composing*: Have the students write a creative story telling the life history of their fossil. Have them tell what their fossil was, where it lived, how it died, how it became a fossil, and how it was discovered. Add to folders.
   A. Share stories. Practice oral reading for fluency. Stories may be recorded.
   B. Save for future editing and publishing.
4. *SSR*.
5. *Additional activities*.

DAY 5

1. *Introduction to dinosaurs*: Chart "What We Know About Dinosaurs" and "What We Want to Know About Dinosaurs." Post these charts for future reference.
2. *Oral reading from literature*: Read the book *Dinosaurs* as an informative text. It discusses the history of life on earth in a relatively simplified manner.
3. *Responding to literature*:
   • Compare new information with our charted information. Discuss and answer questions on the chart "What We Want to Know About Dinosaurs."
   • List words students would like to know more about and add to "Word Wall" for future reference.
4. *Composing*: In groups of three, have students write down things they learned from the text. Add these writings to the students' folders.

5. *SSR*: Have each student select a book from our dinosaur collection for 20 minutes of SSR.
6. *Book sharing*: Have students share their book with a partner.
7. *Additional activities*: Try the sentence combining activity in *Literacy Network Handbook*.

DAY 6

1. *Prereading activities*: Discuss dinosaur names, their origins, and meanings. Add these to the "Word Wall."
2. *Oral reading from literature*: Read poetry from *A Dozen Dinosaurs*. Read poems about the Brontosaurus, Allosaurus, Brachiosaurus, Ornitholestes, and Stegosaurus.
3. *Responding to literature*: Make duplicates of the poetry and use for choral reading. Boys and girls will form groups for this purpose. Tape record the students' efforts.
4. *Composing (SSW)*: Write about your favorite dinosaur. Why is it your favorite? What do you like about this dinosaur? Illustrate your story.
5. *SSR and book sharing*: After 15 minutes of SSR, students will share their book with a self-selected partner for 10 minutes.
6. *Additional activities*: Try a cloze activity using words from the "Word Wall." Have a word-find activity with dinosaur names.

DAY 7

1. *Prereading activities*: Play back yesterday's recording. Have students join in when dinosaur names are stated.
2. *Oral reading from literature*: Read more poetry from *A Dozen Dinosaurs*. Read poems about Pteranodon, Elasmosaurus, Pachycephalosaurus, Triceratops, Ankylosaurus, Tyrannosaurus Rex, and Trachodon.
3. *Responding to literature*: Divide students into heterogeneous groups of four. Have each group select one of the above dinosaurs. Give each group a copy of the poem about their dinosaur. Have each group read the poetry and decide how they could dramatize it. After ten minutes, call the students back. Teacher now reads the poetry aloud while each group of "dinosaurs" act out their part.
4. *Oral reading for fluency*:
   • Have students practice oral reading of poetry with a partner. When they become fluent, they may record a portion of the poem.
   • Play recordings of students' oral reading if they desire.
5. *Composing*: Have the students select their two favorite dinosaurs and

write a paragraph comparing and contrasting them. This can be done in pairs or individually. Discuss comparisons.
6. *SSR.*
7. *Additional activities*: Do a sentence combining activity.

DAY 8

1. *Prereading activities*:
   - Brainstorm "What Happened to the Dinosaurs?" List student responses.
   - Prepare students for the reading of the text by telling them they will be newspaper reporters. Discuss the *wh* questions.
2. *Oral reading from literature*: Read the book *Dinosaur World* and the story "Why the Dinosaurs Disappeared" (*Focus*, Scott Foresman Level 4). Students may take notes.
3. *Responding to literature*: Discuss answers to the *wh* questions. Have a simulated panel discussion. "Experts" will discuss topics related to dinosaurs as well as their disappearance. The experts may also field questions from the newspaper reporters.
4. *SSR.*
5. *Composing (SSW)*: The students will compose a newspaper article with the headline DINOSAURS DISAPPEAR. Add these to the students' folders.
6. *Additional activities*: Students may work on a teacher-prepared or student-generated crossword puzzle. The computer program "Crossword Magic" could be used.

DAY 9

1. *Researching the class booklet*: Each student selects a different dinosaur on which he or she would like to do research.
2. *Organizing the findings*: Each student will organize the research findings on a mapping grid (see *Literacy Network Handbook*). Students may use books from the library, *Dinosaur Flashcards*, encyclopedias, and textbooks to gather the information they need.
3. *Drafting the report*: Have each student write a rough draft of the report in the first person. The writer will be the dinosaur.
   - Have the students proofread and edit the rough copy, in pairs.
   - Edit the students' work, using the proofreader's sheet shown in the *Literacy Network Handbook*.

DAY 10

1. *Polishing the reports*: The students' work is returned to them by the teacher for further refinements.
   - Return rough copies and proofreader's sheets.
   - Students write the final copy of their dinosaur reports.
   - Students make an illustration for their reports.
2. *Publishing the class booklet*: The class reports and illustrations are made into a class booklet and put into the school or classroom library.

Wholistic Day

The following is a description of a wholistic day indicating the events that occurred on the seventh day of our thematic unit *Fossils and Dinosaurs*.

Integrating reading with science (8:45-9:50)

We began our lesson by playing a recording of yesterday's choral reading. As dinosaur names were mentioned, all students joined in with the recording, repeating each dinosaur name.

The class then sat on the carpet in the reading corner for an oral reading presentation by the teacher. Poetry from *A Dozen Dinosaurs* was read to the class. This poetry was informative as well as entertaining.

Following the oral reading, the students were divided randomly into six equal groups. Each group represented one of the dinosaurs that were characterized in the poetry. The students were given copies of the poem about their dinosaur. Each group was instructed to go to a corner of the room, read the poem cooperatively, and decide how they could dramatize their dinosaur. They were given approximately 15 minutes for this task.

The class was then called together. The individual groups acted out their interpretation of their dinosaur in front of the class as the teacher reread the poetry.

Sustained silent reading (10:30-10:50)

Following recess and recorder class (9:50-10:30), the teacher presented a collection of dinosaur books from both the school and public library. Several were shown and discussed with the students to stimulate interest. Each student then selected a book for SSR. Twenty minutes were allocated for this purpose.

Partner conferencing (10:50-11)

Following SSR, the students as a group discussed some of their favorite dinosaurs. The students were then paired randomly and instructed to discuss their favorite dinosaur with their partner. Why is it your favorite? What did you like about that particular dinosaur? What were some of its habits?

Writing (11-11:30)

Following the partner conference, the students began to prepare for a writing activity. The teacher instructed the students to write about their favorite dinosaur. Since each student had discussed this with a partner, background had been established and the students were prepared to begin documenting their ideas.

As the students wrote, the teacher, along with the reading specialist and the learning disability teacher, conferenced individually with the students. Individual encouragement and guidance were given.

Story sharing (11:30-12)

After the writing activity, students were placed in groups of three by the teacher. Students of low progress were grouped with higher progress students. Groups gathered informally throughout the room for story sharing. The stories that the students had written were then read orally to the other members of the groups. As each student read a story, the others illustrated their image of that particular dinosaur. Stories and illustrations were placed into the students' portfolios. The morning concluded with lunch consisting of *Tyrannosaurus Burgers*.

Evaluation

In evaluating our students' progress, we decided to abandon the traditional "teach then test" philosophy. Objective test measures generally lead to memorization of factual material and stifle creative, higher level learning. It became our priority to evaluate each student individually through a process of observation, conferencing, and examining the student's writing. Therefore, we assessed our students' growth in the following manner:

Student Portfolios: Each student kept a folder containing all writing samples, illustrations, and additional activities. These folders were collected and examined daily (see Appendix D for sample portfolio). Progress was noted through a teacher-student dialogue journal.

Conferencing: Individual student conferences were held during writing time to discuss strengths and weaknesses.

Teacher Observation: With the help of the reading specialist and learning disability teacher, students were observed carefully throughout the course of this unit. Notes were taken concerning class participation, peer interaction, and teacher conferencing. Students who demonstrated difficulties were discussed through an informal staff review similar to that suggested by Carini (1982).

Class Booklet: Each student's contribution to the class booklet was evaluated. As this was a published document, attention was given to clarity, form, and convention. However, each student's work was given individual consideration with a very important question in mind—Did this student show progress?

Cloze Test: A brief cloze test was used following both the fossil and dinosaur portions of this unit. Such a test is somewhat subjective and quantitative, but holistically sound.

RESOURCE BOOKS

Dinosaur world by Geoffry T. Williams
Dinosaurs by Colin Douglas
A first look at dinosaurs by Selsam and Hunt
A dozen dinosaurs by Richard Armour
Digging for dinosaurs by W. E. Swinton
Answers about dinosaurs by Frederick Smithline
Wheels and rockets (*Focus* Scott Foresman Level 4)
Fossils: A new true book by Allan Roberts
Fossils: A golden guide by Rhodes, Zim, and Shaffer
Trade books from the school and public libraries
Literacy Network Handbook (Seaver & Botel, 1987)

6
James Learns to Read

James' third grade classroom was a traditional, three-reading-group, subskill-focused, individually oriented one, in which James was frequently described by the teacher as "disturbing." His disturbing, disruptive behavior caused the teacher to send him many times to the principal for discipline, make him sometimes sit outside the classroom door in the hallway, and eventually recommend him for SED (socially and emotionally disturbed) placement.

Since both his previous classroom teacher and remedial reading teacher had him placed at the primer level in reading, this placement was continued in third grade, so that James was below the lowest reading group in the class. The type of instruction offered in this situation involved much working alone on workbook exercises and a short session of oral reading on a very elementary level. For part of the year James was placed with another student (Mike), who was reading very poorly, and together they struggled with decoding primer and first grade material.

The teacher felt she could not spare the time to read to the class very often, since the three-group (plus James) arrangement took much time. Thus James rarely heard whole, connected, meaningful texts read aloud. And since James was regarded as not skilled enough to read on his own, during sustained silent reading time in class James was sent to the remedial reading teacher to do more subskill work with decoding, spelling, and vocabulary. Thus James was rarely expected to read whole, connected, meaningful texts nor was he often asked to read a book of his choice or share it with his classmates.

When social studies and science materials were introduced in the second half of the year, the reading was done by other students in the class, often haltingly and with little expression. Only rarely did the teacher submit James to the frustrating task of reading this material in front of his peers. In this case the system worked to allow those who needed the most practice the least time on task. The class was deprived of hearing fluent reading because the teacher felt the students should read orally, assuming this would help to improve their reading. (Actually it may have improved the oral skill of those who were already the better readers, but it did little more than exasperate the poorer readers, while depriving them all of hearing the text read fluently and meaningfully.)

Often the only social interaction James had with his peers in class was these displays of his inferior oral reading skill. It was rare for there to be time for whole group discussions—the reading groups took too much time. So James had little opportunity to display his critical thinking ability in class in response to literature. And since his access to the social studies and science material was often limited by the mediocre renditions of his peers, he was not equipped to fully respond to this material either.

The primary types of responding to literature activities that James had exposure to were test-like, one-right-answer responses to short pieces of disconnected text. Workbook exercises and skill/drill sheets did not require James to create a story, express his own opinion, explore a concept, or read for any purpose that was meaningful to him. In addition, his responses were limited to silent, individual responses devoid of much meaningful interaction with his peers. There were few peer group or partner activities in the classroom to allow James to display his competence and extend his thinking in interaction with peers.

In James' reading group time, he and Mike were required to decode material they knew was on a first grade level. This sometimes made them even more self-conscious and frustrated with reading. When James was pulled out of the class several times a week to go to the reading resource room, he was given more skills, drills, and phonics rules that were not the same as those he was working on in class. This served to confuse him even more for two reasons: (1) the lack of congruence between the classroom and resource room curriculum, and (2) the abstract cognitive task of having to decipher words and abstract rules removed from meaningful context and functional use.

Essentially James was excluded from the major literacy experiences that carried with them the most potential for learning to read and make meaning in the classroom. Paradoxically, this was not because of bias, malice, neglect, or incompetence; rather it was part of the way the school system worked to solve the problem of reading disability. Learning to read was defined as subskill mastery, and those who did not perform well on subskill measures were given more of the same.

Alternatively, we present in the following activities what we envision as an "ideal day" for James: what might have happened in his classroom if the school district had taken an ecological view, integrated its curriculum with the critical experiences framework, and organized the classroom for collaboration of peers and professionals. The approach is ecological in five major ways.

1. It pulls resources and information from many systems in James' ecology: school, family, community, and the state plan for communication arts.
2. It makes links and connections where there was previously separation and fragmentation.
3. James is viewed as an inseparable and interactive part of his classroom ecology.
4. Dealing with James within the ecology of the classroom has broader implications and benefits for his peers, specialists, and teachers alike.
5. Reading, writing, listening, and speaking continually interrelate in whole language activities that integrate content with skills.

In addition, congruence is achieved between the remedial and mainstream curriculum, and this pedagogy is accompanied by a congruent evaluation plan (see Chapter 11).

In this chapter we describe ecological activities for reading: responding to literature, responding to science texts, and sustained silent reading. Chapter 7 describes ecological activities for writing: oral and written composing, oral and written dialogue, and investigating language patterns. This separation of reading and writing activities, like the separation of the critical experiences from each other, is always somewhat artificial and arbitrary since they continually interrelate and overlap. But for the purposes of discussion, organization, and description we divide them in this way, acknowledging that reading, writing, speaking, and listening are in a continuous interactional relationship. In an ecological approach we attempt to both recognize this interdependence and reduce fragmentation sufficiently to allow for the integration of language learning.

The activities will be divided into before-reading, during-reading, and after-reading activities. A description of the specialist's role before, during, and after the activity follows, after which we extend and analyze the activities to explore the possibilities for creating more ecological learning experiences for all students. Further resources for activities designed for the critical experiences can be found in *Literacy Network Handbook* (Seaver & Botel, 1987).

RESPONDING TO LITERATURE

Mrs. Rinehart has chosen James' story "Bad Luck" as her text for whole group responding to literature.

BAD LUCK

by James

The boy had bad luck
and he never did nothing right
ever since he was born.
And he walked under a ladder
and he got bad luck.
And then the next day he broke a mirror
and he got more bad luck.
And he kept on getting bad luck.

And . . . and one day he decided to join up for baseball.
And . . . the coach picked him for the team
but the team
He's, he's not too good at baseball
cause he's got bad luck.
And he went to hit the ball
and he
and he missed it.
And the bat slipped out of his hand
and hit the coach.
And he said, "Oh, my bad luck.
I'm always getting in trouble."

And then the coach gave him another chance.
He, he, his bat slipped out of his hand again
and hit him
and hit the coach in the same place again.
And then
And then the coach got so mad
he wouldn't let him play anymore.

So he went out for football.
And . . . and . . .
the football coach asked him to go out
he's gonna throw it to him.
So he throws the football to the coach
And he's so much of bad luck
he throws it and he hits the coach in the stomach.
And . . . and
the coach gave him another chance
and he threw it again
and hit him in the stomach.
So he couldn't play football either.

So he went out for hockey.
And this time he got in BIG trouble.
    He was the goalie and he went out to catch the ball
    and he forgot he was playing hockey.
And he got his baseball
and he picked it up and threw it
    and it hit the guy.
    And he got in BIG trouble
        and he couldn't play that.

So he went out for tennis.
    And he forgot he was playing tennis—
        he thought he was playing football.
And he took the ball
And he
    The other guy had the tennis ball
    And he ran up and he tackled him
        And he got in trouble some more
            So he couldn't play tennis.

And so
    And 'bout 50 years later
        his bad luck went away.
And . . .
And he was better at all sports
    And he plays football now
        And he's the best one on the team.

James told the learning disability specialist this story last week, and she tape recorded and transcribed[*] it for him. James has listened to the tape of his own story and read the transcription along with it, so that by now he is nearly fluent in reading his own created text. Mrs. Rinehart and the specialist have worked together on the lesson plan for this text, creating the following before, during, and after reading activities for James' whole class.

---

[*]The transcription attempts to follow the natural speech pattern and rhythm of the student—including pauses, phrasing, and intonation—by using a prose poem form.

Lesson Plan

Before reading

Mrs. Rinehart asks the class what they think of when they see the words *bad luck*—she writes these words on the board. The class then offers many examples, signs, sayings, and myths concerning bad luck, which the teacher maps on the board. Some of the responses from James' classmates include:

> walking along a sidewalk and getting run over by a truck,
> messing up in a big pageant,
> a bigger kid takes something from me,
> getting beat up,
> falling or tripping over ladders.

Mrs. Rinehart also asks the class if they have ever heard any of the superstitions about bad luck: breaking mirrors, black cats, walking under a ladder, or throwing salt over your shoulder.

Mrs. Rinehart asks why students sometimes get in trouble—she writes this word on the board. James' classmates offer:

> They don't have anything else to do.
> They get caught at the wrong time.
> They try to act funny and show off.
> They want to talk—they're social.
> They fight with the teacher.
> They want to take risks.

James says, "They don't do what the teacher tells them to do."

Mrs. Rinehart asks, "Who gets in the most trouble in your family?" After a few responses she asks why they get in trouble and if it is always their fault?

James says, "I always get in trouble at home, but it's not my fault. My brother is always fightin' with me." Other classmates say that happens to them too, and they give many examples.

Mrs. Rinehart asks, "Who gets in the most trouble in this class?" Someone suggests Randy, someone else suggests Mike, and a third student suggests James. James agrees that he gets in a lot of trouble in class. The teacher asks if these students get in trouble because they are bad or because they have bad luck. After some puzzled looks a few students offer:

Bad—there's no such thing as bad luck.

Bad—Mike's a ball hog. He asks for trouble.

Both—If you're with the wrong crowd and you don't know what they're doing, it's bad luck. If they want to take bad risks for fun, they're bad.

Bad—they want to see how far they can get before they get in trouble.

James says: "My mom says me and my dad were born with bad luck. I was born on Friday the 13th."

With James playing the role of the boy in the story and Mike playing the role of the football coach, Mrs. Rinehart has the pair do a simulation of a meeting between the two after the boy has hit the coach three times in the stomach "by mistake" during practice. James insists that he really did not try to hit the coach—he was just trying to pass the ball the way the coach told him to pass it. The coach says he is not convinced, and a lively discussion follows.

During reading

Mrs. Rinehart passes out the story "Bad Luck" to each class member. They are asked to follow along as she reads it, joining in with the words *bad luck* and *trouble* when she comes to them in the text. On their copies of the text she has these words underlined, and as she comes to them she holds up the word cards she has made with *bad luck* and *trouble* on them.

Mrs. Rinehart has divided the class in half with one side of the room taking the role of the coach as she reads, reacting in pantomime to how they would feel and what their actions would be, and the other half of the room being the boy, pantomiming his actions, feelings, and reactions. Periodically she stops reading and asks one of the "coaches" what he feels like saying; then she asks one of the "boys" to respond. She also asks periodically for someone to predict what might happen next.

As each episode in the story concludes, the class is asked to keep score, deciding whether the incident could be called the fault of the boy (is he getting himself in trouble?) or if it was merely bad luck and no fault of his. If they are not sure, they are to score it a question. The score sheets are shown in Figure 6.1.

After reading

Mrs. Rinehart asks for the scores and puts the tally on the board, allowing the students to defend their choices and give evidence from the

FIGURE 6.1.   Scoring the Story: A Sample Sheet

bad luck (no fault)	?	trouble (boy's fault)

text. (She might also have allowed the students to go into small groups to do this activity, reread the text together to find evidence, then report their results to the whole group.)

The students are asked, "What stood out for you in this story?" and they are encouraged to make personal responses based on their own experience and their own feelings about the story.

Mrs. Rinehart puts the class into pairs (one student imagining being a coach and one a boy) to alternately talk nonstop about their side of the story—their thoughts, feelings, reactions. After two minutes of nonstop talking by one student, the teacher turns the light switch off and on to signal that the other student begins to talk. Then each student writes in a journal for ten minutes about what they just said.

The class is then divided into their small work groups, an arrangement that Mrs. Rinehart has worked out with the specialist to include a more advanced reader in each group along with a less advanced reader and an average student. They are to take the role of author and make up a different ending for "Bad Luck." James is in a group with Sue, who writes fluently, and she writes down James' new ending combined with Sam's suggestions. As a group they decide to take the role of actor and dramatize their new story for the class.

The next day the group activity is storytelling, and they sketch the scenario of another bad luck (or trouble) story. James' group has no trouble coming up with another story, which they eagerly tell to the whole class. Mrs. Rinehart tape records it as they tell it, then asks for a volunteer to take the tape home and transcribe it with the help of a family member. This text will then be added to the growing library created by the class.

Mrs. Rinehart has announced that the class is privileged to have in the audience today the author of the famous story, "Bad Luck." She asks Mike to play a Phil Donahue–type television interviewer and ask James to tell the audience something about his background as a famous author/story-teller (for example, How did he get his ideas? Why/how did he write this particular story? How would he describe the boy in the story?).

For both concept building and language study, Mrs. Rinehart asks, "What is the relationship between *bad luck* and *trouble*?" and "How does *bad luck* relate to *trouble*?" After the class wrestles with this for a while, she asks them for examples of *bad* meaning *good*, in colloquial expressions such as, That song/album/group is really bad (meaning it is really good). The class gets into a discussion of how words change meanings over time with particular kinds of use and users. They also talk about the difficulty of making meaning for people who are either learning the English language as a second language or who have not heard some of the various meanings that words can take in particular contexts (as where *bad* is *good*) and how confusing that must be. Juan adds his experiences.

Specialist's Role—Before, During, and After

The specialist first came into the classroom at the request of Mrs. Rinehart when she was having difficulty with James continually disturbing the class and his continued lack of progress in reading. The specialist observed James in the classroom in a variety of learning tasks, documented what she observed, and then met with Mrs. Rinehart to compare notes and to talk about the problem. They both agreed that James was getting nowhere, and Mrs. Rinehart asked the specialist for her thoughts in the matter. Mrs. Rinehart agreed to try the specialist's suggestions in structuring a more integrated, whole language approach to learning in her classroom.

Their first decision was to eliminate the three-group management scheme for reading in favor of more heterogeneous, whole group activities. In this way they felt that James (as well as Mike and, in fact, all the students) would receive more exposure to whole connected texts, world knowledge, higher level thinking, opportunities to extend his thinking in collaboration with peers, and concept building in a community of learners. The elimination of the three separate groups and three separate lesson plans—actually four because James and Mike were in a separate group—left more time for ecological teaching. It meant more time for reading to the class, for concept building and other types of scaffolding before the reading, for more exploration of ideas and building of world knowledge while reading, and for more comprehension activities after reading.

The next decision was for the specialist to work one-on-one with James for a few hours interviewing him, doing an interactive reading protocol (see Chapter 11), and taking his stories. In the process of doing this she discovered that James was an excellent storyteller, so she sug-

gested to Mrs. Rinehart that his stories might be celebrated in the classroom and used to generate more story creation while also serving as the
reading text for the class.

The reading and learning specialists in James' school have been
working with the teachers during inservice workshops and seminars toward
a more integrated approach to language learning across the curriculum.
Because of this exposure to both theory and practice, it was easier for
Mrs. Rinehart to make changes in the ecology of her classroom.

One particular change she had been thinking about, but had not as
yet instituted, was the use of peer tutors—having a more able reader/writer
paired with a less able peer, with each being responsible for the extension
of the other's thinking (see Chapter 8). A similar change involved structuring mixed ability groups, with all members being as responsible for the
learning of their peers as for their own learning.

Mrs. Rinehart and the specialist began working out combinations of
students and types of activities that were dependent on group cooperation
rather than individual competition. She was particularly interested in
placing James in a group wherein he could display his competence and be
a contributing member, while at the same time having the opportunity to
use more advanced peers as resources and models.

Mrs. Rinehart knew, because of the way the specialist's role was
defined in the school system (as colleague of and resource for the teacher
in the classroom), that she would have the support of the specialist in both
planning and executing the needed changes. They worked collaboratively
to plan activities and student grouping, and they decided together at which
times the specialist would be needed in the classroom to assist James. For
instance, she planned to come in during the sustained writing period and
for a reading checkout during sustained silent reading.

The continuing role of the specialist in collaboration with Mrs. Rinehart is performing periodic observational evaluations of James in a variety
of learning activities and group arrangements in the classroom. In this way
the specialist continues to collaborate with Mrs. Rinehart in the improvement of a learning climate in the classroom that will be conducive to
optimal learning not only for James, but for all the students in the
classroom.

During her last observation, for example, the specialist noted that
James was disruptive during the group storytelling activity. She thus arranged to sit in on the next small group activity to help James work more
constructively in the group. She is also considering having James' mother
come in occasionally to sit in during small group activities, and she is
trying to coordinate James' mother's work schedule with Mrs. Rinehart's
teaching schedule so that might be possible.

Analysis

Looking at the differences between the previous fragmented responding to literature activities and the sample activity from our more ecological day for James, we can see how in the latter there were more opportunities for James and his peers to:

1. Hear a whole connected text and respond to it;
2. Interact collaboratively with peers to extend and refine thinking and meaning making;
3. Explore concepts and ideas in a community of learners;
4. Respond personally, both orally and in writing;
5. Call forth and build on their personal knowledge and experiences in and out of school;
6. Use higher level critical thinking.

In addition, James was validated in a way that might allow him to take ownership of his own experiences rather than denying personal responsibility for his own action. Validating the student's voice in the curriculum goes beyond the benefits of self-expression and self-esteem to the benefits of autonomy—ownership, responsibility, and self-governance.

RESPONDING TO SCIENCE TEXTS

During the second half of the year James' class began using a science text, which the students in the class read aloud in a typically disjointed, halting third grade way. This reading was difficult to follow for students like James, and it was boring for the teacher and the better readers in the class. The teacher tried to "spare" students like James from reading orally, but occasionally she would have him read short passages, whereupon he displayed his difficulty with reading.

Several problems emerge in this sort of classroom display of oral reading skill besides the boredom of the better readers and the confusion of those who are not as advanced. First, those who are the better readers tend to get called on to read more often and for longer periods. The teacher tries to protect the poorer readers from embarrassment and frustration in such oral classroom displays of incompetence, so they are called on less frequently and the passages they read are much shorter. Thus we have a situation where the rich get richer and the poor get poorer. Those who read well get more practice, and those who are poorer readers get less practice.

Children are not unaware of the inequity in this process, but they tend to accept the teacher's judgment of their ability or inability. What appears to emerge in this process is a reinforcement of the ability labeling established through the three reading groups in the classroom. So the child labeled as a poor reader (by being put in the lowest reading group or by being labeled as remedial or learning disabled) once again is reminded of his or her incompetence and lack of ability in reading.

A further problem in this process is that none of the students in the classroom get to hear the material read fluently and meaningfully as a whole connected text. They get parts and pieces of often poorly read content material, which makes comprehension more difficult and interest and motivation to learn less likely. So while the poorer readers are subjected to a frustrating task made more difficult by the process, the better readers suffer a loss of interest and motivation. In addition, there is no room in this process for the higher level thinking and reading strategy development that we will describe as part of our more ecological day.

The sequel to the students' oral reading during science periods in James' class was assigned questions from the end of the textbook chapter. These questions typically asked the students to restate, list, define, or recall facts from material that was covered in the chapter. Little was asked that would cause the students to integrate or synthesize learning, to wonder, to ask more questions, or to be more creative in approaching future content information or questions: little, in short, that would teach them to be scientists.

The claim of the textbook companies is that these questions add up to comprehension. The problem is that the questions are isolated elements of vocabulary, main idea, detail, inference, and sequence, which all require recall of one right answer. Such questions aim more at test structure than text structure. They miss text structure because they omit interaction, critical thinking, and the prior experience of the student.

Lesson Plan

Before reading

James' class is studying oxygen, and the teacher begins the lesson by doing an experiment. She puts a lighted match into a glass, and the class watches the flame being extinguished quickly as the oxygen burns up. The class talks about why that happened, raises many questions about the process, and adds this experiment to their science journals.

After letting the students see and do an experiment that gets them raising questions, the teacher draws from the class what they know about oxygen. On the basis of their prior knowledge they arrive at the following list:

It's the stuff you breathe in.
We need it to live.
It's an element (O).
It's stuff that flowers breathe out.

After putting the list on the board, the teacher has the students put some of the words into categories so that they can analyze the classroom community's knowledge of oxygen at this point. The teacher then leads the students in listing what they want to know about oxygen. They ask:

How does it work?
Where does it come from?
What is it used for?
Why is it here?

During reading

The teacher begins reading to the class the text selection on oxygen. She pauses occasionally to predict with the class what might come next from pictures and headings, and to raise questions as they go along in the text.

Today she has decided to focus on a few paragraphs that deal with concepts she wants the class to think about. She stops at the end of each sentence in these paragraphs and says to the students, "What are the things you are thinking about now?" She continues having the students do a think-aloud protocol (see Chapter 11) one sentence after another, and as she reads each sentence she demonstrates some of the things she is thinking about herself.

As she continues to ask the students what they are thinking about, many types of responses are made. Some students simply repeat the sentence, some make predictions, some add their own experience to it, some interpret it in their own way, some analyze it logically, some draw an analogy, others give an example or ask about a word. The teacher writes these things on the board and says to the students, "Do you see how many things we think about? Look at all the interesting things from these very few words—all these different thoughts came out of our reading, and different people had different thoughts. As we were trying to understand the reading, all of these different things were happening in our heads."

After doing this think aloud for a few paragraphs, she continues to read, stopping at the end of each paragraph. She asks the students to predict what is going to happen next, summarize what happened, or raise questions. She guides them through this process, asking them to think about how predicting helped them comprehend, a process sometimes described as metacognitive thinking or learning to learn. This process continually enlarges and expands strategies for reading.

James is very mature and knows a lot of things; so he, along with everyone else in the class, can participate fully in this reading of the science text. They are all hearing each other's thinking processes, and they can learn to appreciate the variety of ways to make meaning from texts.

The teacher gradually moves to larger units of text. She begins with one sentence at a time, then moves to paragraphs, and then moves to whole sections under a hearing. She reads the entire section under a heading and then asks the class to respond. Again she is teaching them strategic reading, emphasizing the comprehension process. She is taking them through the text in a very directed, guided fashion: sometimes modeling, sometimes mediating, but continually leading ahead toward higher level thinking.

After reading

The teacher wants the students to have a purpose for going back to the text so they can more fully comprehend it. So today she asks them to take the role of detective, finding the questions the author had in mind when writing the text. To model their role she takes the students back to the text for several paragraphs and helps them read like a detective, writing the question the author might have had in mind when he wrote the paragraph. She tells them, "Anytime you as an author write something, there is an implied question: You have answered a question in your own mind as an author. The reason you are explaining something is that there is this implied question."

She asks the students to be detectives and see if they can find the questions the author of their text is answering. To do this she has them form small groups of three to four students, find a way to share the rereading, and arrive at the author's questions, which they will write in their science journals. (This activity might also be done with partners.)

Analysis of the Activity/Specialist's Role

The preceding think-aloud protocol and questioning strategies are examples of the fifth critical experience—Learning to Learn. The teacher leads the students through various reading strategies—questioning, predicting, analyzing, building on their own experiences—in successively larger segments of text. Students are led through these experiences and then encouraged to reflect on them. For instance, after the think-aloud activity and the question writing (to discover the author's questions) the teacher might ask such questions as the following:

> What did we do today to learn about oxygen?
> How would this help you in your future reading?
> Where else could this be used?
> How did predicting help you learn about oxygen?

In this way the students are led to reflect on and build their own strategies for learning.

Of course, teachers must also teach themselves how to be reflective first. This is another area in which teacher–specialist collaboration is particularly important. Together these professionals can extend each other's thinking in the direction of looking at the whole of learning rather than at specific elements or subsystems. This is not an easy task, since much of what passes for education is more an accumulation of facts rather than learning to learn. The study of specific, easily measurable facts—the trivial pursuit—is safe and manageable. One need only follow the textbook. But this misses the depth and growth possible in a less linear, less accumulative approach to learning. It also misses the personal professional creativity and growth possible when teachers and specialists take ownership of their own curriculum.

In addition to their role as collaborator with the teacher, helping the teacher select and model reading strategies, for instance, specialists can help plan student groups in the classroom, find and arrange for older student tutors, help plan and execute experiments (or find older students to do so), and help extend the learning of certain individuals in the classroom who need more mediation.

SELF-SELECTED READING

In James' "ideal" classroom, there are at least 100 books from which he and his classmates choose and read for 20 minutes a day. The students choose books and read them in their own way, at their own pace, with opportunities for various kinds of sharing. The books are at a variety of reading and interest levels, and James can read many of them on his own.

Sometimes James chooses an easier book to read, and sometimes he chooses a harder book because he is interested in it.

Before reading

Occasionally, the teacher gives capsule summaries of some of the books in the classroom library and does a form of "bookselling" to motivate interest. On occasion the librarian comes into the classroom to introduce several books that she thinks the students might be interested in. The students in the class from time to time share their books as well, when they read something they particularly like, so James and his classmates have many opportunities to know something about many of the books they may choose from.

During reading

It is sustained silent reading (SSR) time, and the students put everything away and take out books that they have chosen before. Some of the students go to the classroom library because they are ready to exchange books. In a few minutes they are expected to be back at their seats reading quietly like everyone else in the class, including the teacher.

The students know the rule: The only sound allowed is the sound of turning pages. If a student breaks the rule, the teacher points to the sign about SSR time. For the next 20 minutes there is only the sound of turning pages.

Today James has chosen a book about baseball (*The Kid from Tomkinsville* by John Tunis), which is hard for him to read, but because of his own experience and interest in the subject, he is able to make meaning from the text. In addition, the teacher has read aloud from several parts of this book to whet both his and the other students' appetites and thus give them a framework (scaffold) to build from.

After reading

At the end of 15 minutes on this day, the teacher asks the students, "Who would like to share something very briefly that you have been reading?" She has previously asked them to talk for a few minutes about what stood out for them in their reading, so they know it is to be a brief observation only. In James' class this activity has become a sort of bookselling game, with a prize (a book, of course) for the best salesperson.

Today she calls on James, who wants to share a particularly exciting incident from his book. His description is very animated, and several of the other boys in class say they want to sign up to read the book next. If more than four other students read the book because of James' "bookselling," he will get a paperback copy of the book to keep. Usually the students' purpose during SSR time is just to enjoy reading, to become friends with books, to learn about the characters and how they feel, and perhaps to understand themselves better. Today, however, they add to this the purpose of motivating others to read.

7
James Learns to Write

James' ability to orally compose stories went unnoticed in the school system of which he was a part. There simply was no time in the already full day of structured activities geared to the traditional curriculum to allow for oral composing or for the writing of such compositions.

It was presumed that James did not have the necessary skills to write on his own, so it was rare for much writing to be expected of him beyond one-word answers or sentence-level exercises. James' classrooms were not structured for cooperative peer interaction, so the possibility of working with a more competent partner in writing activities or with a group in oral composing, as he did in our responding to literature activity in Chapter 6, did not exist for James.

Through our created day for James we will take a look at the ecological approach to oral and written composing as it might work to the benefit of James' language learning. At the level of the individual activity, we describe a whole language approach to composing that makes use of oral composing as a prelude to (or scaffold for) written composing. At the level of the student, we make use of both cognition and affect as James draws from personal knowledge, experiences, and interests to compose his own stories. At the level of the classroom ecology, we use cooperative peer activities to enhance the learning opportunities of students at all stages of development.

Going beyond the classroom to the wider ecology of the school, we make use of the specialist in collaboration with the classroom teacher to both plan for and intercede in the learning of the individual student. And in the interrelationship between the school and family systems, we suggest the inclusion of the parents (or grandparents) in the composing activities both at home and in the classroom. In this way we hope to establish congruence and continuity of language learning between these two systems in the ecology of the learner.

Essentially, we are attempting to answer the question of how we can operate, given what we know from an ecological approach, to create an optimal learning climate. Theoretically and ideally, we can reduce fragmentation to zero. Practically, it can only be done partially, because we are limited by the way the traditional system is structured. We believe that it is in the classroom that we have the greatest likelihood of making changes at this point. Though political, economic, and cultural changes will be needed for lasting effects, we believe that if we operate within an ecological framework in the classroom—with higher expectations for all students; integrated, whole language learning; and classroom practice that focuses on communication across the curriculum in a community of collaborating teachers, specialists, and learners—we can significantly reduce the number of students who are mislabeled as disabled.

ORAL AND WRITTEN COMPOSING

An Activity in Oral and Written Composing

Today James and his classmates are adding to a list of things they know about and stories they can tell. The list is kept in their writing portfolios, which contain previous personal narratives and a variety of other types of writing they have done. James' list includes football, baseball, basketball, music, and records.

After adding two topics to their writing folder lists, they are to choose one topic and do two minutes of nonstop talking with their partner about this topic. This oral composing activity preceding written composing allows the students to brainstorm ideas with a peer. When the teacher switches the lights off and on, the class knows it is time for the other partner to do two minutes of nonstop talking.

At this point the students will do a first draft of their story or topic. The teacher allows 20 minutes of sustained writing time for this purpose, and the students are encouraged to write continuously about what they have just talked about with their partner. Careful editing is discouraged at this point in favor of a continuous flow of ideas and the creation of a new text. Attention to spelling, sentence structure, punctuation, and other mechanics of writing will wait until the final draft.

On this particular day the specialist is in the classroom to take James' story. She has brought her tape recorder with her, and as James does his oral composing she records the story. Then, while the other students are doing sustained writing, she transcribes the story with James so that he can clarify any words she cannot hear clearly on the tape. They pull two desks outside the classroom door to do their listening of the tape and transcribing so they do not disturb the rest of the class.

THE FOOTBALL PEOPLE THAT COULDN'T SAVE

by James

Once upon a time there was some people who loved football and then they made up a football club. And they were always saving up to buy uniforms, but they always had to—and they never got enough money. And one time they all had a tooth pulled, and they all put it under their bed—under their pillow. They went to sleep, and they woke up the next morning, and there was two dollars under each pillow. And then they had enough money to buy their football uniforms.

But then, while they played football there was these two bad guys—they always tried to mess up the football time. And they kicked the football and the bad guys caught it, and they punched a hole into the football. And then they had to try to save up more money to get a football.

Then every time they'd save up money to get the football they would have to spend it on something. And one time—one time they had enough money to buy the football. As soon as they bought the football for ten—for twenty dollars for one ole measley old football—and then they were mad cause they didn't—it shouldn't have cost that much.

But the bad guys were the ones who did that—they tried to get that football and it was a fake. If they kick it it's gonna blow up—blow up into a balloon and it's gonna pop. And they kicked it and it popped in the air, and they took it back to their thing, and the thing was going. And they said, "It must have been a phoney."

And they went inside where it was, was boarded up. They went inside and it's all empty, and they were lookin' around for some clues and stuff. And they found some blood—they thought it was blood, but it was catsup. The bad guys were tryin' to be ignorant. And they followed the blood into a closet, and the bad guy was hangin' there pretendin' like he was dead. Jumped out and grabbed them and took all their money. And then they went home again cryin'.

Then the last time they saved all the money, and they bought game uniforms for football. And they bought a football. And bad guys had to move, so they had whole football place to themself. And now they all live in New Cumberland where they're all rich. They all saved their money.

James adds this story and tape to his growing collection of stories, which he can listen to and practice with at home to help him with more fluent reading. The specialist has also met with his mother and grand-mother about James' talent in storytelling, and they have agreed to help James with some taping and transcribing of stories. The specialist has asked them in their transcription to be faithful to the way James tells the story, and to just write down exactly what he says without worrying about corrections or perfections in grammar. She has assured them that revision and editing will be attended to when the class prepares final drafts for classroom publication.

At the end of the 20-minute period the class puts the drafts into their writing folders to be worked on at another time. They may choose to add to this particular draft during free choice time, or they may wait until another day when they have a writing workshop period. The piece of writing may also be brought home to work on if they choose.

Extending the Activity

In subsequent writing periods James and his peers may return to this piece of writing and attend to elaboration and clarification of ideas, spelling and punctuation, and other mechanics of writing. Some of this editing work may be done alone, and some of it may be done with a partner, reading the story or composition aloud and asking for questions and suggestions.

The teacher and specialist have done several "fishbowl" demonstrations of peer conferencing for the class, modeled on the teacher-student writing conferences that are part of class writing periods. Following the writer's second reading of the complete text, the partner responds with:

1. What did I hear? (Partner provides a summary.)
2. What do I want to know more about? (Partner asks questions of writer and extends thinking.)
3. What suggestions do I have? (Partner may build on questions, point out where text is not clear, or suggest things to consider.)

As in the teacher-student conference, writers have the power and should do most of the talking as they articulate what they are saying in the text. Writers also retain the final choice in taking suggestions or making changes. The partner may make suggestions, mediate, and extend thinking, but ownership remains with the writer. The conference validates the student by the partner's both understanding and wanting to know more.

On this particular day several sixth grade students were in the class also, watching the specialist tape James' story and then watching as the story was transcribed. The specialist was instructing them as she took dictation and transcribed so that they could do this with other students who needed extra help with writing.

Oral Group Dialogue and the Dialogue Journal

Goodlad (1984) suggests that the most important thing about school for the students who go there is their daily personal and social lives. Sadly, he notes in the results of his study of schooling a gross neglect of exposure to the tragedies and triumphs of human striving in the form of literature. Concurrent with this lack of literary exposure is an inhibition of overt expressions of joy, anger, fear, and other human feelings in the classroom.

Instead of bringing the whole learner into the classroom and attempting to deal with affect as well as cognition, we tend to sanitize the dialogue in the classroom, much as we have sanitized the literature in the curriculum. It is possible to find classrooms with a flat, neutral emotional balance, which have little connection to the fullness of human existence. Critics have claimed that some classrooms and curriculum are filled with trivial pursuits—basic facts, skills, and testmanship—due to the pressures on us to keep the status quo.

Both oral dialogue (in the form of group sharing of thoughts, feelings, and problems) and written dialogue (in the form of personal dialogue journals for the sharing of deeper human emotions) provide a way out of our sterile classroom climate. The power of human dialogue—much like the power of great literature that is not stripped of its dragons, fairies, comedies, and tragedies—can be used to transform the learning environment, particularly for those who find it devoid of meaning for their lives.

Oral group dialogue

The ultimate goal of group dialogue sessions is to have the students work through some of their own experiences, concerns, and problems both in and out of school. The process involves allowing students to talk with the group and the teacher to find out what they are feeling about a problem or an issue, looking at why they are feeling that way, and discovering some ways to handle both their feelings and the problem, experience, or issue.

James' fourth and fifth grade learning disability teacher would call together the class for 20 minutes or longer several times a week, have them pull their chairs into a circle, and allow them to talk about whatever was on their minds. She encouraged them to talk freely, assuring them that no one would judge what they said, and that what they experience emotionally is neither right nor wrong. This was to be a time to talk things out—to share feelings, experiences, and thoughts.

What poured forth frequently during these periods were poignant stories of personal fears, hopes, joys, and tragedies that permeated the lives of James and his classmates. The teacher mediated in the best sense of the word by leading the students ahead to think of options and possibilities in these often difficult situations. She helped them toward fuller understanding and clarity when needed, and she allowed for the full expression of human emotions among James and his peers.

Subjects included dealing with being in a special class, problems and difficulties related to divorce, feelings of needing more attention from parents, troubles with brothers and sisters, and peer problems in and out of school. As the group continued to share, they evolved as a compassionate and caring community, sharing the joy and pain of fellow students.

James' teacher felt that she should not shy away from personal problems, but she did not attempt to solve them either. Instead she mediated, led ahead, modeled, suggested resources, and acted as a caring human being—nothing more, nothing less. Her advice to teachers attempting to begin such oral dialogue sessions is to be objective about what is said rather than reacting with surprise, disgust, or judgment; and to remove personal feelings from the situation, allowing the students to say whatever they want and to talk things out. What follows is her own further description of this approach to oral group dialogue.

As a teacher of learning disabled children I feel that the emotional stability or instability of a child can affect academic performance. If a child is given the opportunity to explore and share his feelings, he seems to be more at peace with his environment. This in turn lends itself to a more consistent academic performance. Oral dialogue can provide the student with a socially acceptable means of sharing, exploring, and understanding his emotions.

Through a group discussion approach each individual functions as a group member. When feelings and incidents are shared, quite often the student discovers he is not alone—that another group member has had a similar experience. Before long the students become a peer counseling group, with the teacher as facilitator. Most often the role of the teacher is only to gently guide the conversation by helping each student express feelings that are difficult for him to share. At no time throughout the discussion can or should the teacher be judgmental. The feelings and experiences shared are neither right nor wrong. They are genuine emotions and must be treated with respect.

James during group dialogue sessions

The following are partial transcripts of James during group dialogue sessions talking about some stealing incidents in the community.

James: Sam comes in town with 10 to 50 dollars. Joe be sayin', "Sam, where'd you get all that money?"

"I went over to the store and took some."

So we'd go up to the store, right. And they'd be just robbin' that place blind. And one time they had these combs and brushes, and put them in the back of their—they had hats on and they put them all around their heads, put their hats on, just like a Smurf—they were all puffed out. They walked out of the store. Then they went up to Sears, took 'em all out, and threw 'em away. They be stealin' just to be havin' somethin' to do.

When we were at [another store] he put $3.95 on a 65 dollar [item] and bought it. We would a got away with it if the lady wouldn't a seen us exchange the price tag.

It's funny though, because when we got caught I had big alligator tears comin' down my face—I was scared. I had tears comin' down my face, my mom said, "You wanna go to a home?"

And then I say, "Yeh, I wanna go to a home."

And she said, "Why?"

And I said, "'Cause I deserve it."

And she said, "No you don't—you're just gonna make up for what you did."

Other student: You didn't do nothin'.

James: That's what I'm mad about.

Teacher: She asked you if you wanted to go to a home, away from her?

James: And I said, "That's what I'm mad about—I didn't do nothin'. But I still got a record."

Teacher: Do you think your mom believes it?

Student: Do you have any offenses?

James: I got a record.

Teacher: Did you have something on you?

James: No. I was just with him and I got a record. I'm 11 years old and I got a record.

(Discussion of peers stealing and giving what they've stolen to others.)

Teacher: When you take something that you know is stolen, that's the same thing as stealing it.

James: What if we didn't know?

Teacher: You can still be punished for it even if you didn't know. I mean it's awfully hard to prove that you really didn't know. It's just like you saying to the police, "Well I didn't know that they were stealin'." Well that's pretty tough to prove to them.

Partial transcript of James talking about his mom not believing him:

Teacher: So lots of times you are telling the truth, and your mom takes somebody else's word and doesn't believe you—feels that you are lying. Do you have any idea why that might be?

James: I don't know—she doesn't trust me.

Teacher: Have you in the past lied to her?

James: Yeh.

Teacher: And gotten caught?

James: Gotten caught lots of times.

Teacher: Remember the old, old story about the boy that cried

James: wolf—I know.

Teacher: She probably brings that up to you all the time, huh?

(James gives example of incident where he was blamed for something that was not his fault.)

Teacher: Do you feel sometimes that your mom expects bad behavior out of you?

James: Yep, she does.

Teacher: That even when you don't do it, that she just figures that you have done it because that's what she expects from you.

James: My mom never believes me—I hate that.

Student: [inaudible]

Teacher: That's an interesting question—maybe you can answer it. He said, "Did your mom ever believe you?" Do you remember a time when your mom used to believe what you were telling her? Never? So, as far back as you can remember she always expected bad things from you?

James: Uh-hm. My grandmom believes me some of the time now.

This excerpt shows that there is a trust relationship in the classroom community between the students and the teacher as well as among peers. Students are validated as they relive even negative experiences. They are allowed to build on their experiences and learn from them.

The teacher or specialist mediates in an understanding way rather than a judgmental way, using dialogue as an opportunity for growth and learning. Books might also be found for students to help them work through some of their concerns.

The dialogue journal

Written dialogue journals (Kreeft, 1984) provide an opportunity to express feelings that are very private, perhaps too sacred to share with anyone else. Dialogue journals are typically kept privately between the teacher and the student, although it is possible for journals to be kept between peers as well. They are an open, continuous dialogue between the two—a sort of written conversation that allows for the communication of anything of interest or importance to the student.

The dialogue journal writing process involves short, 10- to 20-minute writing periods once or twice a week, wherein the student writes to the teacher (after reading her response to the previous journal entry) about a topic of interest or concern. The entries are usually kept in a spiral notebook and passed on to the teacher for a response. The teacher also writes in the notebook when she finds time at school or at home and returns the notebook to the student by the next writing period.

One particularly sacred dialogue journal sharing in James' learning disability class involved Pearl, the author of a moving story about a very small princess (see Afterword). As the end of her story seems metaphorically to suggest, Pearl has considered suicide. She mentioned this on one occasion to her teacher. In her dialogue journal she confided that she hated her mother's boyfriend and that he beat her. Many of her entries were filled with whole pages of hate and anger, which before she had been able to express only through explosive and destructive classroom behavior. It was not unusual for Pearl to swear at the teacher and throw books and other objects in the classroom.

The teacher shared Pearl's problems in confidence with the principal and the guidance counselor so that more help could be provided. Thus the school served as a nexus for collaboration within the ecosystem of the student, in this case by linking to resources within the school system. Ideally, as Heath and McLaughlin (1987) suggest, the school could then connect with community resources (child and family services, community mental health agencies) that would provide more help for the student and the family.

Though we are not suggesting dialogue journals as a method of solving behavior problems, they appear to have value in at least helping teachers and specialists to understand part of the meaning behind some student behavior and alerting them to the need for more help. Some examples of dialogue journal entries from James' peers will illustrate some of their frustrations and concerns.

> *Matthew:* I hate math. . . . I am 8 years old. . . . I can't re
> *Daniel:* I don't no how to handl my big brother he alwas call me that I am stooped because I am in ld
> *Teacher:* I am sorry your big brother is mean to you. He is wrong about being in an LD class—if you are not smart enough to learn (or stupid, as your brother says) you are not put in a learning disability (LD) class. LD classes are for *smart* kids who are just having trouble learning for some reason. What do your parents think about the LD class? What do you think about it?
> *Daniel:* My Partes like it. so do I. But I don't like some of the kids in yer.
> *Teacher:* Who don't you like in the class? Why do you think some of the kids in class get in trouble?
> *Daniel:* I don't like Billy. He gets to smart Nect time he get Bose I am going to kill yem
> *Teacher:* What does he do that bothers you the most? Do you think there is any other way you could get him to change beside killing him?
> *Daniel:* He calls me names. Me and Billy is frinds now.
> *Teacher:* That is *fantastic* that you are friends now. How did you change from wanting to kill him to being friends?
> *Daniel:* I don't no how we did it. I got in a fiht with my big Bother.

In addition to its value for the sharing of personal feelings and thoughts and for written meaning construction, the dialogue journal allows the teacher to model standard written English along with the extension of the student's thinking. As students continue to express themselves in dialogue with the teacher, and as they continue to read the teacher's responses to what they have written, their own writing begins to approximate more closely the teacher's model.

The teacher may spell correctly a word the student has previously misspelled (as in Daniel's *friend* or *brother* above), and use complete sentences in the responses. The student may pick up this spelling in a later journal entry, and may begin to punctuate more logically and reduce the number of sentence fragments. Here again we see how the critical experiences continually overlap and interrelate: An activity in written composing is also an activity in the study of language patterns.

INVESTIGATING LANGUAGE PATTERNS

Although James was exposed to an overabundance of skill exercises designed to teach him to decode, spell, capitalize, and punctuate, he rarely demonstrated competence in any of these skills. Part of the problem, of course, was the fragmented way in which these skills were taught. They were disconnected from any meaningful text, isolated from any purposeful activity, and rarely taught at a point in time that James actually needed them to communicate or make meaning, as in the dialogue journal activity above.

In an ecological approach to language study, the purpose is to understand language systems that will help the students comprehend, decode, and spell in a whole language context that has meaning for them. The students learn about the various features and relationships of language (the basic skills) through using higher level skills of interpretation and communication. For our sample activity we begin with interpretation of a whole piece of language and then give the students an experience in reconstructing the text where there have been some deletions. The students are thus led to take the role of detective, which continues as they arrange and rearrange words from the original text into sentences, and letter patterns into words. The movement is from the whole text, to an analysis of the parts, then back to the whole text.

A Language Study Activity

The teacher begins by reading the following limerick:
　　　There was a young farmer of Leeds
　　who swallowed a packet of seeds.
　　　　It soon came to pass
　　　　he was covered with grass,
　　and he couldn't sit down for the weeds.

She reads it several times so the students can listen to her intonation and emphasis, thereby enabling them to better interpret and understand the meaning. She then has the students echo read with her (she reads a line and they read it back), after which they choral read the limerick together.

The students are then asked to read the limerick to each other in pairs. It is meant to be read orally, and the students now have the opportunity to read and interpret. They are taking the role of actor as they read it to each other and try to interpret it. Remembering the teacher's model, they give the best voice to lines that need to be read a certain way.

Since he has had the opportunity of both hearing the poem and practicing it several times in concert with his peers, James is able to read it to his partner with only a few errors. His partner, a more skillful reader, was chosen to assist James when he needs help.

The students are next asked to take the role of detective in finding the missing words in the limerick. The teacher gives them this cloze activity to do with their partners:

>   There was a young farmer of Leeds
>   who swallowed a packet of _____.
>   It soon came to pass
>   he was covered with grass,
>   and he couldn't sit down for the _____.

James and his partner look for the clues that help them reconstruct the meaning of the poem they have just heard and read. They talk about what the words might be, using a combination of their memory and the context clues in the text.

The teacher then gives the students the following words taken from the rhyme:

a, the, he, it, who
farmer, weeds, Leeds, seed
swallowed, covered, came
of, with, to, from

Their task is to create sentences that make sense. They are to write them, making sure they are capitalized and punctuated properly. James is much quicker than his partner to orally construct the sentences, while his partner is better at capitalizing and punctuating the sentences. With these combined strengths they finish quickly, with the longest list of correct sentences in the class.

The last detective work is arranging and rearranging the parts of words into whole words that mean something. The lesson today focuses on the *ee/ea/e* spelling patterns, and the students are asked to make as many long-*e* words as they can by joining letters from the list of word parts (see Figure 7.1). The partners are to write their own words and/or find them in the chant, then write them in columns, as follows:

e	ee	ee_e	ea	ea_e
he	Leeds	freeze	scream	please

The students thus get practice in constructing words using the *ee/ea/e* spelling patterns.

After this final activity in word making, the students will be familiar with the patterns of spelling the long-*e* sound to the point of being able to

FIGURE 7.1.   How Many Long-e Words Can Be Made from these Parts?

Consonants				Vowels	Consonants	Silent-e
b	sc	br	bl	e	d	e
h	sl	cr	cl	ee	l	
k	sm	dr	fl	ea	m	
m	sn	fr	gl		n	
s	sp	gr	pl		p	
t	sqa	pr			t	
w	st				s	
	sw					
	scr					
	str					

induce the general rule under the direction of the teacher. This rule can then be added to the growing list of conventions of writing that is kept in each student's writing folder.

General Procedures for Developing Activities

Language study activities can be developed for any high-frequency graphophonic pattern. The first step is to find or write a chant for each high-frequency graphophonic pattern. The chant should include a number of words generated from the pattern. Then the activities below can be developed based on the chant.

1. *What Clues Do We Use?* Develop a ditto in which the chant is presented with some words belonging to the graphophonic pattern deleted.
2. *How Many Sentences Can We Make?* Develop a ditto with a set of words from the chant that, when combined and recombined, will generate many sentences. Most of the words should follow the graphophonic pattern being studied.
3. *How Many Words Can We Make?* Develop a ditto with a set of graphophonic elements embedded in the chant that, when combined and recombined, will generate many words and syllables.

4. *Spelling Practice.* Develop a ditto with a list of phrases and sentences comprising mainly words that follow the graphophonic pattern being studied.

5. *Reading Checkout.* Develop a ditto with a set of sentences comprising mainly words that follow the pattern.

(See also the example in the sample integrated day in Chapter 5.)

Analysis of the Activity

The role or purpose for the students has moved from actor (interpreting the text) to detective (finding the missing pieces). As detectives they look for the clues that help them reconstruct the text. From memory and from context, the students talk about what the deleted words might be. They have already heard the whole text and interpreted it, so they are working from a meaningful context. Starting with the whole, the first level of differentiation or analysis is this reconstruction of the whole text.

The second level of differentiation is sentence construction. Taking words from the text on cards, they use the process of arranging and rearranging to construct meaningful sentences, write them down, and punctuate them. In constructing sentence texts, they have to make sense and then punctuate and capitalize properly.

The final detective work is arranging and rearranging the parts of words into whole words that mean something and then reading them. In word making, as well as in sentence making, they are practicing phonics and spelling. The words deleted from the text were selected to illustrate particular graphophonic patterns, so the students are getting much practice in using a certain language pattern. In the word-making activity, the students are working with the same combination of letters and sounds, so that as they manipulate and write down these elements they are getting practice in spelling and phonics.

Meaning has been fundamental. The students are creating meaningful texts at the level of the whole text, the level of sentences, and the level of words. We began with a whole text, and each of the students' created texts have particular significance in relation to the whole. The students are getting practice in the basic skills of phonics, spelling, punctuation, and grammar as they create sentences and words using the higher level skills of interpretation, investigation, and reconstruction of language. They are not just learning one element at a time; and they are taking an active role in the learning process.

8

The Ecological Learning Process

We have referred to the new way of teaching as ecological because we believe that it makes use of the best resources from the total ecology of the student. Resources of the school and family as well as resources of the student are capitalized upon in this framework, and the orchestration of all of these resources into a collaborative approach to integrated language learning creates what we feel is the optimal learning environment for the student. In this chapter we detail certain aspects of this approach that make it more ecological, integrative, and successful for students of all ability levels than the traditional approach.

In the first part of the chapter we return to one of the paradoxes with which we began the book: the solutions offered to deal with individual differences have become part of the problem. We look at what can go wrong with our very right notion of recognizing and accommodating individual differences, and we explain why we sometimes end up with neither equity nor excellence in the traditional system of grouping, tracking, and placement for disability. The ecological solution offered is heterogeneous whole classroom grouping with a variety of small group and partner activities based on the critical experiences framework.

Next, we further delineate important aspects of the new role of the specialist: that of collaborator with the teacher, resource person, and facilitator of content-skill interdependence in the classroom. We view this role as ecological for two reasons. First, it involves continual collaborative interaction between the teacher and specialist, thereby reducing the isolation of both professionals. Second, it increases the congruence in the curriculum between what the teacher and the specialist do, whether the program is mainstream or pull out. This eliminates the fragmentation of learning that often results from the lack of communication between these professionals.

And finally, we look at the family world view and the student's reading of that world, which both precedes and makes possible reading the word. We discuss the family/school connection and the possibilities for drawing on the resources of the family system in the orchestration of the student's learning. Again the focus is on validating the student's voice and, by extension, the voice and experience of the family and community context from which the student comes.

HETEROGENEOUS GROUPING
AND ECOLOGICAL CLASSROOM MANAGEMENT

The traditional view of homogeneous classroom management assumes that, as Sunny's mother said, "If you can't read, you can't do anything." Thus those who are poorer readers are separated into lower reading groups, remedial reading classes, and learning disability classes, wherein they are often excluded from hearing and responding to more difficult texts and from higher level learning activities. It is assumed that if they cannot do the lower level basic skill/drill tasks, they surely cannot do higher level reasoning and communication activities.

Rather than limiting ourselves to the notion that "If you can't read, you can't do anything," we propose that students can very often understand material at a much higher level than that at which they can read. Thus it is possible to begin with higher level thinking for all students in a heterogeneous classroom, while still including the lower level skills in the process. Through such teacher scaffolding as modeling, reading texts to the class, and building cooperative learning structures, all students can learn together in heterogeneous groups. These represent ways that teachers can support students in their learning of difficult tasks: ways that they can continue to teach to the "zone of proximal (potential) development." And through the use of such social interaction resources as partnering, peer tutoring, small group activities, and conferencing, the learning of diverse groups of students can be successfully orchestrated.

The logic of such mediation and support for the student in pursuit of higher level comprehension will not come as a surprise to many reading and learning specialists, who have long noted the greater oral comprehension ability of students labeled as dyslexic, disabled, or poor readers. The ecological approach merely extends this scaffolding to planned classroom practice to develop the potential of all students.

In the paragraphs that follow we will take a look at the history and consequences of high, middle, and low groupings in our school systems. We will see how some of our current problems evolved, including labeling, low expectations, commitment to traditional reading activities, and the exclusion of some students (particularly those labeled as disabled) from higher level thinking activities.

History of Homogeneous Grouping

In the not too distant past in this country there was little structured differentiation of students by classroom teachers. Most classes did not have high, middle, and low groups; there were no learning disability and few remedial reading classes; and the only alternative to the regular classroom was the special education classroom. These special classes were generally limited to those classified as mentally retarded or perhaps physically disabled. Students within each grade level, regardless of their abilities, were taught in heterogeneous groups using the same texts.

One of the problems faced by educators was not being able to meet individual needs of students, who were all expected to master the same texts in the same way. The teacher tended to teach to the middle, so the very able students were sometimes bored and the slower students could sometimes be lost. It was a movement forward from that position to say that we had to differentiate instruction. Students were rightly assumed to have individual rates of learning and different responses to the same texts.

So education moved to grouping to ensure that the needs of the individual were met. Though there were some efforts to totally individualize classrooms, the more practical solution tended to be high, middle, and low groups in reading. It seemed impossible to have all students moving ahead at their own rates in individually prescribed programs. The problem with the solution that followed from these assumptions, however, resulted partly from the language learning theory on which the solution was based.

Educational research, rooted in behaviorist psychology and the stage development work of Piaget, took a linear view of learning and assumed that language learning progressed in stages with a specific skill sequence. It seemed logical, therefore, to separate groups of students into their correct levels and stages so that their individual needs could be better met. But more current research about language learning, rooted in the work of Vygotsky, has informed us that there is neither a linear progression nor a discrete skill sequence that each student follows on the path to language competence. Learning appears to occur more in recursive loops or spirals; the student may drop backwards at times, only to learn something new or enlarge on previous learning. The leap to automaticity in reading, a rapid and unpredictable transformation that may be preceded by what appears to be a regression in ability, seems to be more characteristic of the pattern of language learning than a steady, progressive skill sequence.

Other problems accompanied the educational solution of grouping students. There were problems with keeping students busy when the teacher was not working with their group, and thus many activities tended to be busy work. Dittos and subskill workbooks grew in numbers in the classroom.

Since the reading time had to be divided among three or more groups (some classes had as many as five groups), there was less time to deal with content material. There was little time to really get involved in discussions; explore and make use of the prior knowledge of the students; have dramatizations, panels, debates, and other activities to expand their knowledge; or focus on higher level critical thinking. The teacher tended to use the question and one-right-answer tasks from the basal readers, not only for efficiency but so as not to disturb the other groups. Likewise there was a limit to the collaborative social interaction that could occur in the classroom, and the students rarely benefitted from each other's knowledge. There was little time to think of the text as literature that all students could participate in.

The classroom observation research of Cazden (1981), Allington (1983), McDermott (1974), and Bartoli (1986b), along with our informal interviews with many teachers and specialists, has documented noticeable differences in the actual experiences of the students in the various groups. The activities for the low groups tended to be at a low level, further reducing their chances for meaningful language learning. These groups focused on lower level subskills in isolation from meaningful texts. The teacher's expectations for the students in the low groups tended to be different, and teacher behavior was often more controlling and punitive than it was motivating. Eventually the students' expectations for themselves dropped to match those of their teachers.

Reading groups can become rather rigid, as can the tracking placements that follow from the elementary reading group placements, according to Goodlad (1984) and Oakes (1985). It was their observation that, once a student was placed in a low group, it was unlikely that there would be a movement up and out of that placement. There were exceptions to this, but they usually demanded much effort from a teacher, parent, or student. Other social dynamics complicated the issue (see Chapter 9), and the notion of fixed ability levels and appropriate grouping became firmly entrenched in the American school system.

Our theory espouses Vygotsky's notion of teaching to the zone of proximal or potential development, of learning that is ahead of development, and of the limitations of any present measure of a student's ability. Any estimation of a student's ability can be seen as an underestimation—a fossilization of potential development (see Chapter 1).

The Ecological Alternative

The heterogeneous grouping that we propose as an ecological alternative to homogeneous grouping and tracking is not a movement back to schooling as it was before the focus on individual needs. The ecological framework for classroom management allows for both individualization and interaction in the context of heterogeneous large and small groups. Heterogeneous grouping no longer precludes a focus on the individual, and individualization no longer necessitates isolation from interaction with peers.

Whereas previously all students were asked to master the same text in the same way at the same time, the ecological approach provides for individual differences through the use of teacher scaffolding. The teacher builds on the prior knowledge of individual students, leads them in reading strategy development, and helps them to process the text in a variety of individual ways. They learn at their own rates using their own strategies, while still remaining within the context of the whole classroom of learners.

If a student continues to have difficulty with the text, the teacher may structure peer tutoring or other partner or small group activities that will help the student learn the material. At no point is the learner isolated from peers or relegated to lower level skills. Both the opportunity and the expectation for successful learning are built into the ecological framework.

Along with peer interaction techniques, the teacher uses a variety of individualized activities that allow students to self-select material and proceed at their individual rates. In addition, they have ample opportunities to respond to texts in their individual ways, such as sharing what stood out for them and drawing from their own prior experiences and knowledge (see Chapter 6).

We feel that the new alternative solves some of the previous problems with meeting individual needs. It is more ecologically valid because it connects each student to the classroom ecology and draws on the social interaction resources of that system. Whereas heterogeneous grouping formerly meant a lack of individualization, the new alternative allows for a variety of individual responses within the whole class group. Whereas individualization formerly meant isolation from peers and fragmentation of learning, the ecological alternative allows for individual response connected to the classroom community of learners.

This more ecological type of heterogeneous grouping has several advantages in addition to making the best use of the world knowledge and social interaction resources of the classroom. Because time is not divided among three separate reading groups, the amount of time available to students for both comprehension and content-skill integration is greater. There is more time for concept development, for reading strategy development, for the teacher to more deeply engage the student in learning, and for the student to process the content more deeply and to integrate skills.

In addition, self-esteem of individual students, particularly those who were previously placed in low groups, appears to improve in this type of arrangement. Since student responses are unique and are not judged as right or wrong, and since a cooperative learning climate is encouraged in lieu of a competitive one, all students can be contributing, respected members of the classroom community of learners. They are encouraged to both understand and respect each other, to appreciate the wide diversity of human response to content and concepts, and to learn from the variety of background knowledge brought to the classroom by their peers.

Heterogeneous small group and partnering activities, which stress mutual responsibility for each other's learning, further foster a sense of a caring community of learners. The classroom climate that seems to prevail in this type of classroom management is one of equity and mutual respect. Trusting relationships and increased motivation for learning can also flower in this climate, along with expectations for the greatest potential of each individual student.

In heterogeneous small groups students can also learn from each other, be responsible for each other's learning, and share in the collaborative social interaction that is vital to learning. They can learn interaction skills that will help them to be productive in collaborative work, and they can experience the variety of ways that human beings extend each other's learning: collaborating as equals; enhancing, extending, and encouraging as peer tutors; dialoguing and building ideas above and beyond what individuals might conceive on their own.

Ecological management and the critical experiences

Let us take a look at the ecological alternative to homogeneous grouping in each of the critical experiences. How does individualization occur within heterogeneous groupings? How can an activity be individual but still interactive rather than isolated?

In responding to text the teacher begins with the whole, heterogeneous classroom group, drawing individual responses to such questions as What do you already know about . . . ? What do you want to know about . . . ? And later, What stood out for you in this story/poem/chapter? What the students knows is honored: there is no right or wrong answer. Within the whole group, students respond in their unique ways, but they can also pool the diverse resources of the entire class. Whereas individualization in the traditional classroom often means isolation from peers, ecological management allows for individualization and social interaction at the same time.

The teacher's use of scaffolding or building cognitive supports allows students at a variety of reading levels to interact with and process the same text. Readability stems from the transactions they have with the text and from the strategies, modeled on those of the teacher, that they use. Whereas homogeneous grouping structured around the directed reading activity in the basal reader suggests that meaning is in the text (and thus a student who cannot read the text cannot learn anything), an ecological approach views meaning as derived from the transactions among the reader, the text, and the social context.

In addition to the whole group response to texts, the teacher may structure a variety of heterogeneous small group activities, partner activities, or students working on their own to extend learning. But, in keeping with the ecological framework, these are integrally related to the whole class activity or theme.

Composing activities involve individual students choosing their own topics and working through the writing processes in their own ways. These individual compositions are shared with peers in conferences for drafting and editing. Students collaborate but they also work individually on their own perceptions of things. Small group activities may precede oral or written composing, and presentation to the whole group is always an option. The entire writing process is individualized, but there is also interaction in peer and teacher conferences.

During sustained silent reading the text is self-selected, the reading is self-paced, and the students comprehend on their own in the whole classroom context. There are also opportunities for them to share their reading with peers if they choose. As in the composing activities, there is individualization, but it does not preclude interaction with peers or participation in the classroom community of learners.

Investigating and mastering language activities may involve individual patterns of errors (spelling words and syntax rules from the student's own writing, for example), with students working on their own or with partners. At other times the teacher may use whole group or small group arrangements to teach a pattern or skill necessary for a given project or unit of work. In teaching graphophonic patterns, for instance, the order often flows from whole group choral and echo reading of a text, to partner activities (cloze, sentence-making, and word-making activities), and back to the whole group (see Chapter 7).

To summarize, we suggest that the new ecological alternative of heterogeneous classroom grouping with a variety of small group, partner, and individual activities, all of which are integrated around the critical experiences, provides the optimal classroom climate for learning for students of all abilities. In homogeneous grouping, students placed in lower groups or labeled as disabled were often excluded from hearing and reading more difficult texts, from higher level critical thinking in lieu of practice-drill activities, and from collaborative social interaction with more able readers and writers. In contrast, in the ecological approach, all students are fully integrated into the classroom community of learners. Unlike previous heterogeneous groupings, in which it was difficult to meet the needs of the individual learner, in the ecological approach such teacher scaffolding as partner and small group activities, drawing and building on individual responses, and a variety of self-selected and self-paced activities provides for individual learning within the whole classroom.

TEACHER-SPECIALIST TEAMING AND COLLABORATION

We have described in the previous chapters many aspects of the new collaborative role for the specialist in the ecological approach. Before we explore this new role further, we will describe what specialists are asked to do in the present traditional school system. What are specialists asked to do now, and what will the new specialist find upon entering a traditional school system?

The Traditional Role: Problematic Solutions

Typically the specialist is asked to help with the testing and grouping of students, a practice that is congruent with the system of standardized testing, ability grouping, and tracking that prevails in American schools. Specialists may be asked to write reports based on the tests administered to students. Since these reports, like the psychologist's quantitative reports, are often of little use to the classroom teacher in accommodating the student in the classroom, they are frequently filed away and forgotten.

Learning disability specialists in particular are asked to write an individualized education program (IEP) for each student labeled as learning disabled, and this plan is frequently based on standardized test results. The specialist is also involved in one form or another of teaching outside of the regular classroom. It may be a pull-out program wherein students are removed from their classrooms several hours a week for remedial tutoring; it may be a separate reading clinic or resource room wherein students have scheduled classes to supplement their regular reading program; or it may be a self-contained separate classroom for those labeled as reading or learning disabled.

In any case the specialist is asked to provide a separate remedial program for the students. The program is generally skill oriented and geared to their supposed deficits as diagnosed by tests. The traditional view is that disabled students need skills more than world knowledge, and that we can diagnose these skill needs from testing. Thus there is an abundance of fragmented skill teaching and testing in the traditional program, along with administrative policies oriented toward test results.

The new specialist will also typically find rather strained relationships between specialists and teachers, partly as a result of the system of removing students from class, which even further fragments the learning process. If the specialist has a self-contained learning disability classroom, for instance, the students are mainstreamed (put in regular classrooms) for those subjects in which they are not diagnosed as disabled. The mechanics of working out schedules between the specialist and the teachers for a group of such students are mind boggling, and the result in the LD classroom can look like a continual parade of students going in and out. Trying to integrate learning in such a situation verges on the impossible.

If the remedial program involves reading clinic or resource room tutoring, the students must be removed from their regular classroom at the times arranged between the specialist and the teacher. Many teachers complain that this prevents them from doing more whole class, heterogeneous activities. They are prevented from involving the students who might benefit most from whole language activities and whole classroom events because of the pull-out program.

Strained relations can also occur over the decisions about who will be classified as disabled and who will be removed from the classroom, in addition to when they will be removed. Blame placing among specialists and teachers is perpetuated in the traditional school system, not only because of the above mentioned decisions, but also because these professionals are isolated from each other in separate classrooms and clinics. They rarely have the opportunity to collaborate with each other, profit from each other's professional knowledge and experience, share their understandings about the students they are attempting to help with learning, or establish congruence in the students' program.

The irony in all of this is that, in addition to creating further fragmentation of skills away from content, students away from their peers, and professionals away from each other, we have created the illusion that it is somehow possible to understand students by testing them on low level skills. Furthermore, we continue to operate around classroom management based on such testing.

The Role of Collaborator

The reading or learning specialist can better meet the individual needs of more students by being freed from developing a curriculum separate from that of the classroom teacher. Instead, the specialist can serve as collaborator with the teacher in the classroom to develop a more integrated, whole language curriculum that can meet the needs of all students. In this role specialists can share expertise, problem-solve with the teacher, help plan for the special needs of particular students within the classroom, and continually validate and strengthen teachers in their attempts to build optimal learning climates for all their students.

It is not difficult to see how this could eliminate much of the fragmentation caused by our present handling of students and specialists. What is perhaps less obvious are the many alternative roles and possibilities an ecological approach might open to the specialist in support of the needs of the individual student with a reading or learning problem. Many of these we have previously suggested, but we will outline them here as they relate to the critical experiences.

In responding to literature the specialist may help the teacher develop whole class activities as well as small group task sheet activities to reinforce or extend learning, particularly for students who have difficulty with reading the text. The specialist will be concerned with how those individual students experience and comprehend the text. Therefore, in addition to collaborating in planning for the whole and small group activities, the specialist will observe in the classroom on occasion to diagnose the need for further individual help.

When the teacher and specialist meet together to compare observations of a particular student, they may decide there is a need for more individual help. A variety of options are open for the specialist to extend and enhance the learning of the individual without removing the student from the classroom. The specialist may read parts or all of the text with that student, either alone or in a small group; or the specialist may arrange for a classmate or aide to read with the student. An audio tape of the material could be prepared either by the specialist, an older student, another teacher, or a resource person such as the librarian, a parent, or another member of the community. Alternatively, the specialist might provide the student with a study guide to aid individual comprehension of the material (see Botel & Preston, *Ways to Read, Write, Study: Science*, 1987).

Beyond the classroom, the specialist might contact the parents and ask them to read certain texts at home. Or the specialist and teacher may decide that there is a need for individualized tutoring either by the specialist or by a peer. In either case, care will be taken that the activities are congruent with the classroom curriculum and that they support the student's continued competence as part of the classroom community of learners. Mary MacCracken (1986) gives several examples of her tutoring role in collaboration with the teacher to help a boy (Joey) learn within his own classroom.

In sustained silent reading the specialist can be a partner with the teacher in learning more about the individual interests of the student who is having difficulty. The specialist can then help locate and bring books to the classroom for that student that would be interesting and readable. When the teacher needs assistance, the specialist can conference with students needing extra help with books they read, or can perhaps begin a dialogue journal with students, focusing on their feelings about and responses to books they have read.

During composing activities the specialist can collaborate with the teacher to support and help students who are having difficulty during the various processes of composing. The specialist may conference with a student on choosing a topic; collecting, connecting, or rehearsing information; writing a first draft; revising; or editing. During oral composing the specialist could collaborate with the teacher in taping and transcribing a student's narrative.

Depending on the background and expertise of the teacher, the specialist's collaboration may take several forms. It may be a sharing of competencies, wherein the teacher observes and is made more competent through exposure to new techniques. The specialist transfers personal capabilities to enhance the teacher's competence and leaves the teacher with new skills. The collaboration may also be a sharing as equal partners, wherein the specialist shares the teacher's load and helps take the strain off the teacher by conferencing, connecting with the home, or otherwise giving a hand where needed.

LINKING TO THE FAMILY WORLD VIEW

Parents, teachers, specialists, and administrators are universally aware of the importance of home and school cooperation in the learning success of the student. What they are less aware of are some of the larger ecological dimensions of that cooperation: specifically, the social and cultural perceptions and judgments that may limit cooperation and communication, and the social/ecological processes that operate to maintain the equilibrium or status quo of the system.

The traditional approach to grouping, testing, and labeling fosters the idea that less advantaged (economically and socially) students will not do as well in school as will more advantaged students. It also perpetuates the myth that their less advantaged families are responsible for this lack of success. Typical comments concerning these families are: They don't care about their child's education. They don't value education. They are uncooperative and apathetic. They don't show up for conferences or school functions.

What is missing in this view are the wider social processes affecting the families. The school, reflecting the community social system, places value judgments on certain minority families: black, Hispanic, Mexican American, and American Indian minority groups; poor or "disadvantaged" families; "problematic" (to the status quo) families. The economic system shapes the job opportunities and chances for advancement for certain families. The social system, based in part on financial status, maintains certain families in a particular place relative to the rest of the mainstream society. And the school system, a microcosm of the community/cultural system, operates to maintain the same social groups within the school.

It is these wider ecological dimensions of the problem that have been overlooked in much of the home/school cooperation literature. Yet it is these social processes that continually prevent the full collaboration and cooperation of the home and school in the education of the student.

Problems From the Narrow View

Educators have always known about the importance of home and school cooperation and communication for successful learning. But in our present state of advanced education we seem to be moving farther away from making meaningful and lasting connections between the home and school. Part of the reason is our more-of-the-same solutions to making family/school connections, which negate the realities of the present day family. Heath and McLaughlin (1987) state that only 7 percent of families fit the "typical family" description that is presumed in many of the parent involvement efforts. Part of the reason relates to the consolidation of schools—moving away from the community and neighborhood schools to a less personal context. And part of the reason is a function of the more efficient, production line management of schools, which depersonalizes relationships and leaves little time for getting to know the student or the family.

The case studies of Sunny and James reveal several other barriers to home/school communication. Negative expectations and biased judgments stemming from a narrow view of the students, their families, and their potential limited the possibilities for cooperation and trusting collaboration. In addition, the traditional school system did not have a plan to connect parents with the school as valued collaborators in the student's learning.

What we have suggested about the importance of students' world views and being subjects of their own lives is equally important in looking at the family system. The student world view is an outgrowth of the family world view, so we miss an opportunity for better understanding if we do not try to learn more about the family world view.

In an ecological approach to the family, we connect with the concept of family literacy as described by Freire (1983), Britton (1970), and Taylor (1983). Literacy is mediated through social relationships at home in meaningful interaction with parents, siblings, and friends. Reading the word in school literacy is continually integrated with reading the world that originated in family literacy. Students build their home worlds into their school worlds: The culture and world view of their homes and communities remain a part of their lives when they come to school. Thus it is of utmost importance that schools begin with knowing, understanding, and validating the social experience the student already possesses in the form of family literacy. The family world view is where meaning making begins.

The families of Sunny and James

The tendency in relation to viewing the family is to look for pathology rather than trying to more fully understand. Just as the student is treated somewhat as an object to be studied and judged on test performance criteria, so the family, and especially the family of a problem reader or learner, is frequently studied to find what is wrong. This precludes letting the family tell their own story and be the subjects of their lives.

In the cases of Sunny and James, the assumptions and preconceptions about their families were unchecked by observational data. There were many misrepresentations of family information, many unfounded judgments, and many assumptions that were as inaccurate as they were biased. Sunny's mother was assumed to have been a special education student and a pregnant drop-out with very few capabilities for helping Sunny with school work. In fact, she was never in special education, she earned her high school diploma, she does all the family financial record keeping, and she has a responsible supervisory position at work.

James' mother was judged as typical of the local black community: no long-range goals for their children's academic success and little interest in the value of education in general. It was also assumed that her investment in James was low and that she was not interested in spending time with him or controlling his behavior. The reality was quite different. Her efforts to control James' behavior went beyond those of most parents—requesting to be personally called in to punish James if he misbehaved rather than letting the school handle it. And her future plans for James, as well as for her other son, included a college education.

In Sunny and James' school system the assumptions about poor white families and black families from the community were rather similar. Neither were thought to be interested in education. They did not come into the school for conferences or special programs, they often had difficulty getting to teacher conferences, and they were assumed to have had weak academic backgrounds themselves. School personnel commonly commented that it was a rather hopeless cycle for the student in such a family. These were the disadvantaged families with single parents, working mothers, latch-key children, little education or competence for child rearing, and little concern for their children.

There were many preconceived notions about these families, and rarely were any of them positive or optimistic. Specialists and teachers in Sunny and James' school system cited their belief that between 75 and 95 percent of the learning and reading problems stemmed from the home. Citing family break-ups, incompetent and unconcerned parents, and sad home lives, the school personnel often concluded, "What can you expect?" This created the ideal climate for blame placing and justifying nonlearning. The tendency was to correlate negatives, make excuses for poor behavior, and diminish expectations for successful learning.

Toward Ecological Solutions

Taking an ecological view could broaden the picture of the family to allow for fuller understanding, communication, and eventually a trusting collaboration with the school system. This view begins with the assumption that all parents are among the normal variation of people who care about their children's education. Ethnographic and field study research continues to support the implications from the case studies of Sunny and James: The educational problems of the student stem less from the pathology or inadequacy of the family than from the biased preconceptions and judgments about the family by the community and the school. This problem is often magnified when the family is not mainstream middle-class white.

It is not that there are no problem families. Certainly there are many students who live under very difficult conditions. The problem is with the solution that is offered. Judgments are made from incomplete and sometimes incorrect information, and these misrepresentations tend to result in lowered expectations for the student and justification for nonlearning. This tends to lead to classification in low reading groups and placement in remedial reading classes and learning disability classes. And, of course, such placement results in the fragmented kinds of learning experiences that were offered to Sunny and James—experiences that essentially per-petuate nonlearning.

Rather than rushing to problematic solutions, we suggest a focus on understanding the family world view. Such knowledge and understanding of the wider ecology of the student would give us a much larger context from which to draw resources. It would also give us a greater appreciation for the complexity of the ecosystem of the student.

Knowledge of the wider ecology of any one family will contribute to our understanding of learning. As we become open to the family world view, and as we attempt to both describe and reflect on that world view, we will increasingly widen the ecological lens. First the lens can extend from the school system to the family system, as we seek to understand and communicate more fully. Then the lens may take in the multitude of community/cultural dynamics that invariably have an impact on the family and thus on the school as well.

Understanding Sunny's family world view

Several examples from Sunny's family suggest the value of widening the lens. If the focus of the school system had been understanding this family's world view, school personnel might have come to know the impor-tance of education to the family. Sunny's mother had a tutor come to her home during her pregnancy so that she would not get behind in school work. She feels so strongly that "If you can't read, you can't do anything" that she does everything related to literacy for her husband, possibly making him less competent and confident in his ability to help Sunny and to find a new job. She also has aspirations, thwarted only by finances at this point, of going on to study at the area community college. School person-nel who viewed her as spacy, disorganized, and incompetent would benefit from understanding this part of the family world view.

Sunny's father lost a job he had held for 15 years following a back injury that left him unable to perform that particular job. The job within the same company that was offered him as a replacement demanded night shift work, which he found intolerable for a number of reasons, not the least of which was that Sunny and her brother would be left alone each night and he would rarely see his wife. Since Sunny's mother worked a 3 to 11 PM shift, and since his job would begin at 11 PM, they would barely cross paths in the evenings or at night. In addition, Sunny's father found it impossible to sleep during the day.

Other social factors entered the picture to make Sunny's father feel less competent in the new placement at work, and he became severely depressed to the point of hospitalization for suicidal depression. Eventually he quit the job, and his subsequent search for a new job was hampered by his lack of confidence as well as his lack of literacy stemming from his own experience in special education. School personnel who did not have a fuller ecological picture viewed him as greasy, grimy, and "a cartoon character" who just sat around watching television instead of working or helping his children with school work.

Communication with the family

How can we as educators approach the family so that we can better understand their world view? How can we use that understanding to build better links between the family and school systems? How can we use those links to increase the communication and cooperation between the home and school that is vital to the student's learning? How can we change the tendency to judge, categorize, correlate, excuse, and diminish to an effort toward understanding, collaboration, trust, and mutual respect?

Certainly it will take much effort on the part of specialists and teachers to counteract past and present cross blaming and defensive wall building. The school system's perception of parents who do not show up for conferences and school functions is as firmly entrenched as the attitude of some parents that, "I wouldn't be caught dead going to Back-to-School Night." What is crucial is to explore the multitude of factors, which often include biased judgments, distrust, and a history of negative experiences, that are a part of that attitude. What should flow from that knowledge and understanding is a plan for building a more trusting, collaborative relationship.

The same cooperative climate for increased communication that we are attempting to build in the classroom for optimal learning needs to be extended to the wider ecology of the student. In this way we can link the family and school systems to form an interactive network of mutual support, trust, communication, and growth. An ecologically valid framework for teaching and evaluation, one that fosters cooperation and valuing of all students rather than fragmented teaching and testing, is a necessary first step.

The Role of the Specialist with the Family

Often the family has little or no dialogue with the school except for test results or negative behavior reports. Therefore misperceptions on the part of the family and school often go unchecked. The role of the specialist, in cooperation with the classroom teacher, is to begin the dialogue and establish a relationship with the family.

Several ways that have been successful in understanding more about the family world view and building a more trusting relationship include parent interviews in the home, including the parents in observation and discussion at school, and home/school collaborative plans for the student. In each of these the parent and professional meet as colleagues to learn from each other in an atmosphere of mutual respect. Without a concerted effort by the professionals to remain open, respectful, and positive, and without a sincere desire to understand and communicate with the parents as equals, there will be little progress toward ecological change.

Ideally the new role of the specialist as collaborator with the classroom teacher would leave more time to make connections with the families of students who are experiencing difficulty in reading and learning. But even in the traditional pull-out program or the self-contained learning disability classroom situation, these strategies could be employed at least in part. Though they are time consuming, the benefits to be gained from the broader view of the student far outweigh the time and energy costs.

Family interviews and collaboration

The family interview can be done either in the home or at the school. If possible, we suggest going to the home as a way of showing sincere concern and of beginning a more trusting relationship. The specialist or teacher calls or writes to the parents to make an appointment to talk with them for the purpose of better understanding the student. It should be communicated to the parents from the beginning that the school personnel have much to learn from the family in their attempts to help the student.

The structure and length of the interview depend on the time constraints and openness of the participants. We have used very informal, ethnographic interview techniques that are directed toward a better understanding of both the child in particular and education in general as viewed by the family. Open-ended, unstructured ethnographic interviews (Spradley, 1979) allow the parents to describe fully their ways of looking at the student's problem with reading and learning in the context of their own view of education. They are free to describe their own experiences with schooling, and frequently this is of value in understanding more about the student's learning.

The parents may also be invited to come into the school to observe the student in the classroom. A collaborative meeting with the teacher and specialist following this observation, either after school or while an aide or administrator covers the class, allows all participants to share their observations and understanding. It also allows them to build a base for better communication about the student's learning, and it provides an opportunity for them to share as colleagues in a plan for helping the student. An option in this process is to have students sit in on the meeting and participate in their own plan for learning.

An example of a cooperative plan between James' family and the school system that was successful was a homework contract. The principals, teachers, James' mother, and James all cooperated to ensure that James completed his school work during one marking period in seventh grade. James was required to have his homework assignments listed on a contract signed by each teacher. He was then to have the completed assignments signed by his mother, the teachers, and the assistant principal by the end of the following day. This temporarily linked the family and school systems in support of James' continued involvement in homework, while it served as a continued form of communication between the two systems. The problem, of course, was that the homework was based on a fragmented view of learning.

Home/school dialogue

We know that authentic dialogue is vital to learning, and that dialogue journals can play an important role in fostering more meaningful dialogue. In addition to their use in the classroom, dialogue journals could be an option for increasing communication between the school and the home. They would have the added benefit of allowing for a deeper understanding on the part of both family and school as each party sought to express their views, ask questions, and make suggestions.

Parents and teachers or specialists could write about their own observations of the student: the parents could observe as the student did homework, and the specialist could share classroom observations. If time permitted, each could do cross observations—the parent at school and the specialist at home—and they could compare observations with each other in their journals. As with the informal interview, the possibilities for dialogue journals are limited only by the energy and time constraints of the participants.

Interestingly, once the doors for a more trusting, collaborative communication are opened between the family and school, many important bits of information seem to be shared that are vital to the student's learning. In an almost serendipitous way a specialist might discover that the family definition of reading help is nightly spelling and phonics drills, which have left the student tired, frustrated, and turned off. Similarly, a parent might discover the rationale behind the teacher's focus on meaning in writing and be led to place less emphasis at home on errors in mechanics and more support on the student's expression of meaning. In this way congruence between family literacy and school literacy could develop, just as congruence between the curriculum of the teacher and specialist developed.

Family Dynamics in Reading and Learning Problems

Family systems theorists tell us that it is possible for a student's reading or learning problem to be a signal of family distress: that the student may be looking for help with a family communication or relationship problem. It has been suggested by Peck (1971) and Miller and Westman (1964) that a student may learn the "art of being stupid" and then play a game of "dump the reading specialist" until the school gets the message that the student wants help for the family.

Another possibility suggested by family systems theory and research is that the family system may actually work together to maintain the student's reading or learning problem as a vehicle for help with the troubled family system. The student's problem may also serve as a vent for family tension in a stressful system.

Certain dynamics in James' family might be viewed from this family systems perspective. When James' mother was asked if she thought James could see any advantage in his misbehavior in school, she said, "Maybe he's thinking, 'If I'm bad enough Dad will have to come back.'" And in fact, when his misbehavior twice reached a crisis point, his dad did come back for a day.

There seemed to be a heavy load of stress on both Sunny's and James' families. Certainly Sunny's father's suicidal depression attested to that, and perhaps the learning problems of Sunny and James are related to family stress as well. But whether or not the learning problems are vehicles for help with the family or signals of distress, the school can be instrumental in establishing a more trusting relationship with the family, understanding more about the family, providing for self-expression of the family world view, improving communication skills through oral and written dialogue, and creating a caring community climate for collaboration and cooperation.

Instead of allowing such misrepresentations and judgments as were evident in the case studies of Sunny and James, specialists and teachers can establish a relationship with the family through conversational interviewing and allow this to be the basis for continued dialogue and deeper understanding. An added benefit in this type of collaboration between the family and school is that the student cannot play the parent against the school or vice versa. And greater communication between the two systems will prevent the game of "dump the reading specialist."

Freire (1983) reminds us that the act of reading is part of a wider process of human development and growth based on an understanding of our own experiences and the social world. Reading the world—and of course the world of our first reading is the family, wherein we learn to understand in relationship to parents and siblings—precedes reading the word. So an understanding of the student as reader hinges on an understanding of the family as both subject and author as they write their worlds.

On a further hopeful note, if through our increased understanding of both the student and the family world view we can help students with meaning making and achieving a fuller act of knowing, they may also be strengthened in their ability to transform their lives. Freire sees this dynamic process as central to the literacy process, and we see this as vital for children and adolescents who are searching for meaning in life, particularly those who are experiencing alienation, loneliness, and despair.

Human beings cannot survive in a senseless, meaningless world. In *Man's Search for Meaning* Viktor Frankl observed that the people who survived the death camps in Nazi Germany were those who believed that their life had some meaning. Even such a terrible existence as that could be endured if they saw some sense in life, an aim, or a purpose. But if they had nothing to expect from life anymore—no aim or purpose—there was no point for them in carrying on. Perhaps we should ask if children can learn, through low expectations and differential treatment, to not expect anything. Perhaps, also, we can help build caring communities wherein students can find a meaningful premise for life.

Part III
AN ECOLOGICAL WAY
OF EVALUATING

We begin this part of the book with the central ecological principle that evaluation should not be separate from teaching. As we will discuss in the following chapters, too much time may otherwise be taken up with extracting from the student without helping or putting value in that individual. The more ecological evaluation that we will describe values the individual voice and experience of the learner. It is rooted in contextually valid observation of the skillfulness of the learner in the process of reading, writing, and talking; and it is both congruent with the curriculum and useful in improving it.

In Chapter 9 we note how people have been devalued by tests: how they have been underestimated, reduced to numbers, and labeled. Chapter 10 further explores the issues of the problematic solutions of diagnosis, labeling, and remediation, including the use of tests and activities that presume to focus on underlying neurological functioning, and the use of subtests of reading comprehension to diagnose the reading of students.

Chapter 11 proposes a direction for ecological evaluation in which observations are most critical and information is gathered while the students are in the process of learning. This ecological evaluation takes four major forms: (1) a richly descriptive qualitative account of the student engaged in the critical experiences for learning, (2) a description focused on deeper understanding of the student's world view through interactive observation documented with the student's experiences; (3) a portfolio of the student's finished work and work in progress representing learning experiences, and (4) more valid assessments of decoding, comprehension, and writing. This is followed by a plan for preparing an individualized education program (IEP) that is congruent with the critical experiences framework.

Central to all of these forms of evaluation is the notion of teachers and specialists as researchers and reflective practitioners. As they observe in class, reflect on their observations, and seek patterns and themes in their

FIGURE III.   Ecological Evaluation

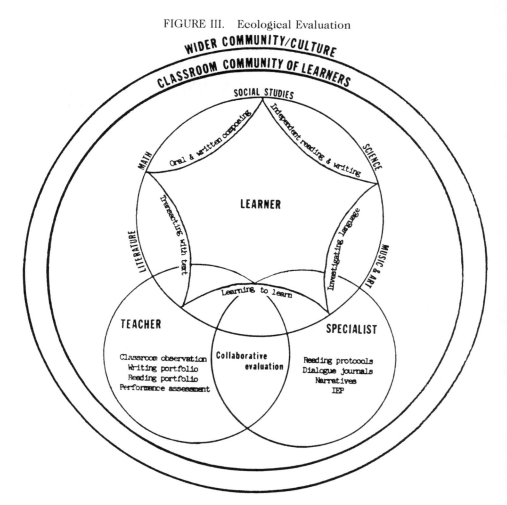

data they are, in fact, qualitative scientists: ethnographers of their own classroom contexts and their own students. This continuous researching of their own settings allows for greater understanding of the learner, greater understanding of themselves as professionals, and a continuous improvement of the curriculum for learning.

The one-on-one interactive observation methods that we will describe are forms of oral and written dialogue, book conversations, and mediation. In the Vygotskian tradition, the teacher or specialist engages the student, leads ahead through supportive encouragement and modeling, and mediates as the student builds on personal experience and knowledge. There is much agreement in education that an observant teacher can evaluate a child's learning progress more accurately than any test can, but these one-on-one interactive methods allow the teacher or specialist to refine that evaluation even more. The methods are as instructive as they are evaluative, so there is no time loss and no threat to self-esteem.

Traditional testing has too often resulted in a fragmented curriculum of testable pieces of information. We often appear to be training technicians and specialists in narrow areas of expertise rather than critical thinkers with broader, integrated knowledge. If we wish to allow more time for concept building, creative and exploratory thinking, and building from the vital experiences of the learner, we need to consider alternative forms of evaluation that are not separate from teaching.

It is not uncommon to hear students complain of boredom in schools. Some see so little value in their assignments and tests that they cheat, drop out, play dumb, or otherwise avoid learning. This is a tremendous loss of human potential that we cannot afford if we are to survive as a democratic country in a complex, technological, ever-changing world.

Could it be that the persistence of failure, cheating, and boredom is a sign of the low value that students place on disconnected learning divorced from personal experience and integrated knowledge? And what if we began to value instead their learning of broader concepts and connected themes? What if we valued their personal responses to texts and literature, their own oral and written composing, their own choices of books and topics for learning? It is not possible to cheat, or to fail, or to avoid learning, with this type of evaluation. It is, however, possible to feel valued as an individual and to learn to learn.

9
A Short History
of the Underevaluation
# of Human Potential

To fully understand the dilemma we find ourselves in with respect to evaluation of reading/learning disability, we must first look at the history of our evaluation methods. The historical path of psychometrics in general and standardized tests of reading/learning in particular is a rocky, convoluted path strewn with invalid data, subconscious (and sometimes conscious) cultural bias, methodological shortcomings, and the refuse of the millions who suffered the lowered expectations, reduced self-concepts, and diminished lives typical of those who were falsely labeled.

THE BIRTH OF STANDARDIZED TESTING OF INTELLIGENCE

We begin our short history in 1905 with Alfred Binet (1857–1911), who was commissioned by the French government to find a way to identify mentally deficient individuals so they could be given individual help in smaller classes. His tests had students calculate sums, establish which face was prettier, and complete a wide assortment of other tasks that he felt would give a rough estimate of cognitive ability. He cautioned against the static, reified use of the test score as a fixed mark of intelligence or inherent worth—but not loudly enough.

The fallacy of reification is that it assumes a test score represents a single, scalable thing in the head called intelligence. And this assumption of intelligence as a fixed quantity may be further perverted to provide a marker of inborn limits—a way to label, sort, and train according to biology. Binet said in 1909 that we must "protest and react against this brutal pessimism" and we must "try to demonstrate that it is founded upon nothing." He feared also the self-fulfilling prophecy of a rigid label setting a teacher's attitude and setting a future path for failure for the student. In 1905 he worried prophetically that teachers might use a reified I.Q. score to say, "Here is an excellent opportunity for getting rid of all the students who trouble us." Thus they might so designate all who were "unruly or disinterested in the school."

Kamin (1974) and Gould (1981) describe the ways that American psychologists perverted Binet's intent, reified his scores, and took them as a measure of an entity called intelligence, which they assumed was largely inherited. One such person was Henry Goddard, who wished to identify people in order to recognize limits, segregate, and curtail breeding to prevent what he saw as "deterioration of an endangered American stock." Of the toiling masses who were doing drudgery in 1919, Goddard said, "As a rule, [they are] in their proper places." He proclaimed that inherited I.Q. levels marked people for an inevitable station in life.

Goddard not only reified the test scores, but he scored and ranked people more strictly than Binet did, labeling as morons many whom Binet would have scored as normal. Goddard collected his data on Ellis Island, where he had women trained to "intuitively" pick out feebleminded immigrants and give them his tests. These immigrants had just arrived in the country after enduring a long and exhausting ocean voyage; they were weak, confused, and fearful; and many were poor and had never held a pencil before. Yet Goddard insisted that their test scores indicated innate stupidity and mental defectiveness. He said in 1917, "We cannot escape the general conclusion that these immigrants were of surprisingly low intelligence." And 70 years later we hear the same verdict passed on poor whites, blacks, Hispanics, Mexican-Americans, and American Indians.

Lewis Terman, father of the Stanford-Binet intelligence test (the standard for all I.Q. tests that followed), likewise wanted to curtail reproduction of feeblemindedness, and he believed that his reified test scores confirmed the biological worth of existing social classes. In 1916 he asserted that the "dullness" of Mexican-Americans, Negroes, and Spanish-Indians seemed to be racial or at least inherent in the family stocks from which they came. He added, "The students of successful and cultured parents test higher than students from wretched and ignorant homes for the simple reason that their heredity is better." His plan for those labeled as feebleminded was to either institutionalize them, as Goddard suggested, or separate them into special classes and give them practical, concrete instruction since they could not master abstractions. And 70 years later we presume that those labeled as learning or reading disabled have difficulty with abstract reasoning.

In 1917 Robert Yerkes gathered together Goddard, Terman, and other hereditarians to write the Army Mental Tests and establish "ultimate validity" for their intelligence tests on the basis of wide-scale testing. Yerkes had succeeded in convincing the government that it would be good for the army and the country to sift the incompetents out from the competents and award rank on this basis. Thus he was permitted to test the vast number of army recruits with the now famous Army Alpha and Beta tests (Yerkes, 1921). These were the first mass-produced written tests of intelligence, and they paved the way for the era of mass testing in which tests could rank and stream everyone.

A closer look at both the tests and the conditions of testing will illustrate the shaky foundation on which standardized I.Q. testing rests. The tests themselves measured familiarity with American culture and were clearly biased in favor of the white, middle-class, Anglo-Saxon majority. An example or two from Yerkes' Army Alpha (similar to Goddard's tests) will illustrate this:

Crisco is a: 1) patent medicine, 2) soap product, 3) food product
Christy Mathewson is a: 1) musician, 2) author, 3) baseball player, 4) artist

Clearly we are not tapping pure thinking ability, but rather cultural knowledge along with socioeconomic access to certain types of information (for example, questions on tennis rules, bowling rules, phonograph equipment, filaments in light bulbs).

The tests were replete with cultural and educational bias. They measured familiarity with American culture and schooling rather than the innate intelligence they were supposed to measure. Recent immigrants were at as much of a disadvantage in these tests as they were when Goddard's "intuitive women" pounced on them on Ellis Island. Minorities, especially blacks, fared no better.

In addition to the bias of the tests, the conditions under which they were given were anything but uniform. Many times the tester could not be seen or heard clearly, recruits were harrassed if they did not conform to the testing protocol, and the original procedure (giving the Beta to all those who failed the Alpha) could only be carried out in part, for various reasons. Thus the tests were invalid even on the basis on which they were devised. But this did not prevent the results from being widely broadcast, nor did it prevent the powerful influence of those results on immigration laws and the eugenics movement, nor did it prevent the wide demand and popularity the tests enjoyed. Hundreds of businesses and schools requested to use the tests in the following years to categorize, group, track, label, and fit people for their determined position in life.

Interestingly, most of the founding fathers (notably Terman and Goddard) eventually recanted, denying the validity of reified I.Q. scores as measures of innate intelligence, and denying their original statements about the inherited inferiority of certain races and the subsequent need for more forceful policies on eugenics to prevent the dominant white race from becoming "contaminated." But that also was too late to prevent the massive spread of the new scientific testing industry. Great damage had already been done in terms of thwarted human lives, stigma and labels where there should have been none, institutionalization and sterilization of many human beings (at the height of the eugenics movement 32 states had mandatory sterilization laws for those tested as feebleminded), and strict U.S. immigration laws that prevented millions of people from leaving Europe before the holocaust.

That is history—a pretty gory one at that—but it is no less devastating than the increasing number of students who are daily labeled as incompetents, shuffled into lower tracks where little is expected of them, or placed in segregated special classes wherein their stigma is sealed. The Grangers (1986) report that close to one million students are being handed "special" labels each year. The evidence is mounting that, along with the growth of the testing industry and labeled students, we are witnessing a growth of institutional practices for getting rid of organizational irritants, and that one of the most common reasons for academic failure is social class injustice. Students are tested on their allegiance to cultural and academic norms and values, and the tests record this educational process—not native intelligence.

SPECIAL EDUCATION LABELING

The history of special education labeling and testing is no less steeped in the shortcomings of cultural and racial bias, methodological deficiencies, and invalid assumptions. Coles (1978), Hobbs (1975), Bart (1984), and Granger and Granger (1986) report the same convoluted history for special education and the tests that now determine the label of "learning disabled"—the most popular label of the 1980s for those who are not achieving well (up to the "norm") in school. Coles reviewed the ten most frequently recommended procedures used for diagnosing learning disability and found them to be replete with methodological shortcomings, invalid applications and conclusions, and omissions that render them essentially useless.

Hobbs described the white, middle-class, Anglo-Saxon values that determined what would be accepted as normal in school and what would be labeled as disabled, incompetent, or deviant. Those who fit the mainstream cultural definition of normal escaped labeling, and the "deviants" were separated out so the "normals" would not be disturbed or threatened.

Bart lists the compulsory education laws, immigration laws, I.Q. testing, and medical and psychological testing as the forces behind labeling in special education.

In short, we are often dealing with a social process rather than learning and reading competence. Our tests are measuring cultural knowledge, familiarity with standard written English, literal comprehension of texts, socioeconomic background, and allegiance to the norms and values of schools (reflecting those of the white Anglo-Saxon majority). Sadly, the more things change, the more they remain the same. We have seen the increase of terminology with a scientific flair (minimal brain dysfunction, dyslexia, hyperlexia, hyperkinetic, attention deficit disorder, learning disabled), but this has served merely to obscure the social origins of the labels.

The Labeling Process

The social process of labeling begins with the identification of students who do not "fit" with the mainstream. They are then subjected to differential interactions and expectations from the teacher. Sensing this, the students begin to act in accordance with the lowered expectations of the teacher. More deviant behavior is produced and tolerated (expected and excused as inevitable), and the testing/placement process begins.

Once a label has been conferred, the student is separated from peers, subjected to more peer rejection, given individualized programming devoid of meaningful social interaction with "normal" peers, and given a fragmented, controlled curriculum. That curriculum prevents the development of higher level thinking as well as personal responsibility for learning (behavior modification techniques particularly work against the development of self-governance).

In this way the label becomes sealed stigma—a social prescription for failure. The student assumes the behavior appropriate to the label and eventually loses self-identity, substituting the identity of the label. Various researchers have referred to this as "learned helplessness" (Dweck, 1976) or "learning the art of being stupid" (Peck, 1971). But it is actually less an individual act than it is a process of "achieving" failure (McDermott, 1974)—a social process performed in concert with the social institutions of school, family, and the community.

Mercer (1973), Cummins (1986), and Rivers (1975) give evidence of the clear bias against Mexican-Americans and blacks in their studies of schools that labeled these minorities as retarded in disproportionate numbers. Schrag and Divoky (1975) cite the cases of hyperactivity labeling and the drugs misused to keep students controlled and conforming to mainstream values and the status quo of the school. And Granger and Granger (1986) add the wider political and economic dimensions that have allowed special education to become a segregation mechanism.

The Process for Sunny and James

What is the process whereby a student comes to be labeled as reading disabled? The answer that emerges from the case studies of Sunny and James is: It is a circular process that appears to be kept in motion through the interaction of the family, school, and community systems in the ecology of each learner. This process can begin with social definitions for family competence, which then lead to school definitions, expectations, and labels for the student. The family is nurtured by the school to accept the label; and if the student assumes the label, it gives the system permission to scapegoat the student. The LD curriculum then maintains the label through more fragmented teaching and testing. As the student becomes increasingly isolated from competent peers and continues to fail, the art of being stupid is perfected. This, in turn, confirms the initial definitions, expectations, and the label; so the process continues on its circular, equilibrium-maintaining course.

The process for Sunny and James seemed to have four basic stages, beginning with the definition stage. Social definitions relative to the white, middle-class community values determined competence and incompetence, set school system expectations, and put a ceiling on the amount of variation that would be tolerated in the system. At this stage both Sunny's and James' families were defined as inadequate, unstimulating, and unsupportive of education. Since their families did not conform to the cultural majority values, both students were subjected to low teacher expectations and biased preconceptions with regard to their potential. This stage in the social process was masked by scientific language disguising the underlying assumptions of incompetence, attributions of failure, and intolerance for variation in the school system.

The second stage in the process involved the family and school systems interactions with respect to the definition of the student as incompetent, and the scientific solutions offered by the school system. The teachers' low expectations and biases were conveyed to Sunny and James through day-to-day interactions in the classroom. Sunny's response to this was to act out the low expectations and do nothing. James reacted by misbehaving in class. The school, in turn, reacted by focusing on both students' supposed deficits and behavior problems to the neglect of the school's role in the process; and the pseudo-scientific, psychological referral chain began. This testing and diagnosis of the individual again masked the ongoing social process (blaming the student, blaming the family) in the politics of everyday life in the classroom.

The third stage in the process of reading disability labeling for Sunny and James was the transitional "learning" stage wherein they learned the art of being stupid. As both Sunny and James continued to meet and confirm the teachers' low expectations for them, the curriculum was adjusted down to their assumed low level. They were viewed as not capable and less was expected of them, so they continued to not learn to read. By the time the tests were completed to allow their label to be conferred, they had provided the teachers with ample evidence of their "unfitness" for the mainstream and their inability to profit from regular classroom instruction. Their labels both justified the teachers', administrators', and specialists' expectations for them, and at the same time functioned to maintain the equilibrium of the classroom with regard to the "normal" (unlabeled) others. At this point the stigma became official dogma, and they were assigned to the LD classroom.

The fourth stage in this process could be entitled "sealing the casket." It is in this final stage that the solutions offered for the disability truly become the problem. Sunny and James were segregated from their "normal" peers and relegated to a context wherein they were subject to mainstream peer rejection and stigma both from the label and from the "special" classroom. They were placed in a context in which *bad* was *good* and *good* was *bad*. Deviation increases in such a context, accompanied by even more labeling by school personnel. Both Sunny and James assumed their labels, and this demanded behavior appropriate to the labels.

The fragmented curriculum offered in the LD classroom exacerbated the problem by teaching and testing subskills instead of providing wholistic language experiences. Management techniques such as behavior modification were used to control the students rather than teaching them autonomy and personal responsibility. The objective of teaching was to "ensure success" rather than to challenge or anticipate the development of potential. And meaningful social interaction in the pursuit of knowledge was discouraged in the name of individualization, which translated into separation and isolation.

The poverty of the curriculum prevented movement up and out, just as the low track curriculum prevented the learning necessary to move up to a college preparatory section. The middle school LD program was created for just such students without the requisite skills to make it in the regular classroom, according to the special services director. At the time of this writing, there are plans for a high school LD program to accommodate and maintain such nonreading students until graduation.

As all of these problematic solutions to the reading problems of students are offered, the students' self-concepts and self-expectations sink lower until their identities finally match the label. It is at this point that learning the art of being stupid is complete. What was once merely a linguistic label, created through social definitions and perpetuated by scientific terminology, becomes sealed stigma. J. Henry's (1965) term, the "bizarre suicide of the soul," seems appropriate for this process.

FROM TESTING TO EVALUATION

In addition to the social bias against the poor, minorities, and those who vary from the tight "normal" range, there is the additional problem of what the tests actually measure, particularly with respect to language competence. The essential meaning-making aspects of reading competence—intention, symbolic/metaphoric meaning, tone, style—demand the use of critical thinking. None of these aspects can be tapped by standardized tests, which measure instead decoding and literal interpretation of texts.

Similarly, the discovery of content and the choice of purpose, audience, and appropriate style and vocabulary are the hallmarks of writing competence. Standardized tests of language measure instead editing skills and mastery of standard written English. Even those tests that include a writing sample do not allow sufficient variation of purposes and audiences for the student's choice-making to be measured. Moreover, one sample cannot validly measure the student's ability to discover, create, and structure content.

Competency tests are yet another degee further away from language competence. According to Cooper (1981), minimum competency tests measure mere parts and fragments of language—the basic decoding skills, which actually have not been declining over recent years. It is higher level critical thinking that the tests do not measure and that has been declining. The deficiency of the competency tests is compounded by the destruction they wreak on the curriculum, desiccating the English curriculum and fragmenting the reading curriculum.

That such tests continue to be used is more understandable when one considers wider political issues along with the history of standardized tests of intelligence. As we have seen, this is a history filled with invalidity and thinly veiled cultural bias serving the function of maintaining the status quo under the guise of scientific validity. Statistics, rendered in such mass projects as the Army Alpha and Beta tests and Goddard's data from Ellis Island, though replete with methodological errors, omissions, and fudged data, served to give support to the racial and social prejudices of the majority. Since the majority rules in a democracy, politicians find it wise to serve their needs and validate their views.

Our position is that any test of reading or learning is an underestimation of competence. Any test freezes or fossilizes human potential at yesterday's level of development, and it tells us nothing about possibilities for future development. Our theory of language learning, rooted in the work of Vygotsky, suggests that it is possible to focus instead on learning that lies just ahead of development. In addition, this theory suggests that we can hold high expectations for the successful learning of all students; and we can successfully meet those expectations through teaching to the zone of proximal development, or scaffolding as it has been termed by Bruner and others.

In Binet's cautions against the use of reified test scores, he spoke of the self-fulfilling prophecy of labels and scores. His original intent was to identify in order to help and improve, and he emphasized the power of education to increase the achievement of all students. Of the notion of fixed intelligence and reified test scores, he said we must "demonstrate that it is founded upon nothing." Chapter 10 will critically analyze tests of reading and learning with this imperative in mind.

The movement from testing to evaluation, from viewing students as the additive sums of their static test scores to evaluating them as in-process learners, avoids many of the problems faced by Sunny and James. Test scores and labels reduced the expectations for Sunny and James, expectations that they most certainly lived down to. Neither was given challenging material, since that was reserved for those who were expected to meet the challenge, which they certainly were not.

We are not suggesting that it is possible to simply expect optimal learning of all students, without providing the sort of classroom climate that is conducive to such learning, or without developing the support or scaffolding that could make it possible. The whole language curriculum, the focus on higher level thinking and learning processes, social interaction, and teacher scaffolding are all integral to the move from testing to evaluation. But we are suggesting that it is possible to return to optimism about the potential of all students, and that it is possible to help them by leading them into what they do not already know.

The Standardized View

Culturally we are dominated in the United States by an efficient American production model. Our standardized tests measure standardized subskills that are taught in a standardized way: same sequence, same pace, same method, same goal. It is an efficient, clean, neat model that allows for little variation from the norm and readily sorts out deviants to be either retrained or removed from the mainstream. Like our American machine model, we examine the parts of a supposedly defective learner, we repair or replace the deficient part (with fix-it methods like subskill work on the deficit), or we remove it from the standardized production line (by labeling it as special and segregating it). Deviation from the norm is equivalent to disability and dysfunction.

There are several problems with this model as applied to human learning. First, it frequently produces standardized thinkers, writers, and readers who lack the higher level critical thinking without which our democracy cannot survive. Second, such a model penalizes individual creative thought (labeling it deviant or disabled) without which true progress cannot occur. Third, it creates a caste society wherein the rich get richer and the poor get poorer, which is antithetical to the democracy to which we aspire.

Though it makes sense from a production viewpoint to standardize teaching and testing, and though it appears to be more efficient to break language learning down into component skills and teach them in a sequential manner, and though it seems more efficient to group and track students according to "ability," it also appears that human language learning operates differently from the production of a Ford. Students learn language more easily and with greater fluency and comprehension when it is taught wholistically in meaningful contexts. Skill needs appear to be unique to the individual learner in both sequence and pace, and they are more meaningfully and lastingly learned in the context of whole language experiences. There is no clean linear sequence appropriate for whole classrooms of students because language learning is recursive rather than sequential. Skills taught apart from their whole language context and the individual student's need appear to be less than efficiently taught. This fragmentation may even cause problems, elsewhere described as "iatrogenic disability" (Sarason & Doris, 1979), in which the solution itself becomes the problem.

In addition to the problems of equity and invalid learning theory, the standardized evaluation view creates such problems as the "tail wagging the dog," in which the fragmented testing of subskills shapes the curriculum to match. There is also the problem of what is actually measured by the standardized tests—lower level basic skills rather than higher level thinking. The standardized view also lacks direction for good classroom practice (apart from more of the same subskill teaching). And standardized testing, continually increasing at the district, state, and national levels, is too often the pawn of political maneuvers to gain popularity and appease the public.

Two Ways of Looking

Again, returning to an ecological perspective, we can see the dynamics of the interacting systems of culture (social bias, economic power, industrial and technological growth—particularly the powerful testing industry and basal reader companies), school (a microcosm of the community), and family (influenced by the commercial marketplace) as they shape the ecology of the student. And again we see the need for a new definition of reading and learning, a new way of teaching, and the congruent evaluation that will be discussed in Chapter 11.

Beyond the powerful forces of the testing industry and subskill material companies, beyond the vested interests of the medical and psychological professions, and even beyond the social biases and perceptions that shape our thinking are the even more powerful (and more difficult to change) forces of habit and tradition: *How else would you do it? That's the way they did it when I was in school 30 years ago. What's wrong with it? It worked for me—I learned and I'm doing well.*

The ecological alternative is not easy in the face of decades of habit and tradition with a less wholistic framework. It is not easy to change perceptions, one's own professional teaching practice, and the well-established (and presumably correct) way of dealing with students' learning. But if professionals can begin to form networks as they come to better understand the implications of an ecological approach to language learning, and as they share their resources with each other in the pursuit of the potential of all students, many meaningful strides can be taken toward a new way of looking, teaching, evaluating, and learning.

10
A Critical Analysis of Diagnosis, Labeling, and Remediation

One of the major premises of this book is that traditional diagnosis, labeling, and remediation of reading and learning problems have themselves been problematic solutions. We explore that view from still other perspectives in this chapter by reviewing what we know from research about dyslexia, learning disability tests, and reading comprehension subtests.

Dyslexic, as a label for seriously disabled readers, preceded the more current term of learning disabled for such students. Many of the same neurological hypotheses have been offered for those labeled as learning disabled as have been advanced for dyslexics. Despite these speculations, Vellutino (1987) states, "Not enough is yet known about how the brain works to enable anyone to devise activities that would have a direct and positive effect on neurological functions." He suggests also that there is a growing consensus among researchers that there is no substitute for a balanced reading program that fosters overall language development in the remediation of reading difficulties.

This wisdom from current research runs counter to much of traditional diagnostic and remedial practice. To explore the origins of some of the problematic solutions that have obscured this wisdom, we turn to a brief review of the evidence behind the term dyslexia, the predecessor of the term learning disability.

DYSLEXIA RESEARCH

Dyslexia is a term that has become a confusing part of educational jargon over the past few decades. The term is used in a wide variety of contexts depending on the biases of those using it. In one frame of reference, dyslexia is said to be organic in nature: the result of a postulated neurological defect, either genetic or induced by minimal, nonobservable brain trauma. In another, it has come to be used in connection with the entire community of those who have difficulty learning to read up to expected capacity, for whatever reason. Given these extremes, dyslexia (like the current term *learning disability*) can be attributed to as little as one quarter of one percent of the population or as much as twenty percent.

The nature and treatment of dyslexia is probably the most exasperating issue in the field of educational disability. The literature on the subject of dyslexia is vast and ponderous; the preponderance of it deals with speculation and assertions regarding the cause of the underachievement and the means for diagnosing it. Too little of the literature has tested the validity of the hypotheses of differential diagnosis as a basis for teaching the underachieving learner.

Our review of the literature attempted to answer the question, What evidence supports the theory that dyslexia is a peculiar and rare organic abnormality, different fundamentally from other forms of reading underachievement? More particularly, What evidence is there that such a diagnosis leads to helping students overcome their underachievement?

A large body of conjecture and research has emerged since the turn of the century that has attempted to establish a clinical definition of dyslexia as an organic disorder. Three hypotheses have been explored. Some believe that dyslexia is a function of a genetic factor. Dyslexia was, in fact, first called "congenital" word blindness. Another organic theory attributes dyslexia to minor brain damage of some sort. It has been found, for instance, that in some cases where brain lesion occurred due to accident or disease, the result is total reading disability. It seems reasonable to such theorists, therefore, that a lesser, nonobservable trauma might have occurred in the disabled reader. Still another organic hypothesis attempts to establish the cause as incomplete brain dominance. This means simply that signals from the subdominant hemisphere of the brain interfere with signals from the dominant hemisphere.

The genetic hypothesis is based on the belief that a certain gene asserts an anomalic influence on the organs responsible for perception, resulting in the inability to read or spell properly. This hypothesis draws on several patterns in clinical observation. First, acute reading disability to some investigators seems to manifest itself in successive generations within a single family. Second, all studies done to date have shown that the afflicted persons are almost always male. Finally, some evidence shows that reading disability occurs simultaneously in identical twins more often than in fraternal twins.

But evidence is sparse and conjecture is highly speculative. No gene or genetic function has as yet been isolated that would account for a neurological dysfunction resulting in reading difficulty. Experimenters who have attempted to establish familial incidence and co-occurrence among identical twins have not taken necessary precautions to ensure the validity of their evidence. For instance, the evidence in this area is limited to interviews with family members, rather than developmental or longitudinal studies in which intelligence and other social factors could be considered. Longitudinal studies that attempt to carefully document the actual learning environment of the student remain to be done. (An ecological study may reveal curricular factors or interactional dynamics that influence nonlearning.)

The second hypothesis, that of minimal brain damage, is open to the same reservations as is the genetic hypothesis. There is little evidence that would allow any final conclusion to be drawn about the actual physical fact of brain lesion or "minimal brain dysfunction." Most evidence in the area of brain damage is based on correlational studies. These include examination of electroencephalographic evidence—that is, the monitoring of brain waves—and the collection of information on the incidence of prenatal anomalies and maternal complications during birth as it relates to later incidence of reading underachievement.

The findings of electroencephalographic testing have not been convincing. In the first place, these studies typically lack controls; and where there have been controls, no differences were found between disabled and normal readers in "spike" patterns. Moreover, different experimenters themselves have obtained different results in separate experiments done with brain wave monitoring. (See Vellutino, 1987, for current studies.)

There is evidence that indicates some positive correlation between the incidence of maternal complications during birth and the student's reading problems in later life. This evidence, however, cannot be interpreted as affirming that any given student with so-called dyslexic symptoms is, in fact, suffering the consequences of prenatal difficulties or maternal adversity.

The third hypothesis, that of mixed laterality, was developed by Samuel Orton in the 1920s. His theory postulates that the two hemispheres of the brain are equal in their development, but that normally one side of the brain remains dominant. The subdominant side, according to Orton, contains a mirror image of the sensory data present in the dominant side of the brain. In normal students, that is, those with no reading problem, the images of the subdominant hemisphere never surface in perception but are suppressed in some way, and only the images of the dominant side of the brain assert themselves. But in readers who have consistent difficulty with reversals, Orton postulated, the perceptive processes cannot suppress the images persisting in the subdominant section of the brain, thus resulting in letter and word confusion. Orton called this anomaly "strephosymbolia" (twisted symbols).

The widespread and long-standing interest in the correlations of brain locale with human functioning, and Orton's hypothesis that dyslexia is caused by lack of unilateral cerebral dominance, has led to a great deal of research in the relationship of laterality and directionality patterns to reading ability. Modern correlates of Orton's thesis propose that brain dominance plays a large part in the proper perceptual and motor development of the student. When, these theories assert, the student is in some way ambilateral—that is, when he or she does not conclusively favor one side of the body or the other—severe retardation in motor and perceptual skills develops. But experimental evidence in the area of directionality and laterality provides little if any support for the position of those maintaining that ambilaterality is a deleterious condition. Correlational evidence shows that there is no positive correlation between hand-eye laterality preference in either reading achievement or intelligence scores for age-alike groups in a random sample of the population. In fact, research does indicate that early inconsistencies with respect to left-right confusion in laterality preferences as well as in perceptual responses continue to decrease from kindergarten to the end of second grade for all pupils.

Several remedial programs have been created that stress the development of motor skills and foster unilaterality as reading-readiness activities. These programs usually demand that students perform various physical exercises that ostensibly give them a greater awareness of their body, improve their sense of balance, and increase their coordination of hand, eye, and leg movements. Remediation employing such techniques is based on the hypothesis that physical maturation and coordination are directly related to and a precondition for the perceptual and cognitive development needed to learn to read. More precisely, it is assumed that by providing a student with the opportunity to exercise motor functions specific to certain stages of development, the student will eventually improve in the coordinate cognitive and perceptual domains. Thus, for instance, creeping or crawling in a stylized way has been proposed as a basis for improving reading.

Some researchers have developed experiments to test the validity of such techniques. One experiment found that training in motor-perceptual development made some difference on a reading-readiness test. However, experimenters have not been able to demonstrate statistically significant differences in reading improvement between groups given various forms of motor-perceptual development tasks and those given none at all.

It seems fairly evident in all this that the problem of dyslexia has never been pinned down. No etiology has ever attained conclusive validity. No experiment has ever definitively isolated any organic factor that could explain the phenomenon called dyslexia. This is not to say that such a factor does not exist, or that in the strictest clinical sense severe reading underachievement does not exist. Indeed, all who work in clinical settings have seen students and adults who, despite good motivation, obvious intelligence, and intact senses, have failed to learn to read beyond the most elemental level. Ralph Preston characterized these readers as being "impaled on a primer" (1950).

To the extent that our analysis of the literature is correct, three conclusions seem warranted. First, since it is today not possible to distinguish organicity from other causes as the basis for reading handicap, the more apt terms *reading disabled* and *learning disabled* seem more warranted, although we would prefer the terms *less-developed* or *low-progress reader* to affirm the potential of the student to become a more skillful reader. Second, instruction based on the findings of motor and perceptual tests has not proved effective in the teaching of reading. Third, neurological, motor, and perceptual tests at present contribute little to our understanding of the nature of reading underachievement. We turn next to this last issue for a closer consideration of the tests used to diagnose learning and reading disability.

TESTS OF LEARNING DISABILITY

The function of tests is to provide their users with valid, reliable, and useful information. In the case of reading disabled and language disabled students, test scores should identify them, distinguish between them and other students, diagnose their problems, and prescribe programs to overcome their difficulties or enhance their strengths. But research findings have repeatedly shown that the two most frequently used test batteries for learning disability and reading comprehension fail in all of these functions.

It is presumed that learning disability tests should identify students who exhibit a

> disorder in one or more of the basic psychological processes involved in understanding or in using language, spoken or written, which may manifest itself in an imperfect ability to listen, think, read, write, spell, or do mathematical calculations. (Federal definition cited in Ysseldyke & Algozzine, 1984)

Furthermore, these tests should be expected to reveal the "specific" underlying difficulties students have, and this should become the basis for prescribing programs designed to overcome the problems.

To determine how well the learning disability tests performed these functions, Coles (1978) synthesized the research on the validity of the ten most commonly used learning disability tests: the Illinois Test of Psycholinguistic Abilities, the Bender Visual-Motor Gestalt Test, the Frostig Developmental Test of Visual Perception, the Wepman Auditory Discrimination Test, the Lincoln-Oseretsky Motor Development Scale, the Graham-Kendall Memory for Designs Test, the Purdue Perceptual-Motor Survey, the Wechsler Intelligence Scale for Children, a neurological exam given by a neurologist, and an electroencephalogram. We refer the interested reader to this very excellent article for further documentation and elaboration of our brief summary.

After an extensive review of the validation studies of these measures, Coles found the tests very weak at best or useless at worst in distinguishing learning disabled students from nonlearning disabled students, or good from poor readers. Furthermore, other research indicated that remedial approaches geared to overcome the difficulties identified by these tests had no positive effect on performance in reading. There was some improvement in subsequent test scores, however, indicating that the approach had some value for learning how to take that particular test, but little value otherwise for reading and learning.

The study by Vinsonhaler, Weinshank, Wagner, and Polin (1983) is an interesting corollary to Coles' research. Looking at the diagnostic and remedial performance of specialists and teachers, they found very little commonality or agreement in diagnostic statements about students. Remediation also appeared to be uncorrelated with diagnosis, which led the authors to conclude that "diagnosis as presently conducted should not be continued."

Part of the problem, of course, is the medical/biological thesis underlying learning disability research, which places responsibility for failure within the head of the student. Other methodological shortcomings in LD diagnosis include the failure to account for variables of social class and race; the lack of construct validity—the tests do not, in fact, measure neurological dysfunction in isolation; and the neglect of context variables—no attempt is made to look at teaching and the school environment for contributions to the problem. Differentiating underachievers from the disabled, or students with emotional problems from those without them is also a problem in the learning disability research. The focus in all of this is away from the learning process and the context of the school, away from the need to change institutions, and away from the need to rectify the social conditions affecting the child. It is a classic example of blaming the victim.

None of this is to say that there are no dyslexic or seriously learning disabled students. In fact, there is considerable agreement, according to

Hynd and Hynd (1984), that there is probably some neuroanatomical malfunctioning in the several interrelated regions of the brain for some small percentage of students. Furthermore, they report that, like any other human trait, this malfunctioning is likely to vary in human beings, rather than being a localized lesion in the brain. That is to say, we are likely to find a continuous gradation from minimal to extreme disability in this small population.

But once we have identified the learning disabled by their low performance on school tasks involving reading and writing, further testing using learning disability tests is clearly a waste of precious time and money—not only the time it takes to give the tests, but also the time it takes to remediate supposed problems identified by invalid tests. In 1971, Balow provided an appropriate footnote to LD research. In a paper critical of neurological explanations for reading problems, he asked:

> If reading disability is at root a medical problem, why is it that the vast preponderance of serious cases come from those geographic areas where the home, community, and school environment are most hostile to academic learning? Why are up to 60 percent of slum area children and only two percent of suburban children severe reading disability cases?

READING COMPREHENSION SUBTESTS

Until there is evidence that so-called underlying auditory, visual, and motor processing are problematic, it seems appropriate to focus attention on reading itself. According to Vellutino (1987), this is consistent with scientific findings regarding the manifestations of reading disability, which invariably have to do with linguistic processing at every level: semantic, syntactic, and graphophonic. Furthermore, many researchers seem to be in agreement that instruction for the reading and learning disabled must involve a balanced, integrated program with both comprehension and graphophonic approaches (Eisenberg, 1979; Hynd & Hynd, 1984; Vellutino, 1987).

Most reading comprehension tests provide a diagnostic profile of a student's strengths and weaknesses in the "subskills" of comprehension. But one of the sturdiest research findings in reading is this: There are many comprehension skills and strategies, but for the individual student we cannot reliably distinguish among these subskills in tests. A further disability could be caused by dealing with a problem that is not a problem.

Consider the following reports. Thorndike (1973) found low statistical probability of reliable differentiation among the subtests of the Davis

Reading Test and the Stanford Reading Test. He said, "Over the realistic range of test reliabilities, and using the kinds of pairs of measures that we are likely to want to use in diagnostic studies, the confidence is often distressingly low." Mason, Osborn, and Rosenshine (1977) synthesized the research on reliability of comprehension subskills on tests and concluded that "no clear evidence was found concerning the distinctiveness of different reading skills." Drahozal and Hanna (1978) studied the issue of identifying subscores on the Nelson Reading Skills Test, using the largest representative sample of third through ninth grade students ever reported in such a study. They found three subtests at all grade levels "to be alternate means of measuring the same things."

All of the tests considered thus far are norm-referenced standardized tests. The question that suggests itself is: Can we get a more reliable diagnosis from criterion-referenced tests, such as basal end-of-unit tests and individually administered informal reading inventories? The research again says no. Schell and Hanna (1981), after researching five recently published Informal Reading Inventories (IRIs),[1] concluded: "The evidence seems overwhelmingly conclusive. Informal inventories do not reveal true strengths and weaknesses in comprehension subskills; therefore they should not be used for this purpose."

Finally, Lyons (1984) analyzed the test results on a study of the Massachusetts Assessment of Basic Skills criterion-referenced test, which has 14 reading comprehension subtests. In his analysis Lyons made the following observation: "Local and commercially developed criterion-referenced reading tests proliferate, each with promises of more precise measurement of comprehension skills. . . . Too often their best efforts, like the pilot efforts in Massachusetts, have no diagnostic value."

SUMMARY

In short, research tells us that there is no valid basis for using a battery of learning disability tests or reading comprehension subtests for identifying, diagnosing, and remediating reading problems. Careful analyses of these tests found them to lack sufficient validity and reliability to be helpful. Many neurological and educational researchers are in agreement that good instruction in reading with a balanced program is best for those with reading problems. The link between neurological deficits and specific remediation geared to those deficits seems logical and has been attempted in good faith by many concerned practitioners. But as we have seen, the

---

[1]Burma and Roe; Ekwall; Johns; Silvaroli; Woods and Moe.

solution has become the problem. Using such tests creates another example of an iatrogenic disability.

The question remains, Is there some way in which we could use the results of comprehension tests to make instructional decisions? The answer is, Yes, we can use the total score of the reading comprehension tests for screening students or to get a general impression estimate of students' ability to read. As teachers have long noted, a test of reading comprehension is a rough indicator of functional reading comprehension. But as we have seen, test results do not indicate real comprehension.

Reading comprehension is a process that involves the orchestration of the reader's prior experience and knowledge about the world and about language. It involves such interrelated strategies as predicting, questioning, summarizing, determining meanings of vocabulary in context, monitoring one's own comprehension, and reflecting. The process also involves such affective factors as motivation, ownership, purpose, and self-esteem. It takes place in and is governed by a specific context, and it is dependent on social interaction. It is the integration of all these processes that accounts for comprehension. They are not isolable, measurable subfactors: They are wholistic processes for constructing meaning.

No one masters reading comprehension. We continue to work at meaning making all our lives. Everyone can comprehend, including the most "disabled" readers. The job of the teacher and specialist is to teach the process of comprehending and to observe, document, and reflect on students as they use the process in reading a variety of texts. From these observations, the teacher and specialist can determine how to help all students, including those labeled as disabled, to reach higher levels of competence.

We need evaluation measures that match our best definition of reading competence and learning, and that also give us useful information for remediation. Recalling that any test is an underestimation of student ability—a fossilization of potential development—we turn in Chapter 11 to modes of evaluation that are built on a broader, ecological way of looking and teaching. The evaluation methods we will discuss attempt to capture the dynamics of the actual learning process of the student, and they are congruent with the ecological teaching practice that we described in Part II.

11
Toward a More Congruent and Ecological Evaluation

The findings reported in Chapters 9 and 10 make clear the potential dangers of testing for understanding the needs of individual students. Teachers and specialists need a broader vision of evaluation, one that will help them see learners in a new way: valuing them by focusing on understanding and bringing out their potential, respecting their personal experience or prior knowledge, and safeguarding them from false labels. Ecological evaluation would be more descriptive of students in the ecology of the classroom and in the process of learning.

In addition to its history of invalidity and bias as described in Chapters 9 and 10, psychometric testing in this century has a history of taking value from the individual—of devaluing rather than placing value in the student's personal experience. In the cases of students from racial minority groups, low socioeconomic classes, and other socially devalued groups, the testing has traditionally reinforced and supported social class differentiation. Tragic and undemocratic as this devaluing has been, there is an even more pervasive problem with our present system of testing. Not only does it devalue certain social classes, but it devalues the voice of the individual student and the autonomy of the teacher, while it limits the opportunity for true learning to occur.

It is not difficult to see how the individual voice and experience of the student are lost in one-right-answer formats typical of standardized tests. Nor is it hard to see how ownership of the curriculum is taken from teachers as they are forced to prepare students to take the required tests. But the danger within all this prescriptive testing, a more pervasive problem actually created by the increase of testing, is that many students may be denied the right to learn to think critically and creatively.

If evaluation is focused on the testable pieces common in a fragmented curriculum, if it forces accountability only for the scores that come from invalid tests, it of necessity limits the possibilities for students to become divergent, exploratory, critical thinkers. Standardized test formats, by their very definition, eliminate the use of the individual background and experience of the student. Yet it is this vital element of personal experience, this prior knowledge, that is central to learning in the fullest sense of the word. Standardized tests also eliminate the integration of skills and strategies: the very heart of the learning process.

So we ask, What is given value in evaluation? Is it testable fragments and testmanship? Is it isolated facts and dates? Is it subsystems of language? If so, then we can expect that the curriculum will be filled with such disconnected bits of information. And we can be sure that there will be little time left over for exploring and developing new ideas, for drawing from the wealth of resources within the individual, for collaborative sharing and further development of those ideas, for concept building, and for integration of knowledge in the pursuit of deeper understanding.

We come, in evaluation, to the very heart of the matter of learning and meaning making in life and in language: What is given value? Should we take value from or should we place value in the individual? Can we respect and value the wider ecology of the student, can we orchestrate a collaborative learning environment within the classroom community of learners, and can we thus create more opportunities for each individual to learn to learn?

We believe that this is possible with an ecological approach to reading and learning. Congruence between teaching and evaluation is achieved by using the same framework for both, allowing teachers and specialists to enrich the curriculum for all students. In this chapter, classroom observation, collaborative observation, interactive observation of the student's world view, and general impression assessment of reading and writing are presented as examples of more ecological procedures for evaluation. We view these as closer to the definition of evaluation as interpretation, a bringing forth of value, and an acknowledgment of the quality or excellence of the learner. They do not preclude other worthy procedures that are available or may be developed, but we view them as more congruent with the critical experiences framework.

What makes the methods described below ecological is their inclusion of experiences from the ecosystem of the learner, their integration of those experiences with the critical experiences that are vital for learning, and the interactions and interrelationships between and among all of those experiences that lead to meaning making. The focus is on the whole learner, in whole language contexts, in integrated classrooms characterized by collaborative social interaction and expectations for optimal growth and learning.

OBSERVATION IN CONTEXT

Ecological evaluation focuses on observing, describing, and understanding the learner rather than extracting pieces from the ecosystem. It is dynamic, constructive, and interactive. Observing disabled learners in the classroom context; documenting what they say, write, and do; and reflecting on these data is the most inherently valid approach to getting to know students. Of course, teachers and specialists in the process of teaching observe learners all the time and continually make decisions about how to help them based on those observations. But documenting their behavior descriptively on a regular basis using 3″ by 5″ cards, a notebook, or a journal helps develop a composite picture of the learner, which the teacher can then reflect on.

Some of the language events the teacher will observe and document are how students participate in class discussions, how they choose books, what books they choose, their collaboration in writing conferences, and what they write about. This process of documentation is what researchers do in all fields. On re-reading and reflecting on their notes, they find patterns and themes not easily discernable while the observations are being made.

The documentation called for is not just a list of errors, miscues, and mistakes. It is more like taking notes on a narrative or a play. Students, after all, are members of a community of learners. What happens to them is not just what goes on in their heads and not just their behavior; it is also what goes on in the interactions with the teacher and classmates. What are the assignments the learners are working on? What time of the day are things happening? With whom is the student working and how are they collaborating? Like a play, then, there are characters, setting, actions, and plot.

More specifically, teachers and specialists can observe students while reading, writing, and talking as they are engaged in the critical experiences. For example, when students are working on their writing pieces they prewrite, draft, revise, and proofread. If running records or notes are kept on the left-hand side of a notepad, the right-hand side can be used to write interpretive notes that serve as hypotheses about the meaning of the observational data for teaching and learning.

Each of the following observational approaches to evaluation—classroom observation, collaborative evaluation, and staff review—is rooted in an ecological perspective. The learner is viewed not as a person with deficits that must be corrected, but as a whole person living and learning in several interrelated systems or communities. Through the documentation of the learner's transactions and interactions taking place in learning events in the classroom, elsewhere in the school, in the home, and in the community, we can gradually come to know learners and their needs.

Observation is the crucial dimension of evaluation. In-class, contextual observation rooted in the critical experiences for learning provides a full and rich description that values the whole learner rather than devaluing the individual. From this base of understanding the student in context, the specialist and teacher can move to more specific individual methods for observing and understanding the needs of certain learners.

Observation during the Critical Experiences

If what we value is indeed the individual, then the most valid evaluation is observation of the individual in the context of those experiences that are critical for learning. As we have explained in Chapter 5, the critical experiences framework provides such an environment for learning broader concepts and connected themes because it links to the experience of each individual student. It is a framework that begins with whole texts and higher level thinking, while at the same time including subsystems of language and basic skills in the learning process. Therefore it is possible to structure our observation of the student's learning around the critical experiences and obtain not only a valid picture of the learning process, but simultaneously a direction for improvement of the curriculum.

As we observe the individual responding to literature and texts, we can ask, How is this student responding to before, during, and after reading activities? If there are difficulties with some of the during reading activities, for instance, we might ask if this signals the need for more or better before reading activities? Often a student who is experiencing difficulty may be a barometer for the general climate of the classroom experience, and this may be a signal to the teacher for a needed change.

The Evaluation Outline in Figure 11.1 is a flexible outline for recording notes or writing an observational evaluation based on the student's engagement in the critical experiences for learning. The form that the outline takes will reflect the classroom curriculum as created collaboratively by the teacher and specialist. The example in Figure 11.1 represents only one way among many of documenting the learning process of a particular student.

When a student experiences a significant amount of difficulty, the teacher would ask the specialist or an administrator to also observe. The same framework could be used to observe the teacher (and also the curriculum) so that congruent changes could be suggested to preserve the ecology of the classroom. An additional benefit from using this framework is that teachers would be credited, and thereby encouraged, as they use the critical experiences framework and continue to be self-reflective professionals.

Dinosaur unit example

The teacher and two specialists who collaboratively wrote and taught the dinosaur unit included at the end of Chapter 5 evaluated one of their students, David, who was labeled as learning disabled, using another

FIGURE 11.1.   Evaluation Outline for Observing Student Learning

	Observations	Interpretation

Responding to Text
    Classroom process
      Before reading:
      During reading:
      After reading:
    Reading process
      Think-aloud protocol:
      Academic journal:
    Performance level (see Appendix A)
    Comments		

Independent Reading and Writing
    Books chosen
    Book conversations
    Types of writing
    Comments		

Oral Composing
    Reports/speeches
    Classroom dialogue
    Narratives
    Comments		

Written Composing
    Portfolio description/analysis
    Prewriting
    Conferencing
    Drafting
    Editing
    Dialogue journals
    Performance level (Appendix C)
    Comments		

Investigating Language
    Discovery/use of patterns
    Performance level (Appendix B)
    Comments		

Learning to Learn
    Awareness and use of strategies
    Approach to difficult text
    Comments		

Collaboration
    With partners
    In small groups
    Comments		

version of the critical experiences framework of the PCRP. Following is the evaluation they submitted for David:

I. Responding to literature
   A. His dramatizations of orally read literature were accurate. He was also thoroughly involved in the portrayals.
   B. His illustrations depicted an understanding of orally and silently read text.
   C. David participated in echo and choral reading activities.
   D. David contributed to word walls, discussions, and question posters.
   E. David played the part of reporter and was able to formulate *wh* questions.
   F. David showed understanding of material by taking part in a panel discussion concerning dinosaurs.
II. Sustained silent reading
   A. David was actively engaged in SSR activities.
   B. Informal conferences helped us determine if David brought meaning to text.
III. Composing
   A. David formulated interesting questions for our guest speaker.
   B. David's journal entries were kept up-to-date and his ideas were expressed thoughtfully.
   C. David was able to sequentially describe steps in "Making a Fossil."
   D. David's "Life History of a Fossil" indicated an understanding of fossil development.
   E. David's research report was evaluated according to accuracy.
   F. David's newspaper article, "How Dinosaurs Disappeared," was evaluated on how well the *wh* questions were answered.
IV. Investigating language patterns
   A. David successfully used words from the word wall in adjective, noun, verb, adverb pattern to make sentences.
   B. David successfully completed a sentence-combining activity.
   C. David edited his report with the assistance of other students as well as teachers.
   D. David published his edited report.
V. Other evaluation
   A. David passed a cloze test on fossils (100%).
VI. General comments

David, as well as the other two LD students, was involved in each activity along with the rest of the class. For the most part, they were as much a part of the group as the others. In fact, David and Jesse outperformed many of the regulars—especially in more creative activities such as dramatizations, panel discussions, and echo readings. SSR was not a problem because they tended to select books they could handle.

Composing was not a problem because we did not emphasize spelling. Children were encouraged to get their ideas down—editing could come later if the works were published. Specialists provided needed help in areas of conferencing, observation during whole group activities, and editing.

Generally speaking, this type of unit was very valuable—particularly for the LD students—because they felt a part of the group. I'm sure they realized that they could progress and learn with the other students—that they really were no different. This had to help their self-esteem and their attitude toward learning.

Observation of Partner and Group Work

Schools are caught in a cultural system that continually endorses and encourages individual competition rather than cooperation and collaboration. As a result, students are less likely to be concerned about or take responsibility for each other's learning in the classroom. They are also less likely to know how to work cooperatively and collaboratively as partners and group members to advance each other's learning. Thus, if we wish to encourage collaborative and mediational social interaction, which we know is important for optimal learning, it may be necessary to structure evaluation of partner and peer group activities into the evaluation plan.

If students know they will be evaluated on the basis of how well they mediate and extend each other's learning in partner and group activities, they may be more motivated to lead each other ahead. Likewise, if teachers and specialists know this is a school value, they will be more likely to structure activities to encourage social interaction in the pursuit of learning. They may also be more likely to collaborate and cooperate not only with each other as professionals but also with the families of particular students who need more help.

At the beginning of the school year teachers and specialists could explain to students that part of their grade for the year will depend on their cooperative work with partners and group members. The students are to take personal responsibility for extending the thinking of partners and group members, they are to share ideas, mediate in the learning of their peers, cooperate as group members, serve as a resource for peers, and help partners to extend and build on their own experience and knowledge.

Simple peer- and self-evaluation forms could be prepared to allow students to evaluate themselves and each other as partners and group members. These might be added to the teacher's and specialist's observations in the classroom. Questions such as the following could be included in some form:

> List those students in the class who have extended your own thinking. (Who in the class has helped you to learn better?)
> In what ways have the above partners or group members mediated in your own learning or collaborated with you? (How have the above students helped you with learning?)
> Evaluate yourself as a partner and group member. To what extent did you mediate in the learning of others, share ideas, collaborate, and serve as a resource for others? (How did you help your partner? How did you share and work with your group?)

The interested reader is referred to D. Johnson, 1981; Gallagher and Reid, 1981; Graybeal and Stodolsky, 1985; Buckley, 1986; and Slavin, 1984 for further information on cooperative peer work.

Collaborative Evaluation and Staff Review

When the specialist and teacher both observe and document the same learning events in the classroom, sharing their notes and tentative interpretations, as did the specialists and teacher in the evaluation presented earlier, they can engage in collaborative problem solving in a spirit of collegiality. The specialist here is not the expert, telling the teacher what to do. Instead there is a feeling of mutual respect for each other's expertise, and both professionals interrelate and build on each other's knowledge. Out of this collaboration may come the need for more information, which can be obtained by further observation, from other colleagues, or from other assessment procedures.

Pat Carini's model of staff review of a child (1982) is a structured process that enables professional colleagues to collaborate effectively in the evaluation of a student. The following is an adapted version of that process, which requires a session of approximately an hour to an hour and a half. The presenting teacher, the chair, and the secretary positions are rotated each time the group meets. No one in the group is considered to be the expert.

1. The presenting teacher portrays the learner from the classroom documentation, beginning with the identification of the presenting problem.

2. The chair, who has taken notes along with the secretary, summarizes and asks the presenting teacher if the essence of the presentation has been captured.
3. The chair then calls for questions from the staff. These questions enable the presenting teachers to expand on their own knowledge of the learner. Since the focus is to be on understanding the learner, the chair gently reminds the staff not to offer solutions during this period. When they do, the chair firmly stops them.
4. The chair summarizes the new information and calls for suggestions from the staff. The presenting teacher may or may not want to respond to these suggestions.
5. The chair summarizes the suggestions.
6. The chair calls for a discussion/evaluation of the process during the session.
7. Plans are made for rotating the positions of chair, secretary, and presenting teacher for the subsequent meeting, for which a date is chosen.

INTERACTIVE OBSERVATION:
THE STUDENT WORLD VIEW

In both reading and learning disability research, one of the most overlooked and underrated sources of knowledge for understanding the problem has been the voice and experience of the students themselves. Yet we know from research in learning that it is the individual's unique way of making meaning that is most important, and we know that meaning making is integrally related to the person's own experiences. New learning builds on the person's experience and knowledge, it occurs in interaction with others in the learner's ecology, and it progresses as a form of self-expression and communication with the wider community of family, school, and culture.

Yet too often students with reading or learning problems are treated as though they can be extracted from their ecosystems and understood as isolated specimens. The ecological dimensions of their difficulties are given short shrift in diagnosis, and the powerful dynamics from the ecology of the individual that could be used for remediation are rarely used to their fullest. Though we know that learning proceeds from the learner's world view, we rarely direct our evaluative, diagnostic, or remedial attempts at giving a voice to that view.

Problematic Versus Ecological Solutions

Student voice is a neglected aspect of the traditional language curriculum in general, so it is not surprising that we should find little of the student's world view in evaluation and remediation. This neglect is due, in part, to the growing removal of curriculum development from the hands of teachers and specialists. We have already cited the problems of deprofessionalization of teachers, prescriptiveness of prepackaged curricula, and the irrelevance of management-type programs to the context of the individual student.

But the absence of a link between student voice and school learning is also a result of the traditional atomistic view of education as a product to be delivered, and the student as a subject to be programmed. This more narrow view ignores the broader ecological dimensions of educating students to become active, critical citizens capable of transforming society, and it prevents teachers from drawing the motivating resources from the learner's experience, background, and interests—resources that give students their own unique voices.

Voice refers to defining ourselves as active participants in the world— to making ourselves understood and listened to. Schools enable students to develop voice by engaging them in self-expression and speculative talk, by focusing on dialogue, and by legitimating their experiences. Thus our ecological approach to teaching draws heavily on students' past experience and knowledge, encourages their individual responses rooted in their own experience, structures dialogue and peer interaction within the curriculum, and legitimates the world view of the individual.

Traditional school systems in this country tend to legitimate the voice of the white middle-class, particularly as it is represented in the values of commercial textbooks and standardized tests. It is uncommon practice for schools to structure the curriculum to enable all students to affirm their voices. But when student voices are denied, the students are also denied the contextual understanding to make the link between classroom knowledge and real-world knowledge. If they are denied the opportunity to affirm their voices within community life, if they are not thus empowered toward creating a more liberating and humane society, we have lost an opportunity to prepare them as active, thinking, critical members of a democracy.

The conventional solution to knowing the learner with respect to reading and learning disability has often been testing. Students are thus objects to be studied rather than the subjects of their own lives. Other individual psychological and medical methods of diagnosis often remove the student from meaningful context, particularly from the classroom, and thus lack ecological validity. In the traditional school system, students with reading and learning problems are removed from the classroom context, given a battery of standardized tests, further clinically tested by a psychologist, and eventually given a label that differentiates and separates them from their classmates. There is little in this type of diagnosis that validates students' world views. Instead, they are often viewed as the sum of their test results, and the entire process of testing and labeling carries with it possibilities for further fragmentation, isolation, and alienation.

In the ecological solution we propose, the student's world view and experiences are validated. Additive sums of test scores removed from the classroom context are viewed as incomplete without a wider view of the whole learner. Students are validated as they dialogue, tell their stories, and strive to understand themselves as learners. The methods used for evaluation and diagnosis say to students that we care about their views, their lives, their experiences, and their unique ways of making meaning. It is interesting to consider what might happen if we could look at students less as objects to be studied and more as subjects of their own lives. Who knows what might happen if we could allow students to tell their own stories rather than relying on someone else's interpretation of them based on test scores, and if we could help students express themselves in an atmosphere of respect, trust, collaboration, understanding, and validation.

Throughout the preceding case studies and classroom activities, we have referred to reading protocols, dialogue journals, and children's narratives. In the following section we will describe more fully these individualized methods of understanding the world view of the student. We see them as more ecological because they are contextual, linking the learner's own experience and voice to classroom learning; they focus on the whole person rather than cognition or perceptual functioning alone; they draw on the various interacting systems of school, family, and community; and they define students as dynamic, interactive participants in the construction and functioning of their own ecosystems.

Children's Narratives

Asking students to tell their own stories is a powerful way to engage them in self-expression and validate their voices. Our procedure for taking stories follows the simple format of asking students to tell an original story about anything they choose. These stories are tape recorded on the spot, sometimes in the school library or resource room. They are later transcribed in prose poem form to follow as closely as possible the pattern and rhythm of the student's own storytelling.

We can understand much about the experiences, perceptions, interests, and meaning making of individuals through their own narratives or folk stories, as Sutton-Smith calls them. In addition to a fuller understanding of the student's oral composing ability, personal story schema, experience and knowledge, and general facility with language, occasionally serendipitous information about barriers to learning and reading comes from the stories.

We know, for instance, that learners construct their own systems of meaning making, and that these represent their own models of social reality. Extending this premise to include the student's construction of personal narratives suggests considering the mind as narrative, and by further extension the possibility of considering analysis of narrative as analysis of mind. There is support for this notion of the narrative mind from psychological, psychoanalytic, and language studies (Bartoli, 1985a); so there is the possibility that some of the students' narratives may be metaphors for their lives (Sutton-Smith, 1981).

James' "Bad Luck" story is a good example of this. Born on a Friday the thirteenth, often perceived by the school to be a troublemaker (though he insists it is not his fault), caught in a negative cycle of school and community expectations and perceptions, relegated to a tracking placement that will preclude his future aspirations, and labeled as disabled despite his competence, James certainly appears to be living a life that is a good metaphor for bad luck.

How much we can extend this metaphor and how often it is part of the student's storytelling is uncertain. But surely there is the possibility for further understanding of the way students learn to define themselves through the analysis of their own narratives. At the least, we will have engaged them in self-expression, given them a voice, and legitimated their experience. Giroux and McLaren (1986), who view classrooms as places where "people come together to speak, to engage in dialogue, to share their stories, and to struggle together within social relations that strengthen rather than weaken," suggest that this should be a central focus of teaching: "Student experience is the stuff of culture and identity formation . . . [and educators must] learn how to understand, affirm, and analyze such experience."

Book and Story Conversations

In this evaluation procedure, students choose one of the books or stories they are reading in class or have read independently and meet with the teacher or specialist to talk together about it. Included in the conversation are such optional questions and invitations to respond as the following:

1. What stood out for you?
2. Tell me the story in your own words.
3. What part would you share with a friend?
4. Which character did you identify with and why?
5. Read aloud a part of the story you liked especially well.

The conversation should be an interactive dialogue, not just a question and answer session. While notes can be taken on the conversation, it is helpful to tape record and transcribe the conversation. After reflection on this dialogue, an interpretive evaluation can be written.

It is important for the students to hear the ideas of teachers and specialists about their responses to the book or story, not only for the scaffolding or mediation this provides but also for the continuation of the dialogue in either oral or written composing. The dialogue may also be continued in written form as an academic dialogue journal. The possibilities for this form of interactive evaluation include responses to informational texts as well as literary texts. Student response to a chapter in a social studies text used in the class, for instance, might take such forms as a personal reaction, an interpretation or elaboration of an idea, an illustration or example from the student's own experience, or the integration of a concept with the student's philosophy.

This type of dialogue centered on written responses to texts provides a full and rich evaluation of the student's reading comprehension. The teacher or specialist can see how well the student is understanding the text, how the student is integrating the learning and constructing meaning, where the student needs more mediation to make meaning, and what the student's personal reactions, attitudes, and feelings are concerning the text.

Evaluation in this context is ongoing, purposeful, and oriented toward growth. It allows for continual and immediate mediation in the learning of the student. There is no failure or falling behind in this procedure, because there are many options for learning if the student has difficulty with a concept or has misunderstood an idea. The teacher or specialist may, for instance, arrange partnering with a peer who understands the concept, arrange a small group activity to extend the learning of the student, or suggest re-reading and more interactive responding in the form of either oral or written dialogue.

Such interactive journals or dialogues centered on classroom texts provide a rich record of the learning process of the student. The teacher or specialist could have a meaningful conference with the student or the parent (or both) based on these interactive journals, exploring ways to improve the critical reading of texts. Rather than waiting for an end-of-unit test to see who has failed to understand, the teacher or specialist can prevent the student from falling hopelessly behind. Collaboratively, they can plan ways to more closely observe and mediate in the learning of certain students who might be experiencing difficulty.

Students should be encouraged or perhaps required to keep book logs on the books they read independently as well. The teacher or specialist may want to respond to the student logs, and thus conduct a dialogue with the student, who may, in turn, want to keep the conversation going.

It would be impossible for any public school teacher or specialist to keep such interactive journals going with all students, just as it would be prohibitive time-wise to attempt to have written responses to all texts. But for a few students, on some text assignments, it might be manageable, and these students could be alternated throughout the year as necessary. Even one student's responses to a text covered in class could provide the teacher with useful information for classroom practice.

Dialogue Journals

Written dialogue journals between the student and the teacher on topics of the student's choosing are another forum for the student's active construction of meaning and the teacher's extension of that knowledge. We have used dialogue journals for the sharing of thoughts, impressions, questions, experiences, and feelings between the teacher and the student. This use of the dialogue journal provides another window on the world of the learner as the student and teacher alternate writing to each other in a notebook several times a week. It is similar to letter writing, but it is continual, ongoing dialogue in which the teacher can model language use, extend the thinking of the student, mediate and encourage if necessary, or perform any of the other language functions typical of human dialogue.

The students benefit from the modeling and mediation of the teacher as well as from the experience of self-expression and finding their own voice in dialogue with the teacher. Students choose what they will write about, though the teacher may suggest topics through questions and comments in the journal. The teacher does not correct the journal entries of the student (for grammar, spelling, punctuation, and so forth). The use of modeling, however, allows the learner to see correct forms of language use and begin to make successive approximations. The modeling extends beyond basic skills of correct language use to critical thinking displayed by the teacher in dialogue with the student.

The difference between the dialogue journal and the previously described book dialogue (academic journal) is that the latter is a more directed use of the dialogue journal: It may be a response to a classroom activity, text, or assigned topic. The teacher may ask the student to respond to certain ideas or concepts presented in class as a way of understanding more about the student's thinking processes. Not only can the teacher gain valuable information about the level at which the learner is understanding certain concepts, but the responses of the students tell the teacher what needs to be further taught in class. Teaching can then be done individually as the teacher or specialist responds in the journal, and it can also be done in small or large groups, depending on the needs of the other students in the class.

Oral Group Dialogue

Oral dialogue centered on student concerns is a logical prelude to written dialogue. Group dialogue sessions, such as those held in James and Sunny's learning disability class, allow for dialogue among students as well as between student and teacher. There are many benefits to some sort of group dialogue session in the classroom. Students in such groups learn to understand each other better, and perhaps themselves as well; and they begin to develop greater trust, better communication skills, and more cooperation.

As understanding, cooperation, trust, and communication develop in oral dialogue while students are in the process of expressing themselves, the class begins to develop into a caring community of learners. In such an optimal climate of trust, caring, and cooperation students' learning potential can flower in a way that is unknown in a less trusting, competitive classroom that does not validate student self-expression. In the more cooperative climate students can be more accepting of their own and each other's mistakes, viewing them as a necessary part of the natural process of learning.

Learning proceeds best when students are free to experiment and make mistakes without fear or embarrassment. Likewise, when diverse student responses are treated with respect, as interesting hypotheses, there is a greater chance for the risk taking that allows optimal learning to occur. The reverse is true where responses can only be right (the textbook answer) or wrong. Respect for the diversity of people, risk taking, and divergent thinking cannot grow in a climate devoid of understanding, trust, and cooperation.

Oral dialogue allows teachers and specialists to build a climate for optimal learning in every classroom. Since it is difficult for the teacher alone to conduct oral dialogue sessions, particularly with large class sizes, the specialist may take half of the class at times or may team with the teacher for some sessions. Certain difficult issues that the class may wish to discuss may at times require the inclusion of a guidance counselor, a psychologist, or an administrator.

Parents or other community members could also be resources for facilitating or mediating in dialogue sessions. If time is short, or if the teacher or specialist thinks it is otherwise advantageous, the sessions could be concluded occasionally by having the students write in their dialogue journals concerning an issue they discussed. The audience for such writing could be a counselor, an administrator, a parent, or another adult, as well as the teacher or specialist. The issues, purposes, uses, and audiences for oral and written dialogue will be unique to every classroom, every student, and every teacher or specialist.

Reading Protocols

Individual read aloud protocols (Lytle, 1982; Brown et al., 1982; Clay, 1985) are used to allow teachers to learn more about a student's meaning-making strategies and definition of reading. The procedure that we have followed is to first explain to students that we are interested in knowing more about what they are thinking when they read, and that this will help us to understand them better as readers. The instructions may be to read the first sentence or a meaningful part of the text (a story, fable, or other text at their approximate reading level), stop, and then talk about what it means, how they figured it out, and/or what it made them think about as they read it. They are asked to proceed in this way to the end of the text, after which they are to give a short summary of the text.

We have found it helpful to tape record these reading protocols, and them make either partial or complete transcriptions so that the student's responses can be analyzed. One way to analyze these responses is to adapt or devise a code for the usual types of strategies used by the student in decoding and comprehending the text, code the transcription, and in this way find both the usual response categories of the student as well as the sequence usually followed.

In a study of three boys labeled as learning disabled, Bartoli (1983) found the following reader responses or strategies to be used by the students as they read the text:

1. Signals understanding: makes sense of it
2. Substitutes another word in the text
   • meaningful substitution: makes sense in the text
   • nonmeaningful substitution: makes no sense

3. Elaborates on the text
   - uses prior knowledge or experience
   - suggests alternatives to the text
4. Reasoning
   - reasoning from prior evidence or text clues
   - predicts what will come next in the text
5. Self-monitoring of doubt
   - monitors doubt about a word or word part
   - monitors doubt about a sentence or central idea
6. Response/strategy following self-monitoring of doubt
   - uses context clues to make sense: reads ahead
   - phonetically analyzes word or word part
   - listens to "how it sounds"
   - uses context or framing hint
   - uses phonetic hint
   - revises miscue
   - re-reads the text
   - gives up or says "I don't know"

The significance of many of these categories is explained by Lytle (1982), and the substitution miscue category is substantiated by Beebe (1980). The use of context or phonetic "hints" was part of the researcher's attempt to mediate in the learning of the student, gain more information about the learner's definition of reading, and conduct a more interactive reading protocol.

The analysis of reading protocols gives us information about the style and strengths and weaknesses of the student in interaction with text, it gives us an understanding of the student as a comprehender in the actual context of reading, and it tells us a great deal about the student's definition of and background in reading. Sunny's protocols, for instance, revealed a definition of reading as decoding isolated letters and sounds. When asked what she was thinking about when she read, she said, "I don't think of anything when I'm tryin' to read . . . I clear my mind out and read." Her definition of reading was to "sound it out," which she usually did one letter at a time, starting from the beginning of the word. Meaning-making strategies were not a part of Sunny's repertoire for reading and learning.

Specialists and teachers, in the process of understanding more about the student as a reader through doing reading protocols, often gain access to much serendipitous information that is equally important for the student's learning. Often the responses provide information about interests, motivation for learning, experiences, and barriers to reading that give the teacher or specialist much direction for teaching that particular student.

A whole class reading protocol session allows teachers or specialists to model strategies that they employ while reading, as well as allowing the students to hear the variety of strategies used by their peers in comprehending texts. One such use is described in Chapter 6. The teacher reads a text line-by-line, pausing and asking for responses by the class, and noting the variety of ways to interpret and make sense of the text. The teacher continues to lead the class in learning about their own and others' strategies for comprehending, and in this way directs an exercise in metacognitive skill development.

THE PORTFOLIO—AN ECOLOGICAL RECORD

The question naturally arises, How is it possible to keep track of all of these diverse pieces of student experiences with learning? In addition to the multitude of papers connected with various daily assignments, thematic units, projects, oral and written composing, in-class and independent responses to texts and literature, occasional dialogues on books, and lists of student books and topics chosen, there is also the issue of following the learning process as it evolves over the course of a year. To give some order to this wealth of information, we propose the use of the portfolio, which may be either a simple file folder or a more elaborate expanding folder with divisions to store the various types of responses, dialogues, composing, and other experiences with in-process learning. The portfolio collection of all valued student experiences provides a view of the ecosystem of the learner: an ecological record of the learning process.

Imagine coming into a classroom where the teacher keeps a portfolio of the writing of each student, with each piece dated. The writing includes the student's responses to reading textbooks and independent reading, original stories and poems, work in progress, essays, reports, outlines, and tests. It is clear that the content of the portfolio is a record involving the interdependence of comprehension and composing at one level and the language process and content at another. It would be quite productive to study such portfolios, describe their qualities, and analyze the progress and needs of the student evident from this cumulative review.

Students also can be asked to reflect on and describe their own portfolios. Like artists, they might be allowed to choose their best pieces after a certain amount of time, make copies, and take them home to share with their families. As students make these choices, deciding what they put value on, they are continually reflecting on and taking ownership for their own learning. This is part of the recursive process of learning: reflecting back on previous work, making choices, refining, and ultimately moving ahead. And much of this learning can involve social interaction with peers, teachers, and specialists in the classroom community of learners.

Parents, of course, should also have access to the portfolios of their children. Particularly at parent conference time, the discussion of the student should focus on the portfolio rather than isolated test scores. Such discussions are by their very nature positive and growth oriented. Appendix D provides an example from the portfolio of a student, David, labeled as learning disabled, who participated in the fourth grade dinosaur unit taught at a public elementary school (see Chapter 5). David's work itself suggests some of the possibilities for discussion with his parents of his strengths, ability, and learning potential.

One way to manage or organize the wealth of material that a student produces over the course of a year is to have several portfolios rather than one. Of course, any structuring or division of the learning process is artificial and ultimately could lead us back into the very fragmentation that we are seeking to remedy with an ecological approach. But good wholistic teachers and specialists continually find ways to achieve a balance between chopping up the ecology into disconnected pieces, and an undifferentiated whole. One such method, illustrated by David's dinosaur unit folder (Appendix D), was used with success to organize the variety of learning experiences of each student during a thematic unit.

Another possible way to organize student material in an ecological teaching and evaluation approach is to use two portfolios—a writing portfolio and a reading portfolio. We will suggest some of the possibilities for this way of organizing, keeping in mind that teachers and specialists will continue to find their own unique ways of organizing the ecosystem.

The Reading Portfolio

The student work found in the reading portfolio might include responding to literature and text activities such as

A map of the key ideas from a social studies unit;
An outline of the main ideas and details from a textbook chapter;
A list of questions suggested by section headings and titles in a science textbook chapter;
A news story based on a book read in class;
A book review of a book studied in class;
A five-minute written reflection on a concept in science.

Academic journals or book/text dialogues might also be in the reading portfolio. These would contain student responses to certain assigned readings, and they would be responses that build from the student's own experience and knowledge. Such journal responses might be evaluated on a scale like the following:

> *Satisfactory/okay*: adequately read and responded to the text
> *Good/better*: made some additional comments of critique, analysis, or elaboration; gave examples from personal experience
> *Very good*: asked challenging questions of the literature; insightfully analyzed and explored ideas; elaborated on theme and concepts; drew many examples from own experience.

As previously mentioned, such responses provide a contextually valid evaluation of reading comprehension. We can learn how well students are understanding the ideas, themes, concepts, intention, purpose, and tone of the text; we can see how well they are using their own experience to understand the text; we can see their strengths and needs in criticizing and analyzing texts; and we can see at what point they have misunderstood a concept or idea. And at the same time that we are understanding more about the depth and quality of the students' thinking, we are validating their own experience, mediating where needed, and continually upgrading our curriculum for learning.

The reading portfolio would also contain a list of all books chosen by the student for SSR. There might also be an SSR log or book conversations in a journal. The difference between the responses in this journal and the academic journal previously described is that all SSR books are chosen by the student. In addition, the student has free choice in types of response (drawing, oral or written dialogue, book advertising) as well as the option not to respond in writing.

Other possible data included in the reading portfolio might be checklists or other records from book conferences with the teacher or specialist. The teacher, specialist, and student might collaboratively devise a progress chart that could illustrate and graph the student's increasing skillfulness in certain aspects of the reading process, such as use of particular reading strategies (personal experience, predicting, questioning) or aspects of critical thinking (intention, tone, purpose).

The reading portfolio of James, our case study student, might include some of his own stories with tape recordings, his science journal with descriptions of experiments and concepts, cloze and maze tests from social studies chapters, lists of questions that the author of his science textbook might have had in mind about oxygen, a list of books that James chose for SSR, and a draft of an advertisement for selling his book on baseball.

The Writing Portfolio

The writing portfolio would contain all free choice writing of the student. A dialogue journal centered on the student's expression of personal feelings, concerns, and experiences could be kept in the writing portfolio. In addition to its benefit for the composing process, such free choice written dialogue responding allows time and space for low risk self-expression and quests for meaning. By allowing the student to make meaning in this accepting, supportive way, we help to create a caring community in the classroom.

Personal narratives such as those by James would also be kept in the writing portfolio. Poems, short stories, essays, or other writing, in which students find their own ideas and topics and draw from their own experience, could all be kept in the writing portfolio. Students might also keep a list of topics they know about, experiences they would like to share, issues they wish to dialogue about, or concerns they would like to express in the portfolio (see Seaver & Botel, 1987).

Prewriting collections of information as well as all of the drafts of various compositions, including peer edited and teacher edited drafts, should be kept in the portfolio. These provide a continuous record of the student's writing process, and they allow the student to go back to earlier drafts, refine, enlarge, or eventually choose to disgard some pieces after a period of time.

The student's own handbook of writing conventions, a personal collection of examples and inductive rules for grammatical and mechanical aspects of writing coming from individual needs and uses of writing, might also be kept in the writing portfolio. This contextual learning of the subsystems or elements of language is supported in current research on the writing process. We are reminded of Vygotsky's (1934) example of the fallacy of studying elements apart from their ecology and the misleading and incomplete information that can result. Of a person analyzing the separate elements of water to understand why it extinguished fire, Vygotsky said, "He would be surprised to find out that hydrogen burns and oxygen sustains fire."

As students reflect back on their own writing process as represented in the writing portfolio, and as they make choices about which pieces are to be more valued, which are to be refined and expanded, and which are to be the focus of teacher evaluation, they are becoming reflective thinkers capable of taking ownership and responsibility for their own learning.

A NEW VIEW OF TESTING AND THE IEP

School leaders, legislators, and policy makers are caught in a double bind in their attempts to find a way to support the exceptional student. They want an equitable way to subsidize schools to help provide additional support, and according to Public Law (PL) 94–142 this means finding objective criteria for identifying the students who need help. But they also want students to be in the least restrictive environment, which most agree ought to be the mainstream classroom, and they want remedial instruction to supplement rather than supplant classroom instruction. So the traditional solution of testing, labeling, and separating students from the mainstream classroom has become more of a problem.

The school system is right to want the money to help students, the policy makers and legislators are right in wanting to ensure that the subsidizing is equitable, and teachers and specialists are right in their attempts to help the individual student who needs more attention. But the school system's response to the state and federal mandates—testing, identifying, labeling, and separating students—has led to the problems of fragmentation which we have discussed throughout this book. One of the purposes of the book is to help school systems that are struggling with this dilemma by providing a way for students to learn within the mainstream.

Although testing seems to be an efficient way to objectively identify disabled students, the research evidence suggests that the tests are neither valid for diagnosis nor helpful in instructing identified students. Too often tests sort on the basis of social factors like socioeconomic level and minority status, and they suggest a prescription that has been shown to have little or no validity. But school systems assume and test makers suggest that the tests are diagnostic, so publishers produce instructional material that looks like the tests, and we find ourselves with another problematic solution.

What Is the Place of Tests?

The law requires that students be identified in very specific ways by a psychologist and/or a team of professionals. Tests probably could help us screen the most likely candidates for additional help, with the understanding that some would be missed and some would be identified who do not belong. The tests could thus help policy makers and administrators determine the proportion of students who need help.

The need to get financial support for students experiencing difficulty is an economic and political reality, and tests may be viewed as the policy maker's way of gathering money and support for students (although sometimes there are other noneducational objectives as well). If that is viewed as the function of tests and it is recognized that they have little, if any, instructional validity and that they must be accompanied by observation as previously described in this chapter, we will avoid further problematic solutions.

An Ecological Education Program

Once a student who needs help has been identified, teachers and specialists could turn their attention back to how students learn: as interactive language users in the mainstream classroom community of learners. The specialist, in collaboration with the teacher, would thus observe in the classroom context as the student is engaged in the critical experiences (see the Evaluation Outline in Figure 11.1). If further information is warranted, the specialist may use any of the interactive observation methods suggested in this chapter. In addition, the specialist and teacher could study together the student's portfolio to understand more about the learning process of that student. A staff review of the child might be a logical next step and/or an interview with the family.

Throughout this book we have suggested ways to create a classroom climate and management system that make it possible for students who vary across the full range of abilities to become successful learners and to advance at their own rates. The job of the specialist in collaboration with the teacher is to make the mainstream classroom the least restrictive environment for all students. Students who need additional help would not be at a disadvantage in this type of classroom.

Observational methods are the prime ways to both know the student and know how to help the teacher make accommodations that will help the student become continually successful in the classroom. Such observation, reflection, and documentation enhance the professionalism of the teacher and specialist as well as the quality of the relationship between these professionals as they problem-solve together concerning individual student needs.

The law requires that all special need students be evaluated, but the evaluation should not use tests that are invalid and unreliable. The evaluation should be the fullest, most richly descriptive, ecologically valid evaluation possible. It should tell us what students are doing while they are experiencing the ways of using language to learn in the classroom. This observational evaluation would then be helpful in providing for the needs of the student, which is also what the law requires.

This more ecological education program, based on collaborative observation in context, provides congruence between evaluation and teaching, and between remedial efforts and the mainstream curriculum. Time and expense are the usual arguments against ecological evaluation, but this type of assessment may be less expensive and time-consuming than the traditional testing, labeling, and placement procedures currently being used. In addition, it has a built-in congruent instructional plan that carries with it the possibility for enhancing both student and professional growth.

As professionals study and document closely particular students in the classroom, they become better observers of all students. It would be impossible (and probably unnecessary) to systematically study and fully document the learning processes of all students. Clearly, the critical ones to document are those who have special needs. But since these students are learning in concert with the classroom community, the documentation relates to all students in the classroom and carries with it the possibility of enhancing their learning as well.

Rather than the special need student taking time away from the teacher and other students, that student provides a unique barometer of the classroom climate. In addition, because the resources of the specialist are brought in, a better learning climate for the whole class results. Instead of separation from the classroom community or separate work sheets and skill work, the focus of remediation is the orchestration of the critical experiences for learning within the classroom. This enables students to read and write more, to do it better, and consequently to do it faster. It allows them to learn at their own levels, write on their own topics more expansively, collaborate and get ideas from others, and share ideas. And it allows them to both use and study language, explore concepts, develop higher level critical thinking, and learn to learn—all within their own classroom community of learners.

These ways of living and working are similar in the families of successful learners. The family does not restrict the learning of their more gifted children because one child appears to be learning more slowly. They do not limit the experiences of that child to separate skill activities. Instead, their collaborative way of living involves opportunities for the development of the capacities and interests of all family members. And so it is with the critical experiences approach to learning in the classroom.

PL 94-142 and the IEP

Public Law 94-142, the Education for All Handicapped Children Act (1975), requires that all special education students be evaluated to determine their unique needs and the services required to meet these needs. School districts must prepare written statements that include:

Annual goals, including long-term and short-term objectives;

Special education services and mainstream experiences to be provided;

Appropriate evaluation procedures and criteria for attaining objectives;

Students' present performance levels.

With the use of the integrative Evaluation Outline (Fig. 11.1), these interrelated requirements can be connected to a more ecological evaluation of student learning, rather than being thought of as discrete and separable statements. The annual goals and special education services can be stated in terms of the five critical experiences (Responding to Text, Independent Reading and Writing, Oral and Written Composing, Investigating Language, and Learning to Learn) provided by collaborating teachers and specialists in the mainstream classroom.

As we have emphasized throughout this book, the collaboration of specialists with teachers is necessary to provide these experiences in a way that encourages students to develop more fully as successful learners. The specialist's role is to facilitate, confer with teachers, bring resources to the classroom to enhance the critical experiences, and promote student engagement in the learning process.

To evaluate the quality of these critical experiences along with the individual student's performance or attainment of the objectives, we suggest the use of the integrated forms of evaluation that we have described in this chapter: observation of the student in the context of the critical experiences, one-on-one interactions with the individual student, portfolio description, and the more wholistic performance level assessment that we see as supplemental to the first three major forms of evaluation.

Figure 11.2 illustrates the interrelationships between the critical experiences and the forms of evaluation. In looking at this outline, one can see how the IEP requirements can be connected with a more ecological framework for learning. The goals, objectives, and critical mainstream experiences to be provided by collaborating teachers and specialists are listed down the left hand side. Across the top are the forms for evaluating the attainment of those goals and objectives.

Long-term and short-term goals

The Evaluation Outline displays the long-term goals and objectives indicating the critical mainstream classroom experiences that we want the student to have. This outline is an adaptable structure that allows the practitioner to meet the requirements of PL 94–142. To write statements

FIGURE 11.2. Evaluation Outline: Interrelationships between the Critical Experiences and Forms of Evaluation

	Observation	One-on-one Interactions	Portfolio Description	Performance Level
Responding to Text				
Classroom process				
Before reading:	✓			
During reading:	✓			
After reading:	✓			✓
Reading process				
Think-aloud protocol:		✓		
Academic journal:		✓	✓	
Performance level				✓
Independent Reading and Writing				
Books chosen	✓		✓	
Book conversations		✓		
Types of writing			✓	
Oral Composing				
Reports/speeches	✓		✓	
Classroom dialogue	✓			
Narratives	✓	✓	✓	
Written Composing				
Portfolio description	✓		✓	
Prewriting	✓		✓	
Conferencing	✓	✓	✓	
Drafting	✓		✓	
Editing	✓		✓	
Dialogue journals		✓		
Performance level				✓
Investigating Language				
Discovery/use of patterns	✓		✓	
Performance level				✓
Learning to Learn				
Awareness and use of strategies	✓	✓		
Approach to difficult text	✓	✓		
Collaboration				
With partners	✓			
In small groups	✓			

that weave the requirements into a unified whole, the outline may be flexibly adapted to the classroom curriculum for learning created through the collaborative efforts of the specialist and teacher.

Thus, the Evaluation Outline can be a flexible outline for writing an observational report that records the student's learning process. This allows the teacher or specialist to make a more valid statement based on the wealth of information and understanding that is possible from the contextual observations of collaborating professionals, and is rooted in evaluation centered on the actual learning process of the individual student.

Students labeled as reading or learning disabled have the same needs as mainstream students for the experiences that are critical for learning. Unfortunately, many students labeled as disabled are further disadvantaged by the poverty of a remedial curriculum that isolates skills from significant content, removes language processes from context, and limits the possibilities for students to integrate and control their own language learning. Thus the ecological approach suggests connecting the language processes to the content of the mainstream classroom, which most agree can be the least restrictive environment.

For example, taking the first critical experience on the Evaluation Outline, Responding to (Transacting with) Text, a long-term objective for James might be stated as follows: James will learn strategies for responding to literature and informational texts with the whole class, in small groups, and on his own. He will learn to draw upon prior knowledge, predict, question the text, retell and summarize, elaborate, and respond from personal, descriptive, analytic, interpretive, and critical perspectives. In Learning to Learn he would not only do these things, but he would reflect on how effective these strategies were in helping him learn.

A short-term objective would connect using the language processes to specific content; for instance, certain stories in a basal reader, a thematic unit on Indians, or a social studies unit. This would go beyond the more narrow view of language processes as isolated from significant content, typical in a traditional disability program that focuses on the decontextualized and separate processes of listening, speaking, reading, and writing.

The ecological approach takes the view that the student is listening to *something* and reading *something*. And it is the *something*—the significant content—that must be connected to learning, or we are left with a group of worksheets or skill exercises on listening with little or no *something*. Thus, the ecological approach begins with meaningful content, to avoid trivializing the curriculum and further disadvantaging the student.

Unfortunately, many special education students like James continue to be disadvantaged by the curriculum. They come to class and are given the experience of listening, speaking, and writing in worksheets and reading kits that have little significant content and no connection to the mainstream curriculum. They are denied access to history, geography, literature, and mathematical content—much like James was denied access to the library—because they are so busy learning only the isolated language processes that were identified as the problem. Once again, the solution has become the problem.

In an ecological program the specialist works collaboratively with the teacher on specific content, connecting it continually to strategies for learning in the mainstream classroom. Learning is viewed as more than the sum total of isolated processes. Without the significant content, the student is left with abstract, decontextualized pieces of language that are difficult to learn. There is a missing link to world knowledge, and there is no connection to the integration of skills that is vital to the reading process.

Appropriate criteria and performance levels

The appropriate criterion for an ecological education program is the observation of the quality of involvement of students in the critical experiences for learning. These experiences must, of course, be fine-tuned by the collaborative efforts of the mainstream teacher and the specialist. Together they can ask:

Are students learning strategies for comprehending texts in every subject?

Are they learning to integrate these strategies into an efficient, self-monitored system for comprehending?

Are they learning to work through the writing processes?

Are they self-selecting books, reading them at their own pace, and responding to them in their own way?

Are they learning to decode, spell, capitalize, and punctuate sentences more effectively—do they use standard English more effectively in speaking and writing?

These and other long-term goals can be converted into objectives by specifying in detail the strategies and the texts to be read, heard, or written. For example, in Responding to Text, the specific texts and strategies can be indicated. In Investigating Language, the spelling or graphophonic patterns can be specified along with the contexts (chant, maze exercise, word making, sentence making, or other writing activity) in which they will be experienced.

Rather than focusing subjectively on the student, a view that has led to biased expectations for certain students, we focus on the larger ecology of the learning process. In Chapters 9 and 10 we have questioned the validity of supposedly objective tests, suggesting the subjectivity involved in the labeling process. The case studies of Sunny and James also give testimony to the subjective bias of traditional approaches to evaluation and diagnosis.

To avoid freezing or reifying the student's present performance level, teachers and specialists can begin observing students while they are engaged in the critical experiences, as suggested in our Evaluation Outline, and define them as in-process learners, rather than as deficient or disabled. In Responding to Text, for example, we are interested in how students are engaged before, during, and after reading. We are also interested in the level at which students can read comfortably, but we do not want to deny them access to more difficult texts.

Although James was found to be reading at a first grade level in the third grade, for instance, he could still experience the third grade text through scaffolding. Rather than denying him access to the third grade literature or social studies text, the teacher and specialist might find ways to use whatever language and thinking processes he had to experience and respond to the content. To do this they might use such scaffolding methods as reading the content to him; providing information to introduce or explain the content through films, pictures, field trips, or discussions in the community of learners; or organizing peer groups to explore and discuss the content.

In the past some have said, If you can't read it, you can't do it. But the new view suggests that reading the text is like reading the world. Reading the word, like reading the world, means experiencing the concepts of the text and context by hearing them, having them explained first, and working with other people. Pulling students out and away from that content and context is to give in to the wrong notion: If you can't read it, you can't do it.

At the same time, it is helpful to know the student's performance level as a rough indicator, as long as the number is enhanced with descriptive comments that show the quality of student involvement in the learning process. Thus, to supplement the broader ecological evaluation we have described, we propose in Appendixes A, B, and C several kinds of performance level assessments that yield a general estimate of student ability.

SUMMARY

Throughout this chapter we have proposed ways of determining a student's present performance levels using objective criteria and appropriate and valid evaluation procedures. Teachers and specialists begin by working collaboratively to observe, document, reflect on, and discuss their direct observations of the student while learning in context. They describe and analyze the student's writing portfolio to determine needs and progress. And if necessary, they further observe through such interactive methods as reading protocols and academic dialogue journals. As a supplement to this, they may obtain general impression performance level scores to meet state and federal requirements.

Not all students need intensive observation—perhaps only those about whom the teacher and specialist have a question or concern. For most students, the reading and writing portfolio, informal in-class observation, a record of small and large group participation, and the performance level assessment would provide a wholistic evaluation of the learning process. It is the interactive, mediational methods that allow educators a larger view of the ecology of the individual student while they are in the process of leading the student ahead toward the zone of proximal or potential development. In each of these methods we see the recursiveness of learning in an ecological approach in which methods for evaluation are at the same time methods for teaching. Such methods preserve the integrity of the whole learner, allow us a wider view of the ecosystem, and feed back into the curriculum for the improvement of the learning of all students in the classroom.

The emphasis in ecological evaluation is on the dynamic development of present student learning in the context of the mainstream classroom. The teacher and specialist observe and attempt to understand the dynamic process of learning those experiences that are critical for learning. Such an emphasis avoids the problem/solution paradox that results from fossilizing student behavior at yesterday's level. Performance levels from tests are viewed as a required part of evaluation, but evaluation is not based on invalid tests that neither help us understand the learning process of the student nor lead us to useful remediation of their learning problems.

Conclusion

We conclude this book by reflecting on the beginning of a lifetime of work for many of us in the educational community. There are many hopeful signs that an evolution is taking place in American education. Research in many fields is converging in an ecological direction, giving support for the paradigm change that needs to take place if we are to significantly reduce our disability, failure, and illiteracy rates. Nationally there are movements toward mainstreaming, higher level thinking, empowering teachers and students with voice and ownership, collaboration of professionals, integration of skills with content, and more valid evaluation methods. It is our hope that the ideas presented in this book will help those in the field who are moving in this more ecological direction: looking at the whole student, teaching with an integrated, whole language approach, using congruent wholistic evaluation methods, collaborating and networking as professionals, integrating all students into the mainstream classroom, and linking to the wider ecology of the student.

For those for whom this approach is not new, we hope to have added a more solid theoretical base, connecting with several converging research traditions, to support work toward a paradigm change. For those who are working in schools that encourage mainstreaming, we have presented an approach that will help in orchestrating both the integration of students into mainstream classes and the collaboration of specialists with teachers in the classroom.

For those for whom the approach is new, we hope to have presented an integrated approach that will help in meeting the needs of students with reading and learning problems. And for those who are working in separate programs, clinics, or classrooms, we have provided more ecologically valid teaching and evaluation methods, which can help students toward the vital integration of skills and knowledge that is critical for the learning process.

The possibility that children like Sunny and James will be successful learners will be greatly increased through the use of the ecological framework presented in this book. And the opportunities for all students to develop their potentials will be increased through greater collaboration of professionals in the school. We believe that at present the greatest possibility for change lies in the classroom wherein the student spends some 25 hours a week. If teachers are given ownership of their own curriculum, if they are given the collaborative help of specialists to deal with the more difficult learning problems, and if the school administration supports their efforts toward more integrated, whole language learning, certainly great strides can be made in reducing the number of reading and learning failures.

Ideally, however, an ecological approach would move beyond the classroom ecology and the school system to the wider family and community systems. Throughout the book, we have presented some ideas for making the family/school connection, and we will conclude with a further exploration of the ecological link between the school and the family system as well as the link to the wider community.

THE CONTINUING PARADOX

When Bateson's group of communication researchers developed the theory of the double bind, they saw it as a paradoxical communication that essentially bankrupts choice itself. They viewed the person as locked into a vital relationship necessary for survival (such as between parent and child), subject to conflicting messages that allow no choice, and prevented from either leaving the context or commenting on the contradictory messages.

Several paradoxical communications are inherent in the LD meta-message of the school system. Students who have difficulty with learning to read may hear the conflicting message, We want you to learn, but we know you have a disability and therefore you cannot learn. Or, You cannot learn, but we will try to teach you. In the traditional labeling/testing/placement system, students are locked into a school context where learning is supposed to occur, but they are told, We do not feel you are fit for mainstream learning. The curricular message may be, Do not attempt to make meaning on a level with your peers because you are not able: Stick with the basic skills you can perhaps handle (with our help).

The student labeled as learning or reading disabled may feel controlled by a prescriptive curriculum, stripped of personal significance, confused about the sense of diagnostic testing and labeling, and inadequate when faced with more-of-the-same decontextualized learning skills, knowing full well that the training wheels are always on. The school tells the student to be responsible, try to improve, and have faith in the scientific diagnosis and remediation. But just beneath the surface of the helpfulness and concern there may lurk hints of preconceived stereotypes; social or racial misconceptions and underestimations, assumptions, or bias; lowered expectations; or other meta-communication (message about the message) that sabotages the learning potential of the student.

It is on this relationship level that the student's sense of competence and self-confidence is shaped. Caught in a paradox of conflicting messages both at home and at school (you need help because you are disabled: You are disabled so you can't learn), students can neither comment on the confusion nor leave the context. To maintain the vitally needed relationship with either teacher or parent, students (and sometimes parents and teachers) must deny that there is a discrepancy between what they do see and what they should see. Instead they usually relate to the teacher, specialist, and parent in terms of the disability message, and eventually lower their expectations for themselves to match those of the adults.

Faced with the absurdity of the situation, yet prohibited from either recognizing the absurdity or leaving the field, students might react in one of several ways that Watzlawick, Beavin, and Jackson (1967) describe as typical of people who are caught in double binds. They may be obsessed with giving meaning to whatever is around them, but shift from the real issues to unrelated phenomena. Externally, this might look like attention problems (deficits) or Sunny's case of "getting off the subject."

A second possible reaction could be to abstain from any independent thinking. Students might focus on the literal or superficial aspect of communication to avoid an otherwise bewildering situation. An observer, struck by students' foolish inability to distinguish between the trivial and the important, might think them to be stupid or disabled. And, in effect, they are in the process of learning the art of being stupid.

A third reaction might be to withdraw from human involvement, blocking input channels of communication as a defense against the double bind situation. An observer might describe such students as withdrawn, unapproachable, or autistic. Watzlawick and colleagues suggest that escape from the double bind may also be achieved by "hyperactive behavior that is so intense and sustained that most incoming messages are thereby drowned out." (One teacher suggested that James might be hyperactive and in need of Ritalin.) Caught in a double bind wherein it is impossible to make sense or find meaning, the student may find cognitive impairment, or learning the art of being stupid, to be the only reasonable response to an absurd paradox.

THE UTOPIAN SYNDROME

An additional villain may enter the scene—the utopian syndrome (Watzlawick, Weakland, & Fisch, 1974)—which shapes many of the preconceptions and assumptions that both parents and teachers have about students and which is a powerful dynamic in the labeling process. In school the utopian ideal for "normal" or "able" is for all students to progress linearly, gradually, and uniformly through the same stage-appropriate curriculum and testing program. There is little tolerance for variation—for marching to the beat of a different drum. At home this syndrome depicts a happy, polite, beautiful, bright child who likes to read and likes to learn. This ideal, when perceived as the norm for all children, makes social cripples and academic failures out of those who are less cheerful or polite, more plain, of average intelligence (make fewer overt displays of competence), slower to develop, or more solitary, or who show less interest in school work. The utopian syndrome makes deviants or disabled learners out of normal students, much like Goddard's tests made morons out of people of normal intelligence.

Without this syndrome we would have less need to label those who deviate from the norm. Without it we could view human variation in all its natural diversity and complexity as normal and interesting. But with the utopian syndrome we are blessed with school labels for those who do not learn on schedule (LD or MR [mentally retarded]), those who are more energetic and more difficult to handle or control than the teacher or parent wishes (hyperactive), those who are more difficult to make conform to classroom/cultural rules of manners and decorum or who do not make the appropriate displays of competence and respect (SED or any of the above).

Watzlawick and colleagues (1967) remind us that "man never ceases to seek knowledge about the objects of his experience, to understand their meaning for his existence, and to react to them according to his understanding." It is the sum total of the meanings coming from interaction with the environment that provides human beings with a unified view of the world—a meaningful premise for existence. And it is the loss or the absence of meaning in life—the horror of existential Nothingness—that these authors see as the most common denominator in all forms of emotional distress. Again we are reminded that human beings cannot survive in a senseless, meaningless world, which is why Friedrich Nietzsche postulated that the person who has a *why* of living will endure almost any *how*.

Because of the utopian syndrome, which, it should be noted, is but a reflection of our cultural values, we are caught in a system characterized by first-order change: The more things change, the more they remain the same. The students are blamed for their learning problems at home and at school, while we continue to maintain these problems through utopian definitions, paradoxical communication, and problematic solutions. What is needed, of course, is a new kind of change that can transform the system. We need a second-order change capable of redefining the problem and lifting us out of the problem/solution paradox, where the solutions to what we think is the problem (but would not be a problem except for our utopian ideals) themselves become the problem.

THE POSSIBILITIES FOR CHANGE

We need to look at our problematic solutions for the source of change. In schools we have invented the problematic solutions of fragmented curricula, invalid testing, and segregated management of students. That these solutions are more of a problem is clear from current research in education and learning. A second-order change would entail a redefinition of language learning (our best definition of language competence and the learning process), a reframing of the curriculum to match this definition (wholistic and rooted in the critical experiences for learning), and classroom management techniques that would reflect a democratic approach to the education of all students.

Two of the major stumbling blocks in education have been our focus on elementary mental functions to the neglect of higher mental functions, and the separation of various subsystems from their meaningful ecosystem. In the language arts this has resulted in a focus on the "basics," translated as subskills or language parts, and skill learning stripped of meaningful content, context, and purpose. In the content areas this has meant a focus on the trivial pursuit of facts, names, and dates divided into separate subject areas to the neglect of critical, exploratory, and creative responses, or concepts integrated across the curriculum. In classroom management this has meant more teacher-owned rules for control of student behavior, more rigid structure and prescriptive individualized activities, and little emphasis on social interaction, student voice, and individual responsibility for learning. In testing it has meant more-of-the-same elementary basics, facts, and parts of knowledge.

A focus on higher mental functions would mean increased use of language to mediate and develop higher level thinking, with language viewed as a tool that shapes, develops, creates, and extends higher mental functions. It would mean more use of social interaction to develop higher mental functions, and the encouragement of voluntary attention and memory through more use of the intellect—more learning to learn. It would mean greater encouragement of self-regulation, with students determining their own behavior through voluntary control. And it would mean tests of critical thinking—application of concepts and theories, analysis, exploration, and expression of ideas—a focus on the integration of skills and knowledge in the pursuit of meaning.

Until recently we have been hindered by an inadequate theory of learning to read—a stage developmental, static, mechanistic theory oriented toward subskills and individual deficits. But there has been a growing convergence of thought and theory to support the priority of learning to make meaning over learning subskills.[1]

In the past we have been hindered by an inadequate theory of disability in reading—an individually oriented, neurological deficit-based, victim-blaming theory that neglected social process dynamics; political, historical, and economic factors; and the ecological interactions of school, family, and community systems. But there continues to be a convergence of theory and research concerned with school and family systems dynamics in the maintenance or perpetuation of learning problems. Ethnographic studies and other research on the culture of the school underscore the importance of school system dynamics.[2] Family literacy and family systems research and theory are increasingly linked to the ecology of learning.[3] And the larger cultural and socio-historical factors in the wider ecology of the learner are increasingly being recognized.[4]

Such a change of view—from traditional to ecological—would indeed be a radical shift or transformation, not unlike the way Vygotsky describes the learning process, or Bateson describes systems change, or Gould describes change in biological systems in the evolutionary process. The shift we envision is toward a more ecological view of student learning, focusing on the changes needed in the ecosystem rather than on the student as sole owner of learning difficulties. But transformations are not easy to accomplish, which is why most change is of the first-order variety.

Many of the forces of fragmentation within the school system, including labeling and subskill teaching and testing, have been counteracted by good teacher and specialist judgment. But the powerful forces of commercial curriculum materials companies and the testing industry (offering easy to teach and test solutions), parental pressures for excellence (at the cost of equity) and/or more of the basics, district level policies, and state

---

[1]See Britton, 1970; Halliday, 1974, 1978; Vygotsky, 1962, 1978; Clay, 1985; Johnson, 1984, 1985; Rosenblatt, 1980; Coles, 1978, 1983; and Cazden, 1981.

[2]See Mehan, 1980; McDermott, 1974; Sarason, 1971; Smith, 1979; and Allington, 1978, 1983.

[3]See Taylor, 1983; Freire, 1980, 1983; Kronick, 1976; and Aponte, 1976.

[4]See Ogbu, 1980; Hobbs, 1975, 1978; Gould, 1981; Mercer, 1973; Bronfenbrenner, 1979, 1986; and Bart, 1984.

and national mandates (offering problematic solutions) can overwhelm even the most valiant individuals.

Within the community/cultural system there are economic and political factors that shape the classification practices and curriculum goals of the school, thereby shaping the day-to-day lives of teachers and students. The scarcity of funds for education in conservative times, the use of problematic, quick-fix solutions by politicians to assuage and appease the public concern over the quality of education, and the subsequent responses of schools to these powerful dynamics are central to our fuller understanding of the learning problems of students and the problem and possibility of change.

We cannot re-design society to eliminate competitive factors that pit students against each other for grades, pit families against other families for acceleration of children, pit parents against teachers and specialists for excellence and demands for more individual attention for their children, and pit professionals against parents and the community in defense of themselves. But we can structure the curriculum in our schools to allow for the collaborative work of professionals, which is the best use of these invaluable school resources.

We can create a classroom climate that is conducive to higher level thinking, is more cooperative, holds high expectations for the potential of each student, and is oriented toward the development of that potential. Freire reminds us that to help students toward literacy it is necessary to have faith in them and to dialogue as equals. It is this new way of teaching—not so much "new" as perhaps renewed—that is the focus of this book. Using this approach while we await further research into chemical, biological/neurological, or psycholinguistic factors in disability, we can operate effectively and less problematically to teach all students to read and learn.

The possibilities for change and intervention that flow from an ecological approach are exciting and challenging for all of us as educators, specialists, and parents. This process-oriented approach allows us to view the larger systems dynamics that are part of the learning process. It allows us to discover and understand more deeply what is happening in the classroom, school, family, and life of the individual student. And it allows us to view the symptom—the rapid increase in disability labeling—as a communication about the need for meaningful language learning experiences and the need for confirmation or validation of the student's experience.

We are preparing students for a world and a time that we will never see, so we must give them our best vision. Together, as collaborating professionals with a broader vision, we can re-shape education. We can build it on a framework of experiences that are critical for learning. We can build within it a view of excellence that does not sacrifice equity, recognizing that true learning, like true communication, demands equality. And we can strive to maintain the expectations, opportunities, and classroom climate necessary to lead all students ahead toward their potential.

Afterword

At some point we as educators must decide how we can best help students to truly make meaning. If, as Britton (1970) has suggested, reading, learning, growing, and living are alternate words for the same process, we need to think about meaning making in life as parallel in importance to meaning making in reading texts.

As we live, we continually create our own texts. Our lives are our stories. As educators, we can encourage the development of these stories, we can stunt their growth and ignore them, or we can watch them be extinguished. The stories may die or disappear, but the meaning is always there.

If we can celebrate these stories in a variety of ways, one of which we demonstrated in Chapter 6, they may lead us to solutions for our more difficult learning problems. If we ignore them, the fantasy may turn to tragedy.

Every little girl dreams of becoming a fairy princess or queen. Will that dream flower into a fantasy of possibilities for happiness, growth, and learning? Or will it be like Pearl's story: neither heard nor responded to—a cry in the dark?

PEARL'S STORY

Once upon a time there was a princess.
She lived in a forest.
But, the princess was very small
and the people of the forest was big.
Her father said,
"When are you gonna grow?"
She was very small—
no bigger than your thumb.
But, one day the princess started to grow.
She grew and she grew and she grew.
She grew bigger and bigger every day.
So one day, she couldn't even fit the palace.

So, she went to the big city.
   And there
      and there she was the giant.
      They made her queen
          queen.
She married and had little ones,
      and they grew and grew and grew.
And then one day
   she shrunk.
      She went down
         down
          down
             down
               and down.
            Until she couldn't go down anymore.

Appendix A
Performance Level Assessment of Reading Comprehension

The most valid portrait of students' reading comprehension is determined by observing and documenting their transactions with actual texts—before, during, and after reading—in literature, science, and social studies. A single score on a test, therefore, cannot adequately represent the richness and complexity of reading comprehension. But we are often called on to provide a performance level score as, for example, on an individualized education program (IEP). This score, however, can only supplement the more valid observation/description.

To assess the performance level of a student, we propose using the *total* score of an informal reading inventory or other criterion-referenced test. The most valid score would provide an estimate of the level of the district basal reader series at which the student can read comfortably, that is, with a considerable degree of oral fluency and comprehension.

"Maze" assessment is one way to obtain such a performance level. A maze assessment can be prepared for a selection at or near the end of each book in a basal series. An example of such an assessment at a high second reader level, preceded by the procedure for constructing the assessment, is presented here.

Procedure

1. Choose a story or coherent part of a story in the last unit of each book level, beginning at the primer level (there are too few words in the preprimer). The story or segment should be approximately 100 to 200 words in length.
2. Delete selectively 10 to 15 percent of the words in the story. Choose words for deletion that were introduced at that book level (words introduced at a book level are usually listed in the appendix to the book).
3. Type the story, leaving a long blank line for each word deleted. The line should be long enough for three words.
4. On each blank line, type the word deleted and two foil words. Take the

foil words from the list of words introduced in this book level or the previous level.

5. Have several teachers read the selection to check for ambiguity or for items showing a bias of any kind.

6. Have the passage typed or printed in readable type.

7. Instruct students on how to read and respond to the passages, using sample paragraphs at a lower level of difficulty. Instruct them to: (1) read the paragraphs or story segment all the way through, sentence-by-sentence, (2) choose the correct word from those on each line, and (3) mark the correct word.

8. Consider a score of 80 to 100 percent on a test to be strong evidence that the student can read independently at that level. Consider the first level at which the student falls below 80 percent to be the student's performance level in reading comprehension.

Published tests that provide a global or performance level score include the College Entrance Examination Board's Degrees of Reading Power, the Metropolitan Reading Achievement Test (Instructional Reading Level), and the Botel Reading Milestone Tests.

Sample Story

BABY HERCULES AND THE GIANT SNAKES*

Little Hercules' mother tucked him and his twin brother into their crabs cribs drawer. "Good night, babies," she said as she put out the light. Then, just as she closed the bedroom door, two giant python snakes, came though throw through the open window.

In the moonlight sunlight bedtime the babies saw the snakes coming toward them. Soon the huddle huge huggable pythons would wrap themselves afraid arrow around the baby boys.

"Mommy! Mommy!" Hercules' brother cried. He tried tied told to get out of his crib. Their mother, hearing the screams, ran quietly quickly queerly towards their room.

"Mommy! Mommy!" Hercules' brother cried again. But the baby Hercules wasn't a bit afraid. He stood up and wasted waited worked quietly. And when the pythons came near, he grapped them by their necks near next and held them.

By the time their mother opened the door, she saw the snakes thrashing their giant baskets babies bodies back and forth. Baby Hercules was holding one in each hand.

---

*Written by Alvin Granowsky, John Dawkins, and Morton Botel.

Appendix B
Performance Level Assessment
of Decoding/Spelling

The performance of students in decoding and spelling is determined by observing them while they are engaged in actual reading or while they are studying the graphophonic system (see the sections on investigating language in Chapters 5 and 7). Assessing students to determine their performance levels is only a supplement to continual observation.

One useful way of determing students' control of the high frequency of graphophonic patterns is to have them read "maze" sentences comprising mainly words from each major pattern group. Ten sentences make a good test, and 90 to 100 percent correctness may be regarded as evidence of mastery. The major high frequency graphophonic pattern groups and two sample assessment sentences for each follow:[1]

1. Decode and comprehend sentences in which most words have the regularly spelled CVC (short vowel) pattern (C = consonant, V = vowel), such as *web, mad, log*.
   Ben fed his pet a <u>win nut net</u>.
   The pig jumped in the <u>mud pat tip</u>.
2. Decode and comprehend sentences in which most words have the regularly spelled CVCe (long vowel) pattern such as *cage, pipe, tide*.
   Jane rides her <u>rode nice bike</u>.
   Pete put the mice in a <u>cage tape cane</u>.
3. Decode and comprehend sentences in which words have the semi-regularly spelled CVVC patterns, including the vowel sounds other than long or short, such as *cow, toy, noon*; the *r*-controlled vowel, such as *tar, dirt, form*; and the alternate spellings of the long vowel sounds, such as *beef, tea, sail*.
   He sits neatly when he eats his <u>loose meals worn</u>.
   The toy rolled in the <u>shout cook dirt</u>.

---

[1]The description of the patterns and examples are taken from the Botel Reading Milestone Tests–Foundation Subtests: Decoding/Comprehension.

4. Decode and comprehend sentences in which most words have the regularly spelled CCVCC (short vowel) pattern and CCVCCe (long vowel) pattern (CC = consonant clusters, V = vowel), such as *twist, crash, shade, slope.*

   The lamp is on the <u>glad twist shelf</u>.

   Stella scratched the <u>crash desk grab</u>.

5. Decode and comprehend sentences in which most words have the semi-regularly spelled CCVVCC patterns, including the vowel sounds other than long or short, such as *mount, shoot*; the *r*-controlled vowel sound, such as *storm, march*; and the alternate spellings of the long vowel sounds, such as *brain, feast, flight.*

   Joyce looked pretty with her red <u>noise cheeks feast</u>.

   I am training a smart <u>knee glow poodle</u>.

These sentences can be dictated to students to determine their performance level in spelling. The performance level would be the percentage of accuracy of the graphophonic pattern words correctly spelled.

Appendix C
Performance Level Assessment of Writing

The most valid assessment of students' writing comes from observing them over time while they are engaged in the processes of writing in various genres for various purposes and with various audiences. But here again, as in the case of reading comprehension and decoding/spelling, we sometimes need a general estimate of a student's writing.

The following six-point scale offers one means for assessing students' overall performance level for writing by scoring samples of their writing. In this wholistic scale the qualities for each score are based entirely on content, organization, and style.

1. One or more unrelated statements
2. Two or more related statements but without a stated central idea or theme
3. Two or more related statements with a stated central idea or theme
4. Elaboration of the central idea(s) or theme(s) with details, examples, arguments
5. Considerable variety in word and sentence choices and/or considerable elaboration
6. Use of such writing devices as unusual examples, metaphor, humor, contrast, logic (if/then, since, therefore, either/or)

Following the wholistic assessment, the writing sample can be evaluated analytically for errors in the conventions of language: usage, capitalization, punctuation, spelling, and handwriting. These mechanical aspects of writing can be described anecdotally and can be compared with subsequent samples.

Appendix D
David's Portfolio

David R

Drawing on folder cover

ASSIGNMENTS

1. Questions — 🙂
2. Words + Sent. – 🙂
3. Paragraph – 😐
4. Test – 100 🙂
5. Fossil Story 😊
6. **Sentences** 😄
7. Combining Sent 😊
8. Dinosaur Story 😊
9. News Article 🙂
10. Class Booklet 😐

ToaTle

ASSIGNMENT 1:   Questions

David   1/12/87

1. Are   all   Things That
are dead Turnd into fossils?

2. How long Do faisls   keep?

3. How l. are faisls   made?

4. How fare   into ~~ground~~ can
faisls form?

5. ————————

ok

ASSIGNMENT 2: Words and Sentences

Front and back of index card

ASSIGNMENT 3: **Paragraph**

On Friday our class made fossil molds! We used some plasters parue and woter, a shell, vasaer and a emtey milk caton we mexed the plasterparone and water together. Put the shell in the gooo, wate and take the shell out!

Boy, you remembered all of your steps! Good! What did you have?

Done

ASSIGNMENT 4:   Test

100%

Name **David**
Date **Jan. 21**

FOSSILS

Fossils are evidence of past **life**. They help scientists called **Paleontologists** figure out what life was like during **Prehistoric** times. By studying **fossils**, we can get a picture of past life on **earth**.

Fossils can be formed in many ways. Many fossils are **imprints** in sedimentary **rocks**. Others may be the remains of animals which have been frozen in **ice**. Sometimes, ancient insects have been found preserved in hardened tree sap called **Amder**. Prehistoric fossils have even been found in black, sticky **Tar** pits.

amber   tar   ice
prehistoric   fossils   paleontologists
imprints   life   earth
               rocks

ASSIGNMENT 5: Fossil Story

A sTory of a fossil

Very interesting, David. Your ideas are great. You may be more careful with your punctuation.

Hellow! my name is Dr. Ray

I'm a PaleonTologisT and I

waNT To Tell you a sTory abouT

a fossil I found. IT was

millons and millons of years ago.

There was a liTTle clame

in The ocon. and loTs of

oTher fish To well ThaTs

a noThee sTory! This liTTle...

clame opened iT's shell and

closed iT agen. And one day

a liTTle beTe of sand

goT in and The clame

did'T   like   iT   so   he
formd   some   oTher   sTuf
around   iT   and   The   wod's
frisT   Pril   was   made! And
The   clam   had   eggs   Thay
hached   and   There   were
more   clams   so   ThaT
Clam   dide. And   The
Shell   was   replased   whiTh
The   miarall   gold !!!   And
when   I   dug   iT   up is
The   year   19 86   iT   was
a $1,000,000.00   fossil

ASSIGNMENT 6: Sentences

Good work

① The ₄ stupid¹ dinosaur² fought³
   Awkwardly!

② They₄ ~~humungous~~¹ eggs¹ flew³
   smoothly!

③ The ugle¹ brain² fought³ rapidly⁴.

④ They₃ Tietanick¹ *Titanic* ₄ Paleontologist²
   croaked Awkwardly!!

⑤ The₄ Plated¹ dinosaur² walked³
   rapidly.

⑥ They₄ bird-Hipped¹ skeleton² fought³
   ~~rapidly~~

⑦ The ₃ ~~stupid~~₄ paleontologist¹
   walked Awkwardly²

⑧ The₄ ugly¹ reptile² fought³
   rapidly.

⑨ The₄ ugly¹ brain² cared³
   smoothly carried

⑩ The ₄ Plated¹ omnivore² stalked³
   furiously.

ASSIGNMENT 7: Combining Sentences

David

good

1. The Brontosaurus plodded along. ~~The Brontosaurus was immense.~~

   Th,e immense BronTosaurus Plddded, along.

2. The Allosaurus attacked. The Allosaurus ~~was~~ fierce.

   The fierce Allosaurus aTTacked.

3. The Brachiosaurus submerged itself. The Brachiosaurus was tricky.

   The Tricy Brachiosaurus submerged iTself.

4. The Ornitholestes hid in a thicket. The Ornitholestes was frightened.

   The frighTened orniTholesTes hid, ih a ThickeT

5. The Stegosaurus flailed its tail. The Stegosaurus was ugly.

   The ugly sTegosaunus flailed iTs Tail.

ASSIGNMENT 8: Dinosaur Story

David

The   Maiasaura   is   my
favorite   Dinasores   it   Toke
kare   of   iTs   youg. Un   like
The   oTher   Dinasores! A   fossile
was   found   in   inglend   of   a
Maiasora..   Maiasoras   mense
(goob   moTher   Lizard)   iT's   my
favoreT   Dinasare   beacus
iT   Toke   kare   of
iTs   youg.

Drawing to accompany story

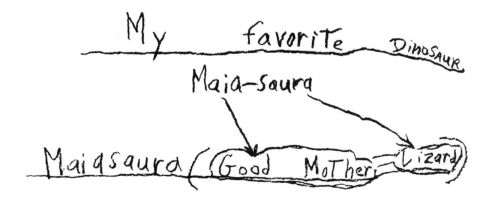

Drawing on back pocket of folder

ASSIGNMENT 9:   News Article

Dinosaurs Disappear!

As we all know Dinosaurs disappeared along time ago. there is a lote of difrent ideaase how they disappeard for insine some people think that meders hit the earth no won nely knows.

Comics

ASSIGNMENT 10:   Class Booklet

The Anchisaurus

I'm an Anchisaurus which means "near lizard". My neck and tail are as long as my body. I have big heavy back legs and short powerfule frot legs too. I have narrow feet with four toes and claws. I walked on all four feet. When I ran I used my back legs. I also was a blunt tooth plat eater. I'm 8 feet long and I lived 225,000,000 years ago. Well, nice Taking to you. Good by.

By, David R

ASSIGNMENT 10:   (Continued)

2: Draft

Teacher edited

I'm a Anchisaurus, which means "near lizard". My neck and Tail are as long as my body. I have big heavy back legs and short powerful front legs too. I have narrow feet, with four toese and claws. I walked on all four feet. When I ran I used my back legs. I also was a blunt Toothed plant eater. I'm 8 feetlong and I lied 225,000,000 x q85 ago. Well, nice Talking to you. Good by.

Drawing to accompany story

Appendix E
Recommended Readings

PART I: AN ECOLOGICAL WAY OF LOOKING

The Ecosystems View

S. Sarason (1971). *The culture of the school and the problem of change.*
G. Bateson (1972). *Steps to an ecology of mind.*
P. Watzlawick, J. Weakland, & R. Fisch (1974). *Change: Principles of problem formation and problem resolution.*
L. Hoffman (1981). *Foundations of family therapy.*
U. Bronfenbrenner (1979). *The ecology of human development.*
N. Hobbs (1978). Families, schools, and communities.
R. Griffore & R. Boger, Eds. (1986). *Child rearing in the home and school.*

A Broader View of Special Education

J. Ysseldyke & B. Algozzine (1982). *Critical issues in special and remedial education.*
S. Sarason & J. Doris (1979). *Educational handicap, public policy and social history.*
L. Barton & S. Tomlinson, Eds. (1984). *Special education and social interests.*

The Broader Social Context of Learning to Read

A. Brown (1982). Learning to learn from reading.
P. Freire (1983). The importance of the act of reading.
P. Johnson, A. McGill-Frazen, & R. Allington (1985). The practical problems of reading failure: Pedagogy and research.
E. Mishler (1979). Meaning in context: Is there any other kind?

PART II: AN ECOLOGICAL WAY OF TEACHING

Language Competence and the Learning Process

L. Vygotsky (1962 and 1978). *Thought and language* and *Mind in society.*
J. Mellon (1981). Language competence.

NOTE: See References for complete citations.

D. Graves (1983). *Writing: Teachers and children at work.*
L. Rosenblatt (1980). What facts does this poem teach you?
M. Clay (1979). *Reading: The patterning of complex behavior.*

A Broader View of the Classroom Learning/Nonlearning Process

R. Rist & J. Harrell (1982). Labeling the learning disabled child: The social ecology of educational practice.
R. McDermott (1974). Achieving school failure: An anthropological approach to illiteracy and social stratification.
R. Allington (1983). The reading instruction provided readers of differing reading abilities.

The Critical Experiences Framework

M. Botel (1981). *A Pennsylvania comprehensive reading/communication arts plan* (PCRP I).
S. Lytle & M. Botel (1988). *PCRP II.*
J. Seaver & M. Botel (1987). *Literacy network handbook.*

PART III: AN ECOLOGICAL WAY OF EVALUATING

Disability Diagnosis and Assessment

G. Coles (1978). The learning disabilities test battery: Empirical and social issues.
G. Hynd & C. Hynd (1984). Dyslexia: Neuroanatomical/neurolinguistic perspectives.
M. Lipson & K. Wixson (1986). Reading disability research: An interactionist perspective.
F. Vellutino (1987). Dyslexia.

The Social Process of Reading/Learning Disability Labeling

D. Bart (1984). The differential diagnosis of special education: Managing social pathology as individual disability.
J. Cummins (1986). Empowering minority students: A framework for intervention.
N. Hobbs (1975). *The futures of children: Categories, labels, and their consequences.*
J. Bartoli (1986). *Exploring the process of reading/learning disability labeling: An ecological systems approach.*

Evaluating the Learning Process

M. Clay (1985). *The early detection of reading difficulties.*

R. McCaig (1977). What research and evaluation tells us about teaching written expression in the elementary school.

S. Lytle (1982). *Exploring comprehension style: A study of twelfth-graders' transactions with text.*

P. Carini (1982). *School lives of seven children: A five year study.*

P. Brown (1987). *Toward a dynamic assessment model for understanding literacy learning difficulties of adolescents.*

P. Johnson (1984). Assessment in reading: The emperor has no clothes.

References

Allington, R. (1978). Are good and poor readers taught differently? Is that why poor readers are poor readers? Paper presented at the annual meeting of the American Education Research Association, Toronto.

———. (1983). The reading instruction provided readers of differing reading abilities. *Elementary School Journal, 83,* 558–569.

Allington, R. & Shake, M. (1986). Remedial reading: Achieving curricular congruence in classroom and clinic. *The Reading Teacher, 39,* 648–654.

Aponte, H. (1976). The family-school interview: An eco-structural approach. *Family Process, 15,* 303–311.

Apple, M. (1980). Curriculum form and the logic of technical control: Building the possessive individual. In L. Barton, R. Meigan, & S. Walker (Eds.), *Schooling, ideology and the curriculum.* Brighton, England: The Falmer Press.

Archer, M. (1984). Foreword. In L. Barton & S. Tomlinson (Eds.), *Special education and social interests.* New York: Nichols Publishing Co.

Balow, B. (1971). Perceptual-motor activities in the treatment of severe reading disability. *Reading Teachers, 24,* 513–525.

Bart, D. (1984). The differential diagnosis of special education: Managing social pathology as individual disability. In L. Barton & S. Tomlinson (Eds.), *Special education and social interests.* New York: Nichols Publishing Co.

Bartoli, J. (1983). Learning from the learning disabled: An exploration into the dynamics of LD labeled students' transactions with texts. Unpublished manuscript. Philadelphia, University of Pennsylvania.

———. (1985a). Metaphor, mind, and meaning: The narrative mind in action. *Language Arts, 62,* 332–342.

———. (1985b). The paradox in reading: Has the solution become the problem? *Journal of Reading, 28,* 580–584.

———. (1986a). Is it really English for everyone? *Language Arts, 63,* 12–22.

———. (1986b). *Exploring the process of reading/learning disability labeling: An ecological systems approach.* Ann Arbor, MI: University Microfilms International.

Barton, L. & Tomlinson, S. (Eds.) (1984). *Special education and social interests.* New York: Nichols Publishing Co.

Bateson, G. (1972). *Steps to an ecology of mind.* New York: Ballantine Books.

Becker, H. (1963). *Outsiders.* New York: The Free Press.

Beebe, M. (1980). The effect of different types of substitution miscues on reading. *Reading Research Quarterly, 15,* 324-335.

Beers, C. & Beers, J. (1981). Three assumptions about learning to spell. *Language Arts, 58,* 573-580.

Botel, M. (1981a). *A Pennsylvania comprehensive reading/communication arts plan.* Harrisburg, PA: Pennsylvania Department of Education.

———. (1981b). Specifying the essentials in an elementary school curriculum. In L. Mercier (Ed.), *The essentials approach: Rethinking the curriculum for the 80's.* Washington, DC: U. S. Department of Education, Basic Skills Improvement Program, 43-70.

———. (1987). *Botel reading milestone tests.* Levittown, PA: Morton Botel Associates.

Botel, M. & Preston, R. (1987). *Ways to read, write, study: Science.* Levittown, PA: Morton Botel Associates.

Botel, M. & Seaver, J. (1985). Literacy network. Graduate School of Education, University of Pennsylvania.

———. (1986). *Language arts phonics.* New York: Scholastic, Inc.

Britton, J. (1970). *Language and learning.* New York: Penguin.

Bronfenbrenner, U. (1979). *The ecology of human development.* Cambridge: Harvard University Press.

———. (1986). Alienation and the four worlds of childhood. *Phi Delta Kappan, 67,* 430-436.

Brown, A. (1982). Learning to learn from reading. In J. Langer & M. Smith-Burke (Eds.), *Reader meets author/bridging the gap.* Newark, NJ: International Reading Association.

Brown, A.; Campione, J.; Coles, M.; Griffin, P.; Mehan, B.; & Riel, M. (1982). A model system for the study of learning difficulties. *The Quarterly Newsletter of the Laboratory of Comparative Human Cognition, 4,* 39-66.

Brown, P. (1987). *Toward a dynamic assessment model for understanding literacy learning difficulties of adolescents.* Ann Arbor, MI: University Microfilms International.

Bruner, J. (1973). *On knowing: Essays for the left hand.* New York: Atheneum.

Buckley, M. (1986). When teachers decide to integrate the language arts. *Language Arts, 63,* 370-376.

Bussis, A. & Chittenden, E. (1987). Research currents: What the reading tests neglect. *Language Arts, 64,* 302-308.

Byers, P. & Byers, H. (1972). Nonverbal communication and the education of children. In C. Cazden, V. John, & D. Hymes (Eds.), *Functions of language in the classroom.* New York: Teachers College Press, 3-31.

Carini, P. (1982). *School lives of seven children: A five year study.* Grand Forks, ND: North Dakota Study Group on Evaluation, University of North Dakota.

Carson, R. (1956). *The sense of wonder.* New York: Harper & Row.

Cazden, C. (1981). Social context of learning to read. In J. Guthrie (Ed.), *Comprehension and teaching: Research reviews.* Newark, NJ: International Reading Association.

Chomsky, C. (1979). Approaching reading through invented spelling. In L. Resnick & P. Weaver (Eds.), *Theory and practice of early reading*. Hillsdale, NJ: Lawrence Erlbaum.

Clay, M. (1979). *Reading: The patterning of complex behavior*. Portsmouth, NH: Heinemann Educational Books.

———. (1985). *The early detection of reading difficulties* (3rd ed.). Exeter, NH: Heinemann Educational Books.

Coles, G. (1978). The learning disabilities test battery: Empirical and social issues. *Harvard Educational Review, 48*, 314–340.

———. (1983). The use of Soviet psychological theory in understanding learning dysfunctions. *American Journal of Orthopsychiatry, 53*, 619–628.

College Entrance Examination Board. (1980). *Degrees of reading power*. New York: College Entrance Examination Board.

Cooper, C. (1981). Competency testing: Issues and overview. In C. Cooper (Ed.), *The nature and measurement of competency in English*. Urbana, IL: National Council of Teachers of English.

Cummins, J. (1986). Empowering minority students: A framework for intervention. *Harvard Educational Review, 56*, 18–36.

Drahozal, E. & Hanna, G. (1978). Reading comprehension subscores: Pretty bottles for ordinary wine. *The Reading Teacher, 32*, 416–420.

Duffy, F. (1987). Personal communication to Morton Botel.

Durkin, D. (1979). What classroom observations reveal about reading comprehension instruction. *Reading Research Quarterly, 14*, 481–533.

Dweck, C. (1976). Children's interpretation of evaluative feedback: The effects of social cues on learned helplessness. *Merrill-Palmer Quarterly, 22*, 105–109.

Eisenberg, L. (1979). Reading disorders: Strategies for recognition and management. *Bulletin of the Orton Society, 29*, 39–55.

Elsasser, N. & John-Steiner, V. (1977). An interactionist approach to advancing literacy. *Harvard Educational Review, 47*, 355–369.

Fader, D. (1976). *The new hooked on books*. New York: Berkley Books.

Frankl, V. (1971). *Man's search for meaning: An introduction to logotherapy*. New York: Washington Square Press.

Freire, P. (1980). The adult literacy process as cultural action for freedom. In M. Wolf, M. McQuillan, & E. Radwin (Eds.), *Thought and language/language and reading. Harvard Educational Review*, Reprint Series #14.

———. (1983). The importance of the act of reading. *Journal of Education, 165*, 5–11.

Gallagher, J. & Reid, K. (1981). *The learning theory of Piaget and Inhelder*. Monterrey, CA: Brooks Cole Publishers.

Gates, A. (1950). American Association of School Administrators Convention. Atlantic City, NJ.

Gibson, H. & Levin, E. (1975). *The psychology of reading*. Cambridge, MA: MIT Press.

Giroux, H. & McLaren, P. (1986). Teacher education and the politics of engagement: The case for democratic schooling. *Harvard Educational Review*, 56, 213-238.

Goffman, E. (1963). *Stigma: Notes on the management of spoiled identity.* Englewood Cliffs, NJ: Prentice-Hall.

Goodlad, J. (1984). *A place called school: Prospects for the future.* New York: McGraw-Hill.

Gould, S. (1981). *The mismeasure of man.* New York: W. W. Norton & Co.

Granger, L. & Granger, B. (1986). *The magic feather.* New York: E. P. Dutton.

Graves, D. (1983). *Writing: Teachers and children at work.* Exeter, NH: Heinemann Educational Books.

Graybeal, S. & Stodolsky, S. (1985). Peer work groups in elementary schools. *American Journal of Education*, 93, 409-428.

Griffore, R. & Boger, R. (Eds.) (1986). *Child rearing in the home and school.* New York: Plenum Press.

Gumperz, J. (1972). Verbal strategies in multilingual communication. In *Georgetown University round table on languages and linguistics 1970.* Washington, DC: Georgetown University Press.

Haley, J. (1981). Towards a theory of pathological systems. In J. Haley, *Reflections on therapy and other essays.* Washington, DC: Family Therapy Institute.

Halliday, M. (1974). *Explorations in the development of language.* London: Edward Arnold.

———. (1978). *Language as social semiotic: The social interpretation of language and meaning.* Baltimore: University Park Press.

Heath, S. & McLaughlin, M. (1987). A child resource policy: Moving beyond dependence on school and family. *Phi Delta Kappan*, 68, 576-580.

Henry, J. (1965). *Pathways to madness.* New York: Random House.

Hobbs, N. (1975). *The futures of children: Categories, labels, and their consequences.* San Francisco: Jossey-Bass.

———. (1978). Families, schools, and communities: An ecosystem for children. *Teachers College Record*, 79, 756-766.

Hoffman, L. (1981). *Foundations of family therapy.* New York: Basic Books.

Hynd, G. & Hynd, C. (1984). Dyslexia: Neuroanatomical/neurolinguistic perspectives. *Reading Research Quarterly*, 19, 482-498.

International Reading Association. (January 1978). Resolutions of the Board of Directors.

Johnson, D. (1981). Student-student interaction: The neglected variable in education. *Educational Researcher* (January), 5-10.

Johnson, P. (1984). Assessment in reading: The emperor has no clothes. In P. D. Pearson (Ed.), *Handbook of reading research.* New York: Longman.

———. (1985). Understanding reading ability: A case study approach. *Harvard Educational Review*, 55, 153-177.

Johnson, P.; McGill-Frazen, A.; & Allington, R. (1985). The practical problems of reading failure: Pedagogy and research. Paper presented at the annual meeting of the American Educational Research Association, Chicago.

Kamin, L. (1974). *The science and politics of I.Q.* Potomac, MD: Lawrence Erlbaum Associates.

Kozol, J. (1985). *Illiterate America.* New York: Anchor Press/Doubleday.

Kreeft, J. (1984). Dialogue writing—Bridge from talk to essay writing. *Language Arts, 61,* 141–151.

Kronick, D. (1976). *Three families.* San Rafael, CA: Academic Therapy.

Kuriloff, P. (1973). Counselor as psychoecologist. *Personnel and Guidance Journal, 51,* 37–62.

Labov, W. (1982). Competing value systems in the inner-city schools. In P. Gilmore & A. Glatthorn (Eds.), *Children in and out of school.* Washington, DC: Center for Applied Linguistics.

Laing, R. (1971). *The politics of the family.* New York: Pantheon.

Lipson, M. & Wixson, K. (1986). Reading disability research: An interactionist perspective. *Review of Educational Research, 56,* 111–136.

Literacy Network Seminar. (1986–87). University of Pennsylvania course taught at Shippensburg Area School District, Pennsylvania.

Luria, A. (1979). *The making of mind: A personal account of Soviet psychology.* (M. Cole & S. Cole, Eds.) Cambridge: Harvard University Press.

Lyons, K. (1984). Criterion-referenced reading comprehension tests: New forms with old ghosts. *The Journal of Reading, 27,* 293–298.

Lytle, S. (1982). *Exploring comprehension style: A study of twelfth-grade readers' transactions with text.* Ann Arbor, MI: University Microfilms International.

Lytle, S. & Botel, M. (1988). *A Pennsylvania comprehensive reading/communication arts plan II.* Harrisburg, PA: Pennsylvania Department of Education.

McCaig, R. (1977). What research and evaluation tells us about teaching written expression in the elementary school. In C. Weaver & R. Douma (Eds.), *The language arts teacher in action.* Kalamazoo, MI: Western Michigan University Press.

MacCracken, M. (1986). *Turnabout children.* Boston: Little, Brown and Company.

McDermott, R. (1974). Achieving school failure: An anthropological approach to illiteracy and social stratification. In G. Spindler (Ed.), *Education and cultural process.* New York: Holt, Rinehart & Winston, 82–188.

McDermott, R. & Aron, J. (1978). Pirandello in the classroom: On the possibility of equal educational opportunity in American culture. In M. Reynolds (Ed.), *Future of education for exceptional students.* Reston, VA: Council for Exceptional Children, 41–64.

Mason, J.; Osborn, J.; & Rosenshine, B. (1977). *A consideration of skill hierarchy approaches to the teaching of reading.* Urbana, IL: Center for the Study of Reading.

Mehan, H. (1980). The competent student. *Anthropology and Education Quarterly, 11,* 131–152.

Mellon, J. (1981). Language competence. In C. Cooper (Ed.), *The nature and measurement of competency in English.* Urbana, IL: National Council of Teachers of English.

Mercer, J. (1973). *Labeling the mentally retarded: Clinical and social systems perspectives on mental retardation.* Berkeley: University of California Press.

Mercier, L. (Ed.) (1981). *The essentials approach: Rethinking the curriculum for the 80's.* Washington, DC: U. S. Department of Education, Basic Skills Improvement Program.

Metropolitan reading achievement test. (1986). Cleveland, OH: Psychological Corporation.

Miller, D. & Westman, J. (1964). Reading disability as a condition of family stability. *Family Process, 3,* 66–76.

Mishler, E. (1979). Meaning in context: Is there any other kind? *Harvard Educational Review, 49,* 1–19.

Myers, M. (1981). The politics of minimum competency. In C. Cooper (Ed.), *The nature and measurement of competency in English.* Urbana, IL: National Council of Teachers of English.

National Council of Teachers of English. (November 1977). Resolutions of the General Assembly.

Oakes, J. (1985). *Keeping track: How schools structure inequality.* New Haven: Yale University Press.

Ogbu, J. (1980). Literacy in subordinate cultures: The case of Black Americans. Paper delivered at the Library of Congress Conference on Literacy, Washington, DC, July 14.

Peck, B. (1971). Reading disorders: Have we overlooked something? *Journal of School Psychology, 9,* 182–190.

Preston, R. (1950). Personal communication.

Purves, A. (1981). Competence in English. In C. Cooper (Ed.), *The nature and measurement of competency in English.* Urbana, IL: National Council of Teachers of English.

Resnick, D. (May 1981). Testing in America: A supportive environment. *Phi Delta Kappan, 62,* 625–628.

Rhodes, W. (1967). The disturbing child: A problem of ecological management. *Exceptional Children, 33,* 449–455.

Rist, R. (1970). Student social class and teacher expectations: The self-fulfilling prophesy in ghetto education. *Harvard Educational Review, 40,* 411–451.

Rist, R. & Harrell, J. (1982). Labeling the learning disabled child: The social ecology of educational practice. *American Journal of Orthopsychiatry, 52,* 146–160.

Rivers, L. (1975). Mosaic of labels for black children. In N. Hobbs (Ed.), *Issues in the classification of children.* San Francisco: Jossey-Bass.

Rosenblatt, L. (1980). What facts does this poem teach you? *Language Arts, 57,* 380–388.

Rosenshine, B. (1977). Skill hierarchies in reading comprehension. In *A consideration of skill hierarchy approaches to the teaching of reading: Technical report #43.* Center for the Study of Reading, University of Illinois.

Rowitz, L. & Gunn, J. (1984). The labeling of educable mentally retarded children. In L. Barton & S. Tomlinson (Eds.), *Special education and social interests.* New York: Nichols Publishing Co.

Rumelhart, D. (1980). Schemata: The building blocks of cognition. In R. Spiro, B. Bruce, & W. Brewer (Eds.), *Theoretical issues in reading comprehension.* Hillsdale, NJ: Erlbaum.

Salmon-Cox, L. (May 1981). Teachers and standardized achievement tests: What's really happening? *Phi Delta Kappan, 62,* 631–634.

Sarason, S. (1971). *The culture of the school and the problem of change.* Boston: Allyn & Bacon.

Sarason, S. & Doris, J. (1979). *Educational handicap, public policy and social history.* New York: Macmillan.

Schell, L. & Hanna, G. (1981). Can informal reading inventories reveal strengths and weaknesses in comprehension subskills? *The Reading Teacher, 35,* 263–268.

Schrag, P. & Divoky, D. (1975). *The myth of the hyperactive child: And other means of child control.* New York: Pantheon Books.

Seaver, J. & Botel, M. (1987). *Literacy network handbook.* Levittown, PA: Morton Botel Associates.

Slavin, R. (1984). Students motivating students to excel: Cooperative incentives, cooperative tasks, and student achievement. *The Elementary School Journal, 85,* 53–63.

Smith, L. (1979). An evolving logic of participant observation, educational ethnography, and other case studies. *Review of Research in Education, 6,* 316–376.

Spradley, J. (1979). *The ethnographic interview.* New York: Holt, Rinehart & Winston.

———. (1980). *Participant observation.* New York: Holt, Rinehart & Winston.

Sproull, L. & Zubrow, D. (May 1981). Standardized testing from the administrative perspective. *Phi Delta Kappan, 62,* 628–631.

Sutton-Smith, B. (1981). *The folkstories of children.* Philadelphia: University of Pennsylvania Press.

———. (1982). The importance of the storytaker: An investigation of the imaginative life. *The Urban Review, 8,* 82–95.

Taylor, D. (1983). *Family literacy: Young children learning to read and write.* Exeter, NH: Heinemann Educational Books.

Thomas, D. (1981). *The social psychology of childhood disability.* New York: Schocken Books.

Thomas, W. & Thomas, E. (1928). *The child in America.* New York: Knopf.

Thorndike, R. (1973). Dilemmas in diagnosis. In W. H. MacGinitie (Ed.), *Assessment problems in reading.* Newark, DE: International Reading Association, 57–67.

Vellutino, F. (1987). Dyslexia. *Scientific American, 256,* 34–41.

Vinsonhaler, J.; Weinshank, A.; Wagner, C.; & Polin, R. (1983). Diagnosing children with educational problems: Characteristics of reading and learning disabilities specialists and classroom teachers. *Reading Research Quarterly,* *28,* 134-164.

Vygotsky, L. (1934). Thinking and speech: Psychological investigations. Cited in J. Wertsch (1985), *Vygotsky and the social foundation of mind.* Cambridge: Harvard University Press.

———. (1962). *Thought and language.* Cambridge: MIT Press.

———. (1978). *Mind in society.* Cambridge: Harvard University Press.

Watzlawick, P.; Beavin, J.; & Jackson, D. (1967). *Pragmatics of human communication: A study of interactional patterns, pathologies, and paradoxes.* New York: W. W. Norton & Co.

Watzlawick, P.; Weakland, J.; & Fisch, R. (1974). *Change: Principles of problem formation and problem resolution.* New York: W. W. Norton & Co.

Williams, J. (1975). *Testing and the testing industry: A third view.* Grand Forks, ND: North Dakota Study Group on Evaluation, University of North Dakota.

Yerkes, R. (Ed.). (1921). Psychological examining in the United States Army. *Memoirs of the National Academy of Sciences, 15,* 1-890.

Ysseldyke, J. & Algozzine, B. (1982). *Critical issues in special and remedial education.* Boston: Houghton Mifflin.

———. (1984). *Introduction to special education.* Boston: Houghton Mifflin.

Index

About the Authors

JILL SUNDAY BARTOLI earned her Ph.D. in Language Arts and Family Literacy from the University of Pennsylvania, where she linked her background in language arts with a family systems/family literacy approach to learning problems. She has taught English, speech, reading, creative writing, and drama at the high school and college levels. Most recently, she conducted a Literacy Network Seminar for the University of Pennsylvania, using the framework developed in this volume.

Dr. Bartoli's latest research involved three years of observation, description, and documentation of the in-context learning processes of students labeled as learning disabled. She has published in the areas of language learning and disability labeling, and has coordinated parent workshops that brought together parents, grandparents, teachers, specialists, and community resources to help children read better.

A certified reading specialist and an English teacher, Dr. Bartoli lives in Carlisle, Pennsylvania with her husband and five children—all of whom enjoy reading.

MORTON BOTEL is the William T. Carter Professor of Education and Psychology at the Graduate School of Education, University of Pennsylvania, in Philadelphia. He has authored, co-authored, and developed over 200 textbooks, activity books, paperback book collections, articles, and tests for students and teachers in reading, phonics, literature, English, study skills, spelling, and mathematics.

Dr. Botel is the author of *A Pennsylvania Comprehensive Reading Communication Arts Plan* (PCRP), 1981, and co-author of its successor, *A Pennsylvania Comprehensive Reading Communication Arts Plan II*, 1988. These action frameworks were commissioned by the Department of Education, Commonwealth of Pennsylvania, to guide elementary and secondary schools in their development and implementation of reading, writing, and oral communication across the curriculum. Dr. Botel and his staff have worked with over 50 school systems to implement PCRP.

Most recently, Dr. Botel has contributed a section in the *Encyclopedia of Special Education* entitled Reading in the Content Areas.